GOD'S PLENTY

GOD'S PLENTY

Chaucer's Christian humanism

Ruth M. Ames

A Campion Book

Loyola University Press
Chicago
1984

© 1984 Ruth M. Ames
ISBN 0-8294-0426-0

Design by Carol Tornatore

Printed in the United States of America

Library of Congress Cataloging in Publication
Data

Ames, Ruth M. (Ruth Margaret), 1918–
   God's plenty.

   (A Campion book)
   Bibliography: p. 261
   Includes index.
   1. Chaucer, Geoffrey, d. 1400—Religion and ethics.   2. Theology, Catholic, in
literature.   3. Man (Christian theology) in
literature.   4. Humanism in literature.
5. Great Britain—Church history—
Medieval period, 1066–1485.   I. Title
II. Series.
PR1933.R4A43   1984   821.'1   83-24812

The illustrations appearing throughout this book are reproduced
by permission of *The Huntington Library, San Marino, California.*

To Ruthie

From The Miller's Prologue

A husband must not be inquisitive
Of God, nor of his wife, while she's alive,
So long as he may find *God's plenty there*,
For all the rest he need not greatly care.

from Preface to *Fables Ancient and Modern* (1700),
by John Dryden

He (Chaucer) must have been a man of a most
wonderful comprehensive nature because, as it
has been truly observed of him, he has taken into
the compass of his *Canterbury Tales* the various
manners and humours (as we now call them) of the
whole English nation, in his age. Not a single character
has escaped him. All his pilgrims are severally
distinguished from each other;
. . . Even the grave and serious characters are
distinguished by their several sorts of gravity: their
discourses are such as belong to their age, their calling,
and their breeding; . . . Some of his persons are
vicious, and some virtuous; some are unlearned, or
(as Chaucer calls them) lewd, and some are learned.
Even the ribaldry of the low characters is different: The
Reeve, the Miller, and the Cook are several men, and distinguished from each other, as much as the mincing Lady-
Prioress and the broad-speaking gap-toothed Wife of
Bath. . . . 'Tis sufficient to say, according to the proverb,
that "Here is God's plenty."

CONTENTS

PREFACE

Heirs to the long-faced Puritan-Catholic Christianity of recent centuries, many readers unfamiliar with medieval religion have a notion that in the old days Christians sang only when being thrown to the lions. Chaucer's joy and mirth, his outspoken discussions of sex and marriage, his criticism of the clergy, and his admiration of the pagans both delight and puzzle these readers. They do not know what to make of the note in editions of Chaucer that says Chaucer was an orthodox Catholic. They understand that like many a cradle Catholic, Chaucer could have been baptized, married, and buried in the Church, without manifesting any desire to amend the Creed or the sacraments. But what they want to know is whether Christianity made any difference in his thinking and in his art.

This book is an attempt to show that Chaucer was an educated medieval Christian who, like many other medieval Christians, loved the world without being entirely engrossed by it, whose sanity about that world was linked to his awareness of eternity, and whose humanism was deeply Christian. It is clear from the whole body of his poetry that Chaucer's Catholicism was an integral part of his outlook, an operative force in his thinking about his fellowman, the world, and the universe. The poetry, rather than biographies of Chaucer or handbooks of theology, has shaped the organization of this study. Instead of looking for passages that illustrate the articles of faith, I have been guided by what seem to me religious ideas in the text, ideas which were important to Chaucer and are still interesting to us, from corruption in the Church to the connection between faith and feminism.

I have tried not to be reductive, not to identify Chaucer with the preachers he listened to or the characters he created, but to remember that he was an artist who maintained a certain distance from his subjects, including this one. On the other hand, he was no alienated rebel but avowedly a member of the community for which he wrote; and in his expressed aesthetic theory, art was not for art's, but for God's, sake.

I hope I have included enough background material to give some notion of what Chaucer was reading and what his contemporaries were thinking. In my experience such hints are welcomed by non-medievalists in general and students in particular, most of whom are not likely to pursue archaic-sounding titles in footnotes. Apologetically consigned to a list at the end of this volume are the names of a few of the many excellent, and excellently documented, studies of the social and religious history of the fourteenth century, as well as detailed analyses of Chaucer's sources; the very excellence of these studies makes most of them overspecialized for the general reader.

I trust that all the medievalists whose brains I have picked without acknowledgement will accept my apologies and thanks. Opinions and interpretations are, of course, my own.

I

Christian Courtier and Poet

ost readers are pleasantly struck by Chaucer's seeming lack of dogmatism. He is so urbane, he is so slow to condemn his characters, and he so often makes us laugh that it is—or was—easy to misread him. The older criticism read him as a jovial fellow, somewhere between Reynard the Fox and John Bull, saved from atheism only by his sound Anglo-Saxon character. The new criticism, based on much wider and deeper knowledge of the Middle Ages, sees the naïveté of the old view. Indeed, some of the new criticism goes to the other extreme of portraying Chaucer as a moralist-theologian, somewhere between the philosopher Boethius whom he translated and the Parson he created for *The Canterbury Tales*. Most scholars today, however, strike a balance; they demonstrate the subtlety of Chaucer's work and acknowledge the complexity of his time.

It is the experience of many teachers that this *new learning* has not seeped down to the average classroom. Even the brightest and best-prepared students—and some of their teachers in other disciplines—assume that the Middle Ages were the Dark Ages, repressed and repressive, intellectually narrow, and more Victorian than the Victorians on sex and language. Such students inevitably misinterpret Chaucer as an exception, if not a rebel; at the very least, as a liberal born "ahead of his time."

Reading the scholars, teaching the students, brooding over the history and the text, I have come to think that whatever the difficulties, interpreters of Chaucer must take the risk of evaluating his religious ideas. Perhaps that is because my own view is that his Christianity influenced not only the way he said his prayers but the way he thought about many of the subjects that were agitating his time and that still concern us, subjects ranging from art to zodiac. It was a complex way, because his was a complex mind and art. Perhaps it is not an impertinence to suggest that interpretations which reduce his religious ideas to a stereotype are unjust to Christianity as well as to Chaucer. To say that his outlook was basically Christian is not to identify him with, say, St. Augustine or Boethius, with Dante or Langland, or even with his own Parson. Like each of these, he believed in the Creed and the sacraments and was influenced by the rich intellectual and spiritual traditions of Christianity; but like each of them, he was a unique person whose faith and works bear an individual as well as a traditional stamp.

I suggest that the picture which emerges from Chaucer's collected works is not that of a philosopher, a theologian, or a skeptic, but of an enlightened fourteenth-century gentleman who held dogma without being dogmatic, of a moral artist whose milieu was ironic humor, of a Catholic who did not find the justification of faith easy, but who believed that God so loved the world that he gave his only son for its redemption. I hope that this view is broad

2

enough to accommodate the seeming contradictions within the poet's work. On the one hand we find Chaucer in some agreement with heretics; on the other, we recognize his markedly orthodox assumptions. The "I" of Chaucer's books frequently disclaims theological answers; but his poems of prayer offer simple and firm affirmations. He asserts a preference for artistic realism over morality and decency; yet his sharpest words are in criticism of the immorality of clergy and laity. With sympathy or humor Chaucer portrays characters who question such matters as the providence of God or the sanctity of marriage; equally sympathetic is his telling of legends of unquestioning saints and martyrs.

As we shall see in later chapters, these diverse strands are woven into the whole fabric of Chaucer's thought. What I should like to establish here is the notion that he and his contemporaries recognized the diversity as clearly as we do; that, indeed, they delighted in multiplicity. This point needs to be stressed because there is a tendency among historians to divide the past into mutually exclusive categories and then fit people into them. Admittedly, medieval terminology encourages this compartmentalization by emphasizing roles: Chaucer himself calls his pilgrims the Miller, the Parson, and so forth. And the Church was so omnipresent that it is easy for us to regard it as having been a monolithic entity, separate from the rest of the world, handing down edicts to laymen who would obediently think as they were told. If such a picture were true, Chaucer, with all of his questions and complexities, would indeed be an anomaly. But the fact that a great many of Chaucer's contemporaries would also have to be judged anomalous suggests that the picture must be false. Certainly medieval society, like most societies, provided neatly labeled boxes, but a great number were open at both ends, and Chaucer, like other interesting people, was not locked in. Then, as now, a man's religion was influenced not only by Sunday church but by weekday work and entertainment, and for every official doctrine preached from the pulpit there were dozens of interpretations in the marketplace. Chaucer's are in his works; looking at what his contemporaries read and said helps us appreciate the way he transformed common knowledge into art.

Chaucer was certainly exposed to a wide range of ideas and experiences, his life-style being anything but narrow. He was a married layman who filled various government posts; the friends we know of were courtiers, lawyers, merchants, theologians, and poets, men and women who comprised a well-educated audience quite capable of catching Chaucer's innuendos.

Like many a prosperous merchant's son, Chaucer began as a page, at the age of fourteen or fifteen, in a prince's household. In 1359 he was in the English army in France, was taken prisoner, and was ransomed, in part by a contribution from King Edward III. Presently, like other young courtiers, Chaucer was serving in diplomatic missions, for which he drew daily pay. Later he was granted government jobs such as Comptroller of Customs and Clerk of the King's Works. These were not just sinecures; as Clerk of the King's Works, Chaucer was responsible for the repair of churches and the erection of scaffolds for tournaments. His wife was lady-in-waiting to the Spanish wife of John of Gaunt, and Chaucer was probably on speaking terms with the Queen. They may well have talked above love, science, or religion, all subjects considered suitable for conversation and versification.

Not only were all things subjects for poetry, but all educated persons were taught to write poetry. Several of the courtiers who served abroad with Chaucer wrote poetry, as he did, in their spare time; and they exchanged writings

4

with poets at the French court, one of whom was the feminist Christine de Pisan. Singing and composing music were also included in a courtly education, and music accompanied Mass, meals, and masques. Whatever the activity, the environment was as ornate as a tapestry. Besides paintings, many beautifully illustrated books survive, especially psalters and Bibles, the colors being like those in stained-glass windows. Even the walls and statues of the churches were brightly painted, and both men and women wore scarlet and ermine—to the despair of moralists and economists.

There was, no doubt, cause to condemn this brilliant society. Poets such as Gower and Langland accused king, bishops, and courtiers alike of corruption, callousness, and extravagance; the same attack was voiced by preachers in church, and by the Parson in *The Canterbury Tales*. Still, the court was not without idealism and serious learning. A certain number of these same courtly persons had studied mathematics and astronomy; Chaucer himself wrote a treatise on the astrolabe. Many of these dancing and singing courtiers had studied logic and philosophy; some of them also wrote pious tracts, and were concerned to live a Christian life themselves and to reform the Church. In brief, this court with which Chaucer had so many ties was an exciting center of affairs and ideas, new and old.

We can deduce from Chaucer's works that he had the basic intellectual training of his time in science, languages, philosophy, rhetoric, and literature, but we don't know where or when he went to school. He was not a university man, but he had ties with Oxford, and he may have spent some time at the famous London law schools, the Inns of Court. Some of the books he read, some of which he translated, will necessarily come into later chapters. Here I should like only to suggest the breadth and variety of his cosmopolitan heritage.

His reading list is likely to sound as dry as a college

catalogue. But this least boring of authors was not bored; in his poems he portrays himself sitting up late at night poring over what were even in his time old books. No professor analyzing trends for Royal Notes, he read for story, meaning, and relevance, works that can still speak to listeners. Chaucer's favorite philosopher was a sixth-century Roman Christian named Boethius, who was himself strongly influenced by Plato, and who wrote his *Consolation of Philosophy* in prison. The fiction Chaucer drew upon includes many of the most famous tales of the western world: Virgil's *Aeneid*, Ovid's *Metamorphoses* and *Art of Love*, Guillaume de Lorris and Jean De Meun's *Romance of the Rose*, Dante's *Divine Comedy*, Boccaccio's *Il Filostrato* (*The Stricken One*), Petrarch's *Tale of Griselda*.

None of these works was written in English; the fact that Chaucer and his contemporaries read them in Latin, French, and Italian gives us a clue to the international quality of their humanism. Indeed, when a work in the vernacular became famous, like the story of Griselda, which was composed in Italian, it was translated into Latin to make it available to all educated persons. An educated Englishman might know Latin and French, at least as languages for literature, better than English. Three centuries after the Norman Conquest of 1066, the language of the London court was still French, although English was coming into its own. It is a sign of the times that Chaucer's friend Gower wrote poems in Latin, French, and English; perhaps more significant, the first masterpieces in Middle English were being written in the late fourteenth century: a jewel of a romance called *Sir Gawaine and the Green Knight* by an unknown author, a magnificent vision called *Piers Plowman* by William Langland, and, of course, *Troilus and Criseyde* and *The Canterbury Tales* by Chaucer.

In brief, the Europe of which Chaucer's England was a

member was, frequent wars notwithstanding, still a community with an international language, an international Church, and a concept of a united Christendom. But the period that we call the Middle Ages was coming to an end, and the full emergence of the vernacular as a literary language may be taken as one of the signs of the new era, which would see the triumph of such modern ideas as nationalism, Protestantism, and secularism. Chaucer and the authors of *Gawaine* and *Piers* lived in what historians call a transitional period, which, it seems to me, gave them certain advantages. Certainly I do not mean to romanticize the wars, plagues, poverty, and greed of their time, but I do mean to point out that their time was also, aesthetically speaking, a time of balance between two worlds. At least, reading them in the late twentieth century, we find in them a mixture of old and new artistic forms, of spirituality and secularity (neither so ascetic as earlier centuries nor so gross as later ones) that we are somehow comfortable with. Through Chaucer's ear we hear what everybody was saying in his time on every subject—the Church and the laity, the Jews and the pagans, sex and marriage, the position of women, even good and bad luck. Chaucer was, in this way, a most "realistic, modern" observer of the human comedy. But his ear was still tuned also to the conventional genres and the traditional values of the medieval Christian world.

Looking back at the religious arguments, observers in recent centuries have tended to emphasize differences, as though there were clearly defined sects. But Chaucer and his contemporaries were neither planning nor praying for the breakup of Christendom, and would have been shocked at the notion. The freedom with which everybody criticized the clergy and argued theology, a freedom which seems surprising to twentieth-century readers of Chaucer, was an old medieval custom. The thoughtful Englishmen who agreed in condemning the worldliness of the clergy and the selling of pardons included bishops, priests, clerks, professors, knights, merchants, and poets. They disagreed on how to accomplish reform, but aside from a very few individuals, they do not seem to have realized how far-ranging were the implications of their positions. Perhaps that is one reason that Chaucer was able to be friendly with individuals at conspicuously opposite ends of the argument.

Chaucer was friendly with the poet John Gower and the theologian Ralph Strode, moderate reformers whose basic outlook Chaucer probably shared. They wished to eliminate abuses in the Church while retaining the structure and the sacraments. Chaucer was also very close with several of those called Lollard Knights, who held radical views. With individual variations, Lollards were followers of John Wycliffe, the famous Oxford scholastic who, among other things, wanted the king to take over Church property, dissolve the orders of monks and friars, eliminate the pope and the bishops, abolish the Eucharist, and end such practices as pilgrimages, cults of the saints, masses for the dead, and celibacy of the clergy.

In the 1380s and 1390s, the argument was carried on with considerable heat, but apparently party lines were not clearly drawn, and the court of Richard II was quite tolerant. It is true that there was official conformity and that heretics could be summoned to ecclesiastical courts for reproof or punishment. But there was no inquisition, no machinery for putting heretics to death, and by their own telling, no heretics. Neither Wycliffe, who died in peaceful retirement in 1384, nor the Lollard Knights, who continued to prosper even after university men were censured, desired to break with the Church or foresaw that in a later century these same arguments would lead to a break. In their eyes, it was the pope and the bishops who were heretics and should be rooted out by the king. The king was super-orthodox Richard II, but his most loyal supporters were these same Lollard Knights. Evidently at this time political loyalties did not necessarily follow religious lines as they were to do later on, about 1410. Orthodox and heretic in Richard's court seem to have been rather like Republican and Democratic senators, members of the same club. They were in the civil service together, they married into each other's families and properties, and they shared in the entertainments at court.

One of the entertainments, as we have mentioned, was poetry, and Chaucer, who had become a famous poet by the 1380s, read his poetry aloud to this society; and he is portrayed doing so in a charming illustration. Poetic ties drew these men together. For example, Sir Lewis Clifford, notable Lollard, probably godfather to Chaucer's little Lewis, brought Chaucer a poem from the French poet Eustache Deschamps. It was to Clifford's son-in-law, Sir Philip de la Vache, that Chaucer's "Truth" was dedicated. Sir John Clanvowe, another Lollard Knight, was probably a poetic disciple of Chaucer; he may have written the Chaucerian *Cuckoo and the Nightingale,* and he certainly wrote a devotional tract. On the other hand, Chaucer's *Troilus and Criseyde* was dedicated to "moral Gower" and "philosophical Strode," both well known for their anti-Lollard sentiments. Apparently this was a court in which a Christian such as Chaucer did not have to be either heretic or heretic-hunter. It was, indeed, a court in which the poet was assured of a knowledgeable audience for his jokes on contemporary religious controversies. As we shall see in a later chapter, the half-serious jokes were unitive rather than divisive.

The picture Chaucer draws of himself in a number of poems is likewise half-mocking, half-serious. Of course,

9

CHAUCER

one must be careful not to take such self-portraits literally. The pilgrim in the Canterbury group named Chaucer who knows only one rhyme is obviously not the creator of *The Canterbury Tales*. And the "I" in the Proem to Book II of the *Troilus* who says that he only follows his Latin source and doesn't know about love at firsthand may be following a literary convention. Still, some of the qualities attributed to literary "I" 's are meaningful. When Dante portrays himself being guided through hell by Virgil, we are not to believe that he took such a trip, but we are to understand, among other things, the Florentine poet's aesthetic and moral indebtedness to his Roman predecessor. Chaucer's frequent pose as a timid, ineffectual man of letters is hard to relate to the successful man of affairs we know from records. But since his audience knew him in both roles, he may have been stating the poet's willed detachment from the courtier, and at the same time signalling his mood of irony.

The Prologue to the dream poem called *The House of Fame*, for example, develops the portrait of a man who can see all sides of an issue and avoid coming down on one side or the other, but who at the same time is comically anxious to convey an impression that he really stands for God, family, and poetry. Discussing the nature of dreams, the poet wonders what causes them, why some come true and some don't. Protesting his inaptitude for analysis, he nonetheless lists the possibilities as they appeared in many a medieval text. Demurring yet again, he concludes that he can only hope that the holy cross will turn every dream to good—for he had a wonderful dream—which everybody had best believe. Most wonderful, in the dream he is carried aloft by an eagle. This sounds like the preamble to various well-known literary and spiritual flights, but Chaucer carefully disassociates himself from the exalted visionaries. He says flatly that he is no Enoch or Elijah, no Romulus or Ganymede, all of whom were transported to heaven. He is rather, he says, a retiring, unheroic person, who goes home after the day's work and sits at his books, living like a hermit—although, the amusing eagle remarks drily, Geoffrey's abstinence is slight.

It is most likely that Chaucer read this poem aloud to the courtly audience in which all were acquainted, and that we perforce miss some "in" jokes. But we can catch some of them. We can accept as true the pleasant picture of Chaucer sitting over his books at night, but we know he was neither a hermit nor an ignorant simpleton. In his audience were men with whom he had probably discussed Macrobius, the authority on dreams, men who would recognize the eagle as borrowed from Dante and would appreciate the allusions and laugh at the notion of Geoffrey's being transported to heaven with the Hebrew and classical heroes.

At the same time, the withdrawn *persona* Chaucer gives himself is more than a joke; Chaucer is no frivolous humorist. His steadfast refusal of the role of hero or prophet, combined with the ironic detachment of the style itself (and duplicated in so many other passages), suggests the detachment of the observer. But he is not indifferent. As he puts it, and as we see it—in his relations with the

11

Lollards as well as in his poetry—he *is* modest, he does see both sides, and at the end he does take a stand for God, family, and poetry. When the layers of irony and indirection in the self-descriptions are finally cut through, what is revealed at the core is a Christian attitude towards God and man.

To take just one more example of this complex simplicity, *The Legend of Good Women* opens with a circular argument. The poet has heard a thousand times, he says with characteristic numerical exaggeration, that there is joy in heaven and pain in hell. He accepts this assertion, he says, but remarks that he knows no one who has been to either place or has any proof of their existence. But God forbid, he exclaims hastily, that men should believe only what they see. God knows that things that are not seen are true. Therefore, he advises the reader, believe what you find in old books, just as does this author.

Simple? Skeptical? One might judge that the writer of such a passage had to be one or the other. But Chaucer is so far from simpleminded that the skepticism he is conveying is probably literary rather than spiritual. It is unlikely that Chaucer and his audience believed in the "thousands" of extravagant legends that purported to describe the hereafter in detail; it is also unlikely that they were altogether serious about the legends of extravagantly faithful women he was about to tell for the benefit of the feminists at court. But putting aside the extravaganzas and conceding the lack of proof, there is reason to deduce from Chaucer's prayers that he did believe in heaven, hell, and old books.

As we shall see in a later chapter, the theme of doubt and belief runs through many of Chaucer's works, and often he takes the position that he is no theologian to answer the questions raised. In this same Prologue to *The Legend of Good Women*, he cannot even answer the god of love on his own behalf; the Queen answers for him, kindly citing his ignorance as an excuse for his supposed crimes against love. The fiction must have amused his friends and may have pacified the ladies who resented his portrait of unfaithful Criseyde and his translation of the *Romance of the Rose.* But this stance of fallibility is useful also in a more creative way. It frees Chaucer from authoritarianism, frees him imaginatively to enter sympathetically into the minds and emotions of his characters. More than a literary device, the presentation of the yeas and nays is a reflection of the way his mind and art work. Behind the self-satirizing cartoons is the quizzically intellectual poet who, in the body of his serious work, goes all around every subject, who is slow to quarrel and slower to pass judgment—and who finally finds something to believe in the old books and traditions. No parson who must preach a sermon, the Christian poet raises the problems of faith through the nay-sayers and demonstrates the Christian yea through the outcome of the story.

Artist and Christian live together amicably in Chaucer's work, but there are signs of a split over the perennial problem of choosing between aesthetic truth and moral teaching. In the Prologue to *The Canterbury Tales,* the artist asserts his right to free speech; in the Retraction at the end of the *Tales,* the Christian repents his use of that freedom.

Plain speaking is the most easily defensible characteristic of realistic art, and Chaucer defends it vigorously near the conclusion of the General Prologue. Before telling about the rest of the journey, he says, he hopes that his courteous reader will not think him coarse if he speaks plainly in describing the behavior of the pilgrims and gives their own words. "You know as well as I," the poet remarks conversationally, that a narrator must set down every word if possible, "however rude and free," lest he falsify his mate-

13

rial. Supporting his thesis with the highest authority, Chaucer observes that Christ himself spoke very plainly in holy writ, in which of course there is nothing shameful, and that Plato also said that "the words must be cousin to the deed."

Quoting the same dictum of Plato, the Manciple in the *Tales* applies it to the way the rich cover their wickedness with fine language. He says that if a lady of high degree and a poor woman are both "dishonest with their bodies" there is no difference between them, although one is called "lady," and the other "wench." Distinguishing further between words and things, he says that the only difference between a respected tyrant and a scorned thief is that the tyrant does more harm.

In the Prologue to The Miller's Tale, Chaucer marshalls further arguments in defense of the dirty story he is about to put in the Miller's mouth. The situation is presumably out of his hands: the drunken, cursing Miller has interrupted the Host to insist that he tell his tale of a carpenter and his wife, and of how a clerk cuckolded the carpenter. Chaucer remarks that the Miller told his churl's tale in his own way. In his own seemingly guileless way, Chaucer answers all the foreseeable objections. He regrets, he says, that he must tell the story, and he begs every gentle person "for God's love" to understand that he is just faithfully reporting what he heard. Whoever doesn't wish to hear it, Chaucer says, shifting his ground, can turn over the leaf and choose another tale; there are enough stories about courtesy, morality, and holiness. Don't blame the author if you choose amiss. It is not his fault that the Miller and the Reeve were churls who told of harlotry. Anyhow, Chaucer concludes on still another note, men shouldn't "make earnest of game."

Enjoying The Miller's Tale, we agree entirely with

Chaucer's defense. Much of our delight is in the extraordinary vivacity of the low-life dialogues. Let the unliterary and the prudish, we feel, "change channels." And surely a joke that is hilarious after six centuries is its own excuse for being; let's not make a sermon of it.

Many a critical sermon has been made of it and of the other dirty stories in *The Canterbury Tales.* It has been pointed out that medieval people were less squeamish than we, not to mention our grandmothers, and that there are hundreds of tales (especially in French, of course) much cruder than Chaucer's. Previous generations thus excused Chaucer's lapse of taste by calling it an unwitting reflection of the coarseness of the times. Taking the opposite tack, one school of contemporary criticism moralizes the tales, classifying them with clerical attacks on the sins they describe. And it is true that preachers were very outspoken in their sermons, and that illustrators of devotional books did not stop short of portraying bedroom scenes the reader was not supposed to emulate. Neither of these views, however, accounts for the fact that Chaucer found it necessary to apologize in the Prologue to The Miller's Tale and to repent in the Retraction at the end of The Parson's Tale.

While the fabliaux have been attributed to the barbarous license of the Middle Ages, this Retraction has often been written off as medieval superstition. Poor Geoffrey, it has been said, must have fallen into the hands of the priests, who terrified him with hell fire, and handed him pen and paper on his death bed. An unlikely story; but Chaucer does seem to have been thinking of the end of his own earthly pilgrimage when he took his leave of the Canterbury pilgrims. Chaucer begs those who read or hear this work to thank our Lord Jesus Christ, "from whom proceed all understanding and goodness," for any good in it. If anything displeases them, he asks that it be attributed to his

15

lack of ability, not his will. His intention, he says, has been to follow the biblical injunction that "All that is written is written for our instruction." He therefore beseeches the reader to pray that Christ will have mercy on him and forgive him his sins, namely his "translations and enditings of worldly vanities," which he revokes in his retraction.

Chaucer names a considerable number of his works, including segments of *The Canterbury Tales*, which "tend toward sin," for which he asks Christ to forgive him. There are other works for which he thanks God: his translation of Boethius's *Consolation of Philosophy*, and his books of legends of saints and homilies and devotion. Finally he prays in a most orthodox formula for the grace of true penitence and confession, so that he may be saved at the day of judgment.

Scandalized more by the Retraction than by The Miller's Tale, modern readers often do not see the validity of Chaucer's aesthetic-moral problem; in fact, it is closely related to later conflicts between art and society. Semantic and moral styles change, but the arguments over censorship remain quite stable.

The prevailing medieval view was that coarseness should be described coarsely. Although an occasional lady objected, preachers and moralists used language which shocked and distressed Victorian men, and which still seems strong to us. In one of the most famous medieval works, Jean de Meun's *Romance of the Rose*, it is a lady named Reason who refers to Jupiter's testicles in telling the story of the birth of Venus. Answering the objections of the polite, but immoral, Lover, she says she learned the correct term from God. Her critics, she adds, are shocked by the word, not the thing. At the beginning of our century, Bernard Shaw used much the same moral argument to justify discussing prostitution in public. And some years later in a famous court case involving the censorship of James Joyce's *Ulysses,* the judge worked out a highminded union of moral and aesthetic principles. Opining that Joyce's work is not obscene, the judge distinguished between pornography, which is intended to titillate the senses, and art, which depicts sexual immorality as part of a serious criticism of life. The distinction is increasingly difficult to make as the definition of sexual immorality slides into oblivion. Most contemporary writers feel no defense is necessary, their sole criterion being, to use Chaucer's words, that the tale must not be untrue. But a practical consideration has arisen to fill the place of the moral one. If the portrayal of rape and murder in a television presentation of, say, *Clockwork Orange* leads to increased rape and murder on the streets, do we choose aesthetic truth or the safety of society? If one is both artist and citizen, the choice may be difficult.

Chaucer was both artist and Christian. He may well have argued that the sexual immorality depicted in The Miller's Tale is part of a serious criticism of life. But apparently when he wrote the Retraction, he conceded that such tales might indeed titillate the senses. It is not the plain speaking that he censures, but the tending to sin. And the fact is that such funny, clever, dirty stories are not told in Scripture or by Plato, and that part at least of our enjoyment is pornographic according to the definition of the judicial verdict of *Ulysses.* The effect of the spicy details is not to make us hate the sin but to enjoy the illicit sex vicariously. That, at least, is the response of college students who, along with the professor, are more entertained than edified.

That is not to say (as it sometimes has been said) that Chaucer thought he would go to hell for telling these tales and the others listed in the Retraction. According to The

17

Parson's Tale, which immediately precedes the Retraction, no man is entirely free of such sins as idle talk and gluttony, but these are not serious sins like envy, pride, and anger. "Worldly vanities," as Chaucer calls many of his works, is a relatively mild term, suggestive of venial rather than mortal sin. Mortal or deadly sin is defined by the Parson as loving creatures more than Jesus; venial or less serious sin is defined as loving Jesus less than you ought. In examining his conscience with the thought of death, Chaucer did not recommend burning his books, but he was sorry that in his writing he had loved Jesus less than he should have.

How much should he have? It is unlikely that the Parson, much as Chaucer admires him, is himself a measure for Chaucer. Man and priest, the Parson singlemindedly pursues his goal. He reprimands the Host for swearing, and he refuses to tell a story. Why should he sow chaff, he asks, if he can sow wheat? Instead, he preaches a long sermon on Confession and the seven deadly sins. While Chaucer's ultimate goal was the same as the Parson's, his had to be reached by telling stories, for that was his vocation. Artists were expected to use their gifts for the greater glory of God, as did Dante in his *Divine Comedy,* a work which Chaucer knew. In certain moods Chaucer may well have felt that he had fallen short of the goal and had not sufficiently studied the salvation of his or his readers' souls.

As he points out in the Retraction, Chaucer's subjects had been both religious and worldly. He had translated the *Consolation of Philosophy,* and written saints' legends and homilies. He had also written romances and love poems and fables; indeed, he had enjoyed portraying himself as a love poet, a dreamer, a reader of old books, and an observer of the human comedy. Is it possible that in the two tales told by the pilgrim Geoffrey, the sophisticated author is satirically portraying these two faces of himself? Such an adroit maneuver would be entirely in keeping with the spirit of the piece.

The humor of the situation is apparent to the most casual reader. Turning to the pilgrim Chaucer, the Host mocks his way of riding as though looking for a hare on the ground, and laughs also at his fat waist and "elfish" face. Poor Geoffrey apologetically explains that he knows only one rhyme. His Tale of Sir Thopas, a most witty satire on metrical romances, is such bad doggerel verse that the Host interrupts, complaining that his ears ache. Why will you stop me more than another man, asks Chaucer, since it's "the best rhyme" I know? By God, the Host replies, because "your filthy rhyming is not worth a turd!" Humbly accepting the literary criticism of the Host, Chaucer offers to tell instead "a little thing in prose."

Before he tells his second story, Chaucer gives a bit of gratuitous Scriptural exegesis, by way of explaining that his telling may differ from other versions they have heard. In fact, he expresses a theory of independence in approaching the Bible that, as we shall see later, some of his characters enjoyed practicing. You know, the pilgrim Chaucer says to the group, that there are differences in the accounts of the Evangelists, Matthew, Mark, Luke, and John; nonetheless, all agree in meaning. Therefore, Chaucer continues long-windedly, he feels free to add proverbs to the "little treatise" from which he took "this merry tale." The merry little treatise, The Tale of Melibeus, is one of the longest and most somber of the *Tales*. The gist of it is that Dame Prudence counsels her husband not to take revenge against enemies who had beaten her and wounded their daughter. Anti-women and pro-war, Melibeus objects. After a series of lengthy arguments, adorned with Scriptural and classical allusions, Prudence persuades her husband to forgive the attackers, and the enemies become his friends.

It is a commonplace of Chaucerian criticism that the tales told on the pilgrimage fit the tellers. Chaucer himself observes that the churlish Miller tells a churl's tale; the Prioress tells a miracle story, and so on. Here, however, the technique must be extended outside the framework to the poet. The Tale of Sir Thopas obviously burlesques not only a certain kind of verse but the teller; and the teller is named Chaucer. On the other hand, The Tale of Melibeus has been related not to the pilgrim teller but to the courtly poet. Chaucer may, in fact, have intended it as a piece of propaganda to dissuade John of Gaunt from going to war to enforce his claim to the throne of Castile.

Subtle, analytical Chaucer may have intended still another level of meaning. It is typical of the pilgrims, including the one who tells these two tales, that they do not see their own faults; it is the poet who makes us see the truth about them. Perhaps here we have Chaucer's wry comment on himself in a kind of double mirror: on the one hand, a trivial poetaster reciting a foolish romance; on the other, a solid, prosy Christian teaching good doctrine. This is, at least, the division of his works that he makes in the Retraction. The deep humility presupposed by such a self-satire appears not only in the Retraction but in the other self-portraits of the poet, and is essential in understanding his religious spirit.

In the old manuals of Confession, humility is always allied with truth and distinguished from false modesty. In ironically identifying himself with the teller of The Tale of Sir Thopas, Chaucer is not belittling his talent; on the contrary, the tale itself is a superb demonstration of his metrical virtuosity. But looking at himself *sub specie aeternitatis*, he could recognize the humiliating truth that the romances of the fat poet were less important than his sermons. And although he mocks his own theological pretensions in the introduction to The Tale of Melibeus, the tale itself is not a mockery. It is not an incongruous choice (as The Parson's Tale would be) for a Christian layman. The enthusiastic praise of the Host, who wishes his wife had heard it, suggests, albeit comically, that it is a suitable layman's guide to good conduct in the world. The Tale of Melibeus is certainly one of the homilies Chaucer thanks God for in the Retraction and it is preferred to The Tale of Sir Thopas by all the sensible persons on the pilgrimage.

I mean to suggest not that Chaucer's was a split personality, but a many-sided one, and that like intellectual and sensitive Christian laymen of any time, he had to pick his own path between the claims of God and the world. Apparently he felt there was danger to his soul from too much love of the world, but it seems to me that he struck a balance that made for sound religion and great poetry. Indeed, it may be a failure of historical imagination that leads us to insist on a categorical division between them. The same Christian virtues of compassion, humility, and love which are stated overtly in, for example, the devotional poems to the Virgin Mary, inform the rich fictional world he created. Perhaps the world came first, and it might be true to put it the other way round and guess that the personality he was born with, or the good digestion he was blessed with, drew him from love of creatures to love of their Creator, both loves appearing in so much of his work. Similarly, Chaucer, like other fourteenth-century poets such as Gower and Langland, does not divide truth into religious and secular; Chaucer's musings on the nature of truth mix aesthetics and religion and politics in a manner that is both intellectually and spiritually complex.

We have seen that Chaucer defends the use of rough language as making the word cousin to the deed, and the low-life stories themselves as truthfully portraying reality.

In a confessional mood, brooding on the influence of his work, Chaucer apparently felt that he had gone too far, and we may as well concede that he could never resist a joke. When he was composing poetry, however, he may well have thought, as we do, that truth is one, that art which is "true to life" cannot conflict with the truth of God. Indeed, in a short moral poem called "Lack of Steadfastness," he points to the disparity between "word and deed" as an example of immorality, and an indication of the "upside-down" condition of the world. "Truth is put down," he says further, "reason held a fable," and "the world has made a permutation from right to wrong, from truth to fickleness." And in the Envoy, he beseeches King Richard to fear God, do justice, and "love truth."

It is apparent from this and other poems and stories that Chaucer, like other medieval thinkers, considered truth to be sacred. "Keeping your word" and "keeping faith" are two ways of expressing the same inherent principle of human and divine relations. Truth is also an appellation for Christ, and this is its primary meaning in a poem called "Truth," which was the best known of Chaucer's works in his own time. The refrain at the end of each stanza, "And Truth shall deliver thee, do not fear," is based on the verse in the Fourth Gospel, "You shall know the truth and the truth shall make you free" (Jn 8:32).

Courtier, Christian, and poet are clearly seen together here. Addressed to a friend named Sir Philip de la Vache, the poem begins by advising him to flee from the "courtly crowd" and "dwell with truthfulness." Chaucer's meaning is unfolded in the lines following, in which he tells him to be satisfied with whatever means he has, to "rule himself well" so that he can counsel others, not to distress himself trying to reform the whole world but to seek peace and cultivate acceptance. The detachment for which Chaucer is famous is here elevated to a precept. And why is Vache advised to avoid the struggle? Because, the poem goes on, this is not home but only a "wilderness" in which we are pilgrims. "Hold the high way," advises Chaucer, and be not a "slave to the world"; ask mercy of Him who made you of nothing, and pray for heavenly reward for yourself and others.

In what it says, in what it leaves unsaid, this little poem epitomizes Chaucer's religious spirit. "Flee from the crowd" is not a recommendation of the monastic life, but advice from a court poet to a courtier, who may have been in political danger at the time, on how to live in the world and yet not be enslaved by the world. And in the midst of this solemn piety is a little joke: the pilgrim is called a "beast in a stall" because his name Vache means cow in French.

The poem also reinforces the suggestion of the historical record that Chaucer's religious spirit was what we call ecumenical. Vache, who was son-in-law of Chaucer's Lollard friend Sir Lewis Clifford, was most probably a Lollard sympathizer himself. Perhaps out of respect for the good faith of his Lollard friends, Chaucer chose to emphasize the theme of contempt of the world, a theme most congenial to the Lollard Knights, as we know from their devotional works. Further, Chaucer did not refer to the sacraments here as was his wont elsewhere, possibly because he and Vache did not think alike on the Eucharist and Confession. Instead, Chaucer affirmed that central Truth sought by all men of good will, that Truth which was, as orthodox Strode had said, the common goal of orthodox and Lollard.

Chaucer's own orthodoxy is plain enough in other works, but it is relaxed rather than aggressive. Elsewhere he makes no secret of his belief in the necessity of confession to a priest, of his reverence for saints and sacraments, his acceptance of pilgrimages, all practices condemned by the

Wycliffites, but never argued by Chaucer. Everything we know about Chaucer—the body of his work, the records of his life, his self-image—contribute to a picture of a man who held orthodox views without worrying about conformity, who practiced intellectual freedom, who was zealous for truth and charity, and who had great breadth of humor and humanity.

The fictional world Chaucer created with such skill and art reflects this inclusive Christianity. The reason there are no Wycliffites on the Canterbury pilgrimage is probably because the Wycliffites disapproved of pilgrimages rather than because Chaucer excluded them. On Chaucer's way there was room for men and women of all classes, lay people and clergy, saints and sinners, all needing to be delivered by the same Truth. As Chaucer portrays the road to Truth in his various works, it is long and winding, rough and uncertain, and those who should be guides, the priests, often give little help in avoiding the holes and detours. Nonetheless, the trip is worth taking; there are love and pity, high talk and low laughter along the way, and the end is eternity.

II

The Church and
the Clergy

o equate the Church with churchmen, as some historians still do, is to give a misleading idea of medieval religion. Described practically, the Church was composed of clergy and laity; considered more mystically, the Church transcended both these sets of sinners. Not itself the City of God (which, according to St. Augustine, was known only to God), the Church was the sacramental organ of that City. More emotionally personified as Holy Mother and Bride of Christ, the Church was also called the Guardian of the Scriptures, the Teacher of Morality, the Refuge of the Poor, the Fulfillment of the Synagogue and the Light of the Gentiles. Small wonder that those who cared most deeply about such an ideal were dissatisfied with the medieval clergy! Chaucer's dissatisfaction is evident enough, but hard to judge without a little background. While his ironic style precludes final interpretations, we can begin to place him in his time if we recognize traits of the widespread medieval anti-clericalism in his work. Modern critics have come to

25

think that different as he is from, say, Langland and Dante, Chaucer's views were not notably different from theirs, or from numerous less famous reformers and poets.

It was generally agreed that the obligation of disinterested love, which presumably bound all Christians, bound the clergy most tightly. While lay members of the Church had other legitimate ties, clerics had chosen, or been chosen by God, to follow Christ alone. Their position in the community was thought to be parallel to that of the ancient Hebrews in the world. Like the Hebrews, the clergy were a chosen people, set apart not to grow fat on the sacrifices but to bear the mark of God in a specially consecrated way. And like the Hebrew prophets, medieval reformers believed the chosen should be judged most severely if they, who knew the law of God, did not obey it. Gifted with grace, knowledge, and power, the clergy had to be better than ordinary people, not only because they knew better, but because their example was so potent for good and evil. So said the priests themselves, as the collections of sermons reveal.

Whatever medieval Christians thought of the clergy in their own time, they saw the role of the Church as crucial in history, because the Church was founded by Christ and the Apostles for the salvation of all mankind. The subject was embodied and embroidered in many a volume of "historical fiction," most of which has been long forgotten. However, we still read *Piers Plowman*, a best-seller by Chaucer's contemporary Langland, of which more than fifty manuscripts survive to testify to the good taste of our ancestors. To the Dreamer in this extraordinary poem, the Church appears personified as a fair lady who comes down from a mountain to teach the people the way of salvation; her text is "God is love," and her treasure is Truth. In the historical part of the poem, Langland uses a quite different set of images in an allegorical account of the origin of the Church: the foundation, called Mercy, was laid by Grace, who used a kind of mortar made with the blood Christ shed on the Cross; the walls were made of Christ's pains and Passion; the roof was made entirely of Holy Scripture. So it is that Holy Church is the source of all holiness and truth, which spring from her through honest men who teach God's Law.

When priesthood is corrupt, however, the Church can be the source of all evil. One of Langland's characters explains that priests are the roots of the true faith, on whom the people depend; where the roots are rotten, the flowers, fruit, and leaves will never be healthy. If only the clergy would practice what they preach, their example would fill the world with love of Christ and neighbor. If only they followed the way of perfection, every monk and friar would be on a level with the Twelve Apostles. If only the leaders were truly holy, they would be the salt to preserve Christian souls; but "if the salt has lost its savor, with what can it be salted?" Alas, cries Langland, these "blind buzzards" do not even try to teach the folk. "Bloated round-bellied chamber pot" he calls a Master of Divinity who preaches mortification and is himself a glutton. Such prelates are traitors with Judas who kept the purse for himself; if they did their duty, no Christian would ever be without bread and soup.

Like satirists of all times, Langland looks back to better days when a few holy men converted the world, when bishops shared with the poor, when friars were like St. Francis. Now Avarice keeps the keys; now, with tens of thousands of preachers and a pope to rule them, nobody goes forth to preach to the Saracens and Jews, who would be converted if priests were holier. Instead, the pope sends armies to kill the very folk he was meant to save.

27

Whether or not they advocated the disestablishment of the Church (as did orthodox Langland), most medieval reformers blamed the corruption on the Church's possessions, and they regretted the so-called Donation of Constantine, by which presumably the first Christian emperor in the fourth century transferred his sovereignty over Italy to the Papal See. Langland repeats an oft-told story that when Constantine made his gift of temporal power, an angel was heard to cry in the air over the city of Rome, saying, "This day the wealth of the Church is poisoned and those who have Peter's power have drunk venom."

A greater poet than Langland, indeed, one of the greatest of all poets, Dante Alighieri, had made the same point some seventy years earlier. "Ah Constantine," grieved Dante, "What ills were gendered" when you made "the first rich Pope your heir!" Like *Piers*, Dante's *Divine Comedy* is an allegory of man's salvation that draws on the intellectual and spiritual riches of medieval Christianity. And like Langland, this most famous singer of Catholicism raged against those who in his words raped the Church, the "Fairest among women."

It is because they perverted their high office that Dante puts several popes in hell—upside down because they reversed the proper order. In the eighth circle of hell, these "miserable pimps and hucksters" are thrust into holes head first, with only their feet protruding. Dante names them. One is the shade of Nicholas III who died in 1280, and he tells Dante that his predecessors lie beneath his head, and that the next comer, Boniface VIII, will enter the same hole head first, thus pushing Nicholas in further. Dante bitterly reproaches the former pope for having followed Simon Magus, who thought he could buy the keys to the Kingdom. Such pastors, laments Dante, sadden the world with their avarice and commit idolatry by their wor-

28

ship of gold. Even Dante's heaven is troubled by this iniquity. In the *Paradise*, St. Peter recalls the great martyr popes of the early Church who shed their blood to foster Christ's bride, not to ensure gain; and he denounces Boniface and others whom he calls wolves in shepherds' garb.

St. Peter does, however, have many later clergymen in his company, and it should be observed that they outnumber their counterparts in the more widely read *Hell*. There are, for example, many scholar-saints such as Aquinas and Bede in the two circles of lights comprising spirits characterized by the gift of wisdom (Old Testament Solomon and Nathan the Prophet are also among the wise). To show how heavenly light has further illumined these wise men, Dante places side by side in heaven savants who honestly disagreed on earth. In Paradise also are the founders of the orders of monks and friars, notably Benedict, Dominic, and Francis.

It would be easy to multiply examples of similar eulogies of the past and attacks on the medieval clergy; they appear in stories and in sermons written by clerics and laymen. Indeed, the same phrases appear in so many places that one begins to suspect the presence of a convention copied from other writers as much as from life. Without going so far as the historian McFarlane, who concluded that there were more reformers than abuses to be reformed, one must conclude that condemning the clergy was entirely acceptable, perhaps stylish, certainly orthodox.

Looked at against this background, Chaucer's clerical portraits seem moderate; his details, sometimes derivative, but nonetheless powerful and convincing. Chaucer was generally less polemical than Dante and less prophetic than Langland, and his attack on vice is usually more indirect and considerably funnier than theirs. When the offender is a cleric, however, Chaucer too sounds like a Daniel come to judgment. Apparently he agreed with the good Parson of *The Canterbury Tales* that whatever the sin, it is worse if committed by one in religion; and the higher the rank, the greater the sin. In his sermon-tale, the Parson calls simony, the selling of Church office, the greatest sin because it places in the Church thieves who steal souls from Jesus Christ; simony sells the souls of sheep, he says, to the wolf that strangles them.

It is in this mood of judgment that the clerics are portrayed in *The Canterbury Tales*. Ten of the twenty-nine Canterbury pilgrims are either members of the clergy or minor functionaries in the Church, and another cleric briefly joins the party en route. Only four of these, the Parson, the clerk, the Nun's Priest, and the Second Nun, pass without criticism, the last two not being described at all in the General Prologue. Further, the priests, monks, friars, and clerks who figure in the tales told by the pilgrims are a notoriously sinful group; indeed, in these stories there are more good pagans than good clerics. And yet, to judge from these same charcters, Chaucer was neither an atheist nor a heretic, but a Catholic who desired the reform of the Church in an orthodox way.

The fourteenth-century heretic way, as was mentioned in the previous chapter, was to demand that the government dissolve the monasteries, expropriate Church lands and goods, and desacramentalize the Church. Agreeing with the Lollards that the Church was sick, Chaucer apparently disagreed with the proposed cures. Chaucer never recommends any of the "new" remedies; always, as we shall see, his medicine is to be found in the old Church. He offers no easy solutions, but like many orthodox reformers, from Old Testament Micah to medieval Dante and Langland, to sixteenth century Thomas More, he exposes the evil, setting beside it the beauty of the ideal, both within the Church.

Like all of the reformers, Chaucer saw that the very success of the Church in the world had corrupted it by placing the clergy among the mighty and giving clerics privileges denied the lowly. Designed as the straightest road to heaven, the Church had become, through a combination of historical forces, the most labyrinthine institution in the medieval world. Chaucer shows it as the principal organization in which a smart man of low birth could win money and prestige. While the Church still attracted saints, it thus drew also the worst, or at least the most ambitious, sinners for whom it was a calling not to God but to the king's court, to a court of law, to a good "living" somewhere in the Church.

Chaucer consistently deplores this professionalism, but he does not give us a simplistic picture of evil churchmen among good laymen. Instead, he give us glimpses of an amorphous Church in the city of the world, variously respected, condemned, interpreted, questioned—even on such topics as clerical celibacy and monastic vows. Chaucer's ironic technique is so subtle that the modern reader is in danger of attributing the views of his characters to him, especially when they sound most "modern." But the technique itself reveals the basic conservatism of Chaucer's criticism.

All the clergy, both pilgrims and characters in tales told by the pilgrims, are identified first by the station in life they have chosen. We remember them by their position as the Parson, the Monk, the Friar, the Prioress, the Second Nun, the Clerk, the Nun's Priest, the Summoner, the Pardoner, and the Canon, rather than by their names, even when they are given any. This medieval custom of identifying a person by means of a professional label serves as a constant reminder of the requirements and expectations of the person's job. Whether an individual monk, say—or a reader—thinks the monastic rule beautiful or ridiculous, the fact that the Canterbury pilgrim is "The Monk" means that he and we know he has vowed to observe that rule, which Chaucer takes pains to define, and which binds all monks.

With most of these clerics, we must deduce Chaucer's views from his treatment of their faults. But in the person of the good Parson, Chaucer has given us a standard by which to judge all the rest. A better priest could nowhere be found, says Chaucer.

Unlike the priests condemned by all the reformers, Chaucer's Parson does not care about money; indeed, he gives away what little he has. Poor himself, he is no respecter of persons, and he reprimands sinners regardless of rank. He is especially harsh with priests, from whom he feels a great deal should be expected. To the Gospel words so often quoted, "If the salt lose its savor . . ." he adds the proverb, "If gold rust, what will iron do?" It is a shame, he says, to have "a shitten shepherd" and "clean sheep." "Rich in holy thought and work," he preaches Christ's Gospel and gives a noble example to his sheep. Most important, he practices what he preaches.

The overt criticism of mercenary shepherds, the indirect criticism through listing the sins not committed by the Parson, and the stress on the Parson's apostolic poverty and simplicity echo many of the reforming tracts of the time while, I think, carefully avoiding controversy. Lollard priests had a reputation for simplicity, but orthodox as well as Lollard reformers condemned the abuses singled out here, and praised simple Christianity. On controversial matters, the Parson is entirely orthodox. Not only does he never express a heretical view, but no Lollard would have been on a pilgrimage or preached the sermon that is his tale. A large part of the sermon concerns the sacrament of penance; the Lollards were hostile to the sacraments in general, and private confession in particular was called by Wycliffe a device of the devil. The Parson's Tale is a model of theological orthodoxy as the teller is a model of an old-fashioned priest. That is not to say that his function is to serve as propaganda against the Lollards. That possibility is forestalled by an involved joke that is at least partly a tribute to the virtues of Lollard preachers.

When the Man of Law has finished his tale, the Host calls on the Parson, sprinkling his request for a story with "for God's bones" and "by God's dignity." When the Parson in reply asks what ails the man to swear so sinfully, the Host "smells a Lollard in the wind," and satirically warns the pilgrims that this Lollard will preach something. The cause of orthodoxy is supported further by that even less likely doctor of disputation, the blasphemous Shipman, who swears by his father's soul that the Parson will not "expound the Scriptures" here. "We all believe in the great God," the Shipman says piously, but this man will sow some difficulty or spread "some cockle" in our "clean corn." He offers to tell instead a dirty story.

Should we deduce from this passage that the Parson was one of those preachers the Lollard Knights were accused of protecting? But the only information the text gives us about the Parson is that he didn't like swearing. Now it is true that the Lollards were reputed to frown on swearing, but the Host notwithstanding, there was never any orthodox defense of the custom. Indeed, in France the laws against blasphemy were so cruel that they were unenforceable; after a futile argument over modifying the law, a royal decree in 1397 reestablished the old penalty of lip-splitting. And even the rascally Pardoner, blasphemous enough in

33

practice to keep the other rogues company, preaches an eloquent, orthodox bit against swearing.

What the Host and the Shipman are really talking about is preaching. There were orthodox objections to Lollard sermons, and the Shipman, no doubt to the amusement of the court, knew them well enough to paraphrase them. It was a frequent complaint that the Lollards "glossed," that is, interpreted, the Scriptures to suit their doctrine. And a Papal Bull in 1377 charged English bishops with, in an image much like the Shipman's, allowing "tares" to spring up amidst the pure wheat in the fields of the Church.

What this extraordinarily perceptive passage reveals is not the Lollardry of the Parson but the rude ignorance of the rednecks. The ironical joke is that the blasphemous and ignorant Host and Shipman, setting up as exegetes, consider the virtue of the Parson proof of heresy and their own vice proof of orthodoxy. Taken with what we know of Chaucer's friendships with both Wycliffites and anti-Wycliffites, the passage may be understood also as pointing to the folly of religious controversy. The good Parson himself does not answer the accusation of the Host, nor does he attack the Lollards. Putting together what he says and does not say, with what Chaucer says and does not say about him in the General Prologue, I take him to be an orthodox reformer concerned more with correcting sinners than arguing with heretics.

There are two other parish priests in *The Canterbury Tales*. One, called the Nun's Priest, will be discussed with the Nun Prioress's group to which he belongs. The other is only sketched in the background of The Reeve's Tale, but the few lines devoted to him reveal not only his vices but the curiously mixed attitude of the laity to him, and no doubt to others like him.

34

The social pretensions of the miller and his wife in The Reeve's Tale are derived from her birth, her father being the parson of the town. Although, as the Reeve says, her name was "somewhat sullied" and she was really "as noble as water in a ditch," she was full of pride and pretension. Further, she expected her daughter to be the heir of the parson, who himself put difficulties in the way of ordinary suitors because he wanted a higher social alliance. The Reeve, himself in a class with the Host and the Shipman, perceives with considerable bitterness the priest's disgraceful conflict of interests. He tells us ironically that "holy church's goods must be spent on holy church's blood, as it descends. Therefore he would honor his holy blood, even if it devoured holy church."

Nobody in the Reeve's audience had to be told that the blood of a priest's daughter was anything but holy, and that ultimately they, the parishioners, were paying for the dowry. The good Parson says in his sermon that sins of fornication are far worse when committed by the clergy. Since the vow of chastity is a special sign of God, he says, those who break it are special "traitors to God and to the people"; for the people support the priests so that they will pray for them, but such prayers as theirs cannot help anybody. Instead of an angel of light, such a priest is an angel of darkness; and a wicked priest, says the Parson, corrupts the whole parish. The father of the miller's wife in The Reeve's Tale is just such a source of corruption; his respected position gives status to his illegitimate child and to adultery itself.

The concubinage of the clergy alluded to in this tale was a widespread scandal, and one of the cures suggested for it was a married clergy. The subject was warmly debated in the fourteenth century, and there is one avowed enemy of clerical celibacy in *The Canterbury Tales*, the Host. The champion of orthodoxy against the Lollards in the dispute over swearing, the Host here takes the Lollard side; both sides would do better with him as an enemy. But the ludicrousness of his argument has not kept later readers from attributing his view to Chaucer, in part because the Host slyly remarks that many a truth is said in jest.

Asking for a tale and apparently looking over the Monk with a keen eye, the Host jocularly remarks that the Monk has a fair skin and must live in a fine pasture; certainly he doesn't look as though he fasts. Working around to the subject that is never far from his mind, the Host proceeds to a lengthy harangue in which he laments the Monk's choice of career, speculating that he would have been a great rooster if he had as much "permission as power" to propagate the race. If he were pope, the Host generalizes, not only this Monk but every mighty man, "though he were tonsured," should have a wife. All the world suffers, he says, because religion has taken up all "the corn of copulation," and laymen are only "shrimps." Since from feeble trees come wretched grafts, he proverbializes, the heirs of laymen are so weak that they can barely procreate. That's why, the Host winds up, wives try these religious, for they pay "Venus's charge" best.

The Monk takes "all in patience" without replying, and Chaucer leaves his audience to separate the corn from the shrimps. The Host's proposal, I think, ridicules the controversy over celibacy by parodying the various views propounded.

Although the celibacy of the clergy was warmly argued, there was never any suggestion that monks should marry, coed monasteries obviously belonging to the realm of Rabelaisian ribaldry. Wycliffe did think that priests were "wifeless against the authority of God," since he could find no Scriptural injunction in favor of celibacy. But unlike the

Host, he thought marriage would restrain, not foster, clerical engendering, of which, according to reformers and comedians, there was already more than enough. Indeed, Wycliffe said that celibacy was a device of the fiend to kindle the fires of lust. And one would think that nobody ever seriously argued for a married clergy as a means to improve and increase breeding, anymore than one would seriously argue today for an unmarried clergy as a means of population control.

But behind the Host's lament for the loss of a fine begetter is an argument over whether or not celibacy is against nature. In answer to the argument that celibacy would lead to the end of the race, St. Jerome in the fourth century had pointed out sardonically that the future of the race was not likely to be jeopardized by the multitudes practicing abstinence. But in the twelfth century there seemed some semblance of reason for alarm: a flourishing heretical sect called the Catharii believed all sexual intercourse wrong and required celibacy of all true believers. It was largely in response to these heretics that a number of priestly defenders of orthodoxy took to praising Nature and fecundity, and to playing down celibacy, which anyhow had always been considered a vocation for the few.

In the thirteenth century, Jean de Meun, in the *Romance of the Rose,* carried the argument a long step further. A character named Genius, who is Nature's priest, says that Nature, as deputy of God, has her own Scripture, which exhorts fecundity, and which curses, excommunicates, and damns to hell those who refrain. Genius offers two arguments. One is that if all refrained, the race would end in sixty years. Second, if it were God's will that some lead virgin lives, then all should. If not all, then God wants all to generate. So Nature's spokesman counsels lords to get on with the work: "Plow, barons, plow—your lineage repair!"

37

Forget about celibacy and do as did your fathers and mothers. Now Jean de Meun was probably being ironic, but there really were anti-celibate zealots, some of them college students. In 1277, the bishop of Paris denounced certain ideas which were being discussed by liberal arts students at the university. Understandably, the bishop didn't like the proposition that read: "Total abstinence from the work of the flesh corrupts virtue and the species."

The corruption of the species is what the Host says he is worried about. Feeble trees, he says concernedly, produce weak offspring. But Chaucer typically adds a line with an unmistakeable leer; when the Host says laymen's wives therefore "tried these religious," nobody is expected to believe that he means they were concerned for the future of the species.

Chaucer may have been alluding also to two curious arguments against celibacy held by certain followers of Wycliffe. In a list of "Conclusions" published by some Lollards in the 1390s was a condemnation of the law of continence enjoined on priests, since it "was first ordained to the prejudice of women." Poor girls! As the Host says, religion has taken all the best. A more startling resemblance to the Host's diatribe appears in the recantation of Chaucer's Lollard friend Sir Lewis Clifford. In 1402 Clifford testified that Lollard preachers said that unmarried priests and nuns are not approved by God, "for they destroy the holy seed of which shall grow the second Trinity." It is likely that Chaucer had heard such apocalyptic talk; it is not unlikely that he would try to laugh it out of court. It is possible that a satiric reduction of the "holy seed" would come down to the Host's "corn of copulation."

Finally, as the cancelled Epilogue to The Nun's Priest's Tale indicates even more strongly than the Prologue to The Monk's Tale, it is not celibacy but sex that preoccupies the Host. Blessing the Nun's Priest for his merry tale of Chanticleer, the Host looks over his brawn and build with professional approval. We have not been led to suspect this priest's morals, but the Host remarks gratuitously that if he were not a priest, he would be a great cock who would need more than seven times seventeen hens. That Chaucer is not here recommending matrimony for priests is suggested by, among other things, the Host's image of the rooster with a hundred and nineteen hens. The barnyard image was commonplace, but not as a figure of marriage. In a typical discussion of the nature of man, Gower, in the *Confessio Amantis,* uses the cock metaphor to describe the amoral sex life of primitive man; Gower considered monogamy a significant step forward in civilization. Nor did the Wycliffites advertise marriage as an orgy. Drawing on other domestic animals, Wycliffe wrote that married couples were not intended to "have fleshly lust without reason and fear of God, as mules and horses and swine that have no understanding."

In brief, Chaucer uses the device of *reductio ad absurdum* to mock the controversy over celibacy. He does not tell us his own conclusions, but surely if he had favored a married clergy, he could have found a more respectable spokesman than the Host, whose notorious partiality for dirty jokes disqualifies him just as his habitual swearing destroys his credibility in the argument over blasphemy. The model priest, the Parson, combines orthodox precept and practice; celibate himself, he bitterly condemns clerical unchastity. As an old-fashioned remedy for lechery, he counsels love of Christ, which first he practices himself. But again, as in the argument over blasphemy, the Parson does not dispute the Lollard view.

Chaucer's basically conservative view against updating faith and morals is shown plainly in the description in the

General Prologue of the prosperous Monk admired by the Host. This Monk not only breaks the rules of his order but throws out the rule book as outdated. How "shall the world be served?" he asks, if he "pores over a book in the cloister" and labors with his hands. He says that he ignores the rule of St. Benedict because it is old and strict, and the old must pass away in favor of the new freedom. He cites two texts famous in diatribes against monks, one that hunters are not holy, the other that a monk out of the cloister is like a fish out of water. Our Monk doesn't give a plucked hen for the first or an oyster for the second. And his fellow-pilgrim, Chaucer, "said his opinion was good."

The author, Chaucer, however, is criticizing the Monk in the same phrases as all the other reformers, from Wycliffe to Gower. And like Dante and Langland, Chaucer uncovers the Monk's vices by an implicit comparison with the founders of monachism. His technique is to turn the verses in such a way as to show that the Monk serves only himself by accommodating the monastery to the world and the times, and that this Monk is no theorist working from within to reform the institution but an unprincipled man of the world who has made a good thing out of the Church. By telling us that when he rode, the bells on his bridle jingled as clear as the chapel bell, Chaucer is telling us that the Monk ignores prayer, the essence of the monastic vocation. He prefers horses, greyhounds, expensive clothes, and a fat swan. This is the way he "serves the world," which is paying for all on the supposition that he is following the rule of St. Benedict. Such extravagance was condemned by the Parson even in laymen, who might otherwise give the superfluity to the poor. Instead, the Parson grieves in his sermon, all goes for expensive horses, for the pay of boys to care for them, for carved harnesses and elaborate saddles. All of this, when Jesus rode only on an ass.

The monk in The Shipman's Tale who also spends his time hunting fair game is an even more slippery character than the Pilgrim-Monk. In the story, the monk is contrasted most unfavorably with a merchant. The merchant is honest, faithful, trusting, and generous; the monk is dishonest, disloyal, adulterous, and contemptible enough to woo the merchant's wife with the merchant's money. We ought not to take this pat contrast altogether seriously, because The Shipman's Tale is a fabliau, a kind of dirty story that traditionally took cynical pleasure in portraying the adulterer as a cleric. Told by the rough Shipman, the story may reveal more about the teller than about monks. But certain details which seem beyond the Shipman's range of subtlety suggest how much Chaucer was irked by the worldliness of the socially acceptable cleric. This smooth monk makes friends of all in the merchant's household by his pleasant manners and little presents. When he meets the wife of his friend in the garden in the morning, he rallies her on looking pale, and makes a little joke about how hard her husband must have been working her all night. The breviary which he had been reading before she came is most convenient for him to swear on, when he is in fact forswearing his friendship with the husband and planning to cheat the wife. Adultery, as the Parson says, is both breaking of faith and theft.

While monachism goes back many centuries in Church history (the Benedictines were founded in the sixth century), the orders of friars were begun only in the thirteenth century. They performed a most valuable service, carrying out not only the "renewal" that all institutions need perennially, but the "updating" that is useful periodically. Their mission was quite different from that of the monks who were dedicated to a life of work and prayer within the monastery. The dramatically "new" vocation of friars was to go out into the field and marketplaces—like the apostles of old—and preach the Gospel to the poor. Dominic and Francis, the most famous, captured the imagination of their time, and thousands of young men followed them into what were at first austere, self-sacrificing lives. But like the Church of which they were a part, they were too successful, and it seemed to many observers in the fourteenth century, and to historians ever since, that the world had converted them instead of vice versa. They were accused of neglecting the poor for the rich, of sexual immorality, and most of all, of deceiving the populace with their hypocrisy.

No doubt the charges were true. Still, the case for the friars seems to me not entirely closed. For one thing, the attacks are so massive and so uniform that after the first dozen one gets the impression of collusion, if not conspiracy. And for another, in spite of the fact that literally everybody must have heard these exposés, great numbers of individuals continued to endow the orders and leave money for them in their wills. In Oxford, the very hotbed of anti-fraternalism, one third of the local citizens in the second half of the fourteenth century left bequests to the Franciscans. And we know from other sources that, as historian May McKisack says, there was no "general support for attacks on the religious life."

It is possible that the friars' bad press was not altogether a moral matter. On the one hand they made enemies of parish priests by competing with them; on the other, they offended the intelligentsia by popularizing religion. In fact, the inadequacy of parish priests was a prime cause of the growth of the orders. Some local clergy were so ignorant that they had to be ordered by the bishops to learn the Ten Commandments. Many of them were so poor that they could not be distinguished from the most oppressed, with whom, indeed, they united in the Peasants' Revolt of 1381. The friars made them poorer by encroaching on their prerogatives of preaching (and taking the collection) and of burying the dead (for a fee). Further, the friars were specifically trained to preach emotional sermons; and they were sympathetic confessors (too sympathetic, says Langland of Friar Flatterer) who did not hesitate to eat and otherwise fraternize with the laity.

Fraternize, fraternal, frere, fra, friar—brother—the "just folks" approach always succeeds with the lowbrows and irritates the highbrows. Often sincere and heartwarming, the cozy approach easily becomes false and, traditionalists say, it bends to the common man instead of bringing him up. Partly, perhaps, it is a matter of taste. The twentieth century has not been without popular preachers who were scorned as housewives' philosophers by the university. So in the Middle Ages, a notable lover of books, Richard de Bury, complained that the friars relied on "apocryphal imbecilities" not for the refreshment of souls but for "tickling the ears of the listeners." A reader of medieval sermons can testify to the imbecilities; on the other hand, the works of the professors are hardly all sweetness and light. One William of St. Amour wrote a really vicious attack on the friars as precursors of antiChrist, a diatribe that has tickled the ears of subsequent generations of admiring professors. In any event, many bystanders paid no heed. According to Gower, who also detested the friars, there was no king or great man who didn't confess to them, thus making them mightier than lords.

Chaucer apparently shared the university view. His two friars could easily have been drawn from current attacks, rather than from life. But Chaucer does a masterly job of bringing together all the criticism and endowing it with life.

43

In describing the Pilgrim-Friar on the way to Canterbury, Chaucer uses the same literary technique as for the Monk: as he shows the Monk reversing the rule of St. Benedict, so he portrays the Friar parodying the founder of his order. Chaucer's audience would have recognized the satiric parallels because everybody knew the story of St. Francis of Assisi. Francis, a lover of music before his conversion, became a troubadour of God, playing and singing hymns he composed himself. Chaucer's Friar sings and plays musical instruments as he "lisps with wantonness." Francis, a barefoot hippie type, had not only thrown away the middle class comforts he was born to but was determined to be free of all possessions. The crowds of young men who were first drawn to him lived as he did by begging, dependent on the charity of other poor men, to whom they preached the good news of liberation through Christ. Chaucer's Friar is the "best beggar" of his house; he can get a farthing from a widow even if she has no shoes. Francis, in one dramatic moment of truth, had carried the Gospel to its logical conclusion, and kissed a leper. Chaucer's Friar knows hostlers and bartenders "better than lepers"; he thinks the poor beneath his dignity and prefers rich franklins. Francis wept for his sins and moved the hearts of others to repentance. Chaucer's Friar pretends to believe that if a man is hard of heart, it is a sign of contrition if he makes a gift to the order.

In his unworldly wisdom, Francis had wished to ban not only private but communal ownership of property by his followers. Chaucer, I think, sympathized with that dream. The worldly wise argued that the brothers needed permanent homes, that if you're building you might as well build well, and that anyhow, the whole enterprise was for the glory of God and the service of men. But as Chaucer (and Wycliffe and Gower) saw it, the establishment had become an end in itself. The Friar of the Prologue, like his brother in The Summoner's Tale, commits all the sins, but is a pillar of his house because he is a great fund raiser (even if he keeps a share for himself). What especially irked Chaucer was that the worldly success of the friars was ensured by their hypocritical protestations of imitating the unworldliness of their founder. He portrays them preying on the gullible piety of the laity and glorying in the status which they disclaim. And even those who see through their role-playing treat them with respect because of the role.

The Summoner's Tale reflects the various contemporary attitudes toward the friars. By way of Prologue, the rough Summoner says that the Friar knows so much about hell (to which this fellow-pilgrim had sent the Summoner in his tale) because millions of friars have their nest under Satan's tail. In the story which follows, the Summoner, with the subtle cunning of a Chaucer, gives friars high marks for zeal, business acumen, hypocrisy, vainglory, and manipulation of women. He shows his friar busily rushing from church to private homes, preaching, and lying, and collecting. Rather like the cat he dispossesses from the bench in Thomas's house, he values his comfort. He enjoys his work of greeting the wife with a kiss and ordering a simple dinner for a "spiritual man," who, he says, is "nourished by the Bible" and "wants no beast hurt for his sake"— just a "capon's liver, a roasted pig's head, and soft bread."

In a long dramatic monologue, part sermon, part exhortation, the friar claims for himself and his order all the virtues they lack. Having just demonstrated his gluttony, he has the audacity to claim the abstinence of Moses, Aaron, and Jesus. With singular lack of humility, he says the friars' prayers are more acceptable than those of Thomas, his host. He blames Thomas's continued sickness on his dividing his contributions to the various orders in-

45

stead of giving all to his, "not for himself," but for the building of a new church. The final irony is that he preaches against anger to the bedridden old man just before he becomes enraged "as a lion" by the trick Thomas plays on him.

The vulgar trick is perfectly appropriate not only because it defeats his greed while exposing it but because it humiliates the proud friar and his whole convent. And the way the jest is mixed with earnest in the following scene conveys the psychologically curious relationship between the friar and the household of a man of high rank. From their own words it is clear that the lord and his lady perceive the lack of Christly savor in this friar, and they go along with the final joke at his expense, even rewarding the squire who devised the insulting plan. In spite of the mockery, however, all treat the friar with superficial courtesy, and there is no suggestion that they will change confessors or disinherit the order in their wills.

Moving from the friars to that little group within the group, the Prioress, the Second Nun, and the Nun's Priest, we are a bit startled at the notion of the nuns listening to these fabliaux. Certainly there is no coarseness in the two women, and the worldliness of the Prioress is a far cry from the Friar's. The deference with which the Host treats the Nun Prioress is much more sincere than that accorded the Friar, partly because of the generally better reputation of nuns, partly because of the particular elegance of this Prioress. Every detail of Chaucer's description suggests elegance, from her romantic name to her genteel table manners and handsome clothes.

All the innkeepers in the world would respect such a lady, but did Chaucer? As the clue to the Monk's character is the bells on the saddle which ring as loud as the chapel bell, the clue to the Prioress's character is her effort to imitate courtly behavior. In his poem called "Truth," Chaucer advises even a young nobleman to flee the court, and everybody knew that a nun was supposed to imitate Christ and Mary, not Guenevere or even the good Blanche in *The Book of the Duchess*. This nun is so successful in her copying of court manners that if we omit the first line of identification, we might not guess that the lady described is a nun; even her rosary is the type carried by well-to-do ladies outside the convent. It is "respect" such as theirs that she covets; but the Parson says in his sermon that the world's respect is reversed in hell, where no more reverence is given to a king than a knave. This lady may not be on her way to hell, but she has certainly adapted the rule of poverty and obedience to her personal tastes, and her order of priorities is not quite that of the founder of her religion.

Chastity, however, is high on her list, and I do not think that the ambiguous motto on her rosary, "Love conquers all," implies that she has broken her vow of chastity. In the light of the development of her character and personality in her prologue and tale, it appears that while her "love" falls short of Christian charity, it is not lechery. She simply loves dogs and children better than men and women. There is no reason to doubt the sincerity of her praise of virginity; indeed, when it is of the seven-year-old martyr in her tale, it seems excessive to us. Whether or not it seemed excessive to Chaucer, it perfectly suits the Nun. If she does not have charity, she has chastity, and I think Chaucer would not have said, as did Langland, that chastity without charity will be chained in hell. Chaucer's subtle handling of the Prioress shows that he well understood the difference. The Prioress's devotion to Mary, limited but sincere, is a redeeming quality.

It may indicate something of Chaucer's view of nuns that he nowhere portrays an unchaste one, as he might easily have done in one of the fabliaux told by the rough-necks. The only other nun in *The Canterbury Tales* is the Prioress's assistant, called the Second Nun, and she too praises virginity sincerely. Since she is not described in the General Prologue, and since the tale she tells was probably not written or adapted for her, we cannot tell much about her, and indeed, Chaucer may not have given her much thought. But perhaps it is not going too far to say that the attribution to her of poetry, which he probably wrote in his own voice, reflects certain favorable assumptions on his part. It is likely that Chaucer assigned her the tale of St. Cecilia because a legend of chastity and martyrdom seemed suitable for a nun. In this, the nuns and their stories are alike. On the other hand, their prologues and stories are dissimilar enough in style to suggest that Chaucer did not think all nuns were alike.

In her prologue as in her tale, the Prioress is attracted to the infantile. She begins by saying that God is praised not only by men of dignity but by the mouths of children, sometimes by babes sucking at the breast (an allusion to the legend of St. Nicholas, who allegedly took the breast only once on Wednesdays and Fridays). Therefore she will do the best she can to tell a story in praise of Mary. But her learning is so weak that she is like a child of twelve-months-old or less who can hardly speak a word; therefore she prays that Mary will guide her song. Some of her lines are charmingly lyrical in a convincingly childlike way.

The very movement of the verse of the Prologue to The Second Nun's Tale is more rugged. While the Prioress begins, "O Lord, our Lord, thy name how marvellous/ Is in this large world spread," the Second Nun begins "The minister and the nurse to vices,/ Which men call in English idleness." This devotee of Mary needs help, not because of childish incapacity, but because she is a mature and intellectual person, who is troubled by the body, by the weight of earthly desires and false affections, and who therefore asks for wit and time to accomplish the works without which faith is dead.

One of the characters in The Second Nun's Tale is the highest member of the hierarchy, the pope. Pope Urban is a saint of the early Church, who loves chastity and charity, who preaches, baptizes, and buries the dead. Persecuted for the faith, he lives with "light heart" in a cave among the poor. Since Urban was martyred in the year 230, we cannot deduce Chaucer's opinion of the fourteenth-century papacy from this portrait, but taken with the rest of his work, it does tell us something of Chaucer's views. What is remarkable, by contrast with the attacks on the popes by other medieval writers, is that there is nothing derogatory about the papacy in Chaucer's works.

Orthodox critics did not go quite as far as Wycliffe, who desired to reform the "anti-Christ" and his office out of existence. But as was observed earlier in this chapter, orthodox Dante, Langland, Gower, and countless others criticized the popes with at least as much enthusiasm as they did friars and monks. Nor were the popes beyond the range of comical satire. In that most famous collection of stories called the *Decameron*, written only a few decades before *The Canterbury Tales*, Boccaccio told the story of the odd way in which the pope contributed to the conversion of a virtuous Jew named Abraham. Abraham's Christian friend, who sincerely desired his conversion, was appalled when Abraham decided to go to Rome to see the way of life of the pope and the cardinals, but could not dissuade him. This intelligent and sober-minded Jew, says Boccaccio, saw how prelates were sunk in lewdness—gluttony, wine-bibbing, and open simony. Returning to his friend in France, Abraham surprisingly announced his conversion.

He said that having considered the papal zeal for destroying Christianity, he concluded that only the presence of the Holy Spirit could explain the continued growth of the religion.

There is no trace of this tone in Chaucer. He does not even use his technique of negatives on this subject. He could easily have said in the Second Nun's Tale, for example, that this early Pope Urban was *not* a luxurious simoniac; but there are no such thrusts, although there are many openings. In the General Prologue, it is observed that the wicked Pardoner has come with his false pardons from Rome, but no mention is made of the pontiff. The other references to the papacy are uniformly respectful. In The Man of Law's Tale, the pope arranges the marriage of Constance to the converted Sultan, and later in the story, King Alla goes to Rome to ask penance of the pope, both acts right and proper. The Clerk's Tale contributes a brief episode which implies considerable confidence in Rome. When Walter wants to calm the indignation of the people over his proposed remarriage, he decides that a papal bull approving his divorce will satisfy his subjects. Whereupon Walter forges a counterfeit bull. Again, the possibilities for innuendo are obvious, but Chaucer does not avail himself of them. The impression conveyed by Chaucer is that popes are at least honest and competent, at best, brave and saintly.

Besides the Second Nun, a Priest is also accompanying the Prioress. Chaucer tells us very little directly about him, but apparently he is a not especially esteemed member of the Prioress's entourage. The Host, who so often gives us the clue to the status of the pilgrims, treats him with condescension, even using the familiar "thou" when calling on him for a story. Shrewdly evaluating his situation, the Host tells him to be happy even if his horse is a lean jade; just make sure, he counsels, that your heart is always merry. The Nun's Priest, as he is always called, is apparently accustomed to doing as he is told. "Yes, sir," he replies, "unless I am merry, I know I will be blamed."

That the person who might blame the Priest is the Prioress is apparent in the course of his merry tale of Chanticleer. The Prioress is the boss; the Priest grumbles at his dependence but is a little afraid of her, whether of her tongue or her ability to fire him we do not know. He takes revenge, I think, with a deliberate mistranslation of a Latin phrase in the midst of his tale. "In principio, mulier est hominis confusio," cock Chanticleer tells Pertelote; hastily mistranslating, he says that that means that woman is man's joy and all his bliss. Now the Prioress, who knew the Latin liturgy, could surely read Latin well enough to understand that the line means, "In the beginning, woman is man's confusion." But might it not slip by her orally? The Priest was in a position to know if her protestations of ignorance were not due to modesty alone.

Sir John himself seems knowledgeable enough, but there is not much on which to judge the quality of his priesthood. There are no slurs on his moral conduct, and he is apparently living in poverty and obedience of a sort. His tale is one of the few that is funny without being ribald, and he moralizes it at the end, saying it is not just a fable of a cock and a hen. "Take the meaning, good men," he says, "for St. Paul says that all is written for our instruction. . . . Take the fruit and leave the chaff." A delightful story, we think, a good enough man—a good enough priest. But if the Parson represents the ideal, the Nun's Priest represents the mediocre. So far from cringing before what the Parson would have called the "high estate" and the "pomp" of the Prioress, the Parson, in the Nun's Priest's place, would have rebuked the head of the convent herself for her fine

51

clothes and pet dogs. And in the prologue to his own tale, the Parson pointedly refuses to tell a "fable"; also citing St. Paul, and using the same imagery as the Nun's Priest, he says that Paul reproves those who tell fables. Why should he sow chaff when he can sow wheat? We are expected to enjoy the fable more than the sermon, but Chaucer lets us know the Parson is the better priest.

Monks, friars, priests, all have clearly defined ranks, with corresponding regulations. Chaucer's "clerks," however, are a most diverse assortment, some being "clerics" in our sense, that is, priests, others being university students at large. Gower, in the *Vox Clamantis*, raises the question of why scholars want to be priests. The reason he advances sounds like one sometimes cynically suggested by postulants for the teaching profession in the twentieth century: they want a job with "position" and plenty of free time. In fact, many medieval students never went as far as holy orders, but filled the lower ranks of the civil service instead. But higher education, which had begun as training for the priesthood, remained ecclesiastical in organization and orientation. Even a man who left the university to go home and marry, like the Wife of Bath's fifth husband, was still called a "clerk." A frequently cited, and most illuminating, fringe benefit of the title was that law-breaking clerics escaped the common law since they were tried by notoriously more lenient ecclesiastical courts.

Emerging from this heterogeneous picture, the Clerk of Oxford supplies a model of the medieval university man. Apparently a priest who qualifies for a post, he is still pursuing his studies, probably for a Master's Degree. The proverbial poor scholar, he is thin, his overcoat is threadbare, and even his horse is "lean as a rake." The fact that he would rather have "twenty volumes of Aristotle" at his bed's head than "rich robes" or a "fiddle" tells us about his way of life and tastes. Austere and philosophical, he is too unworldly to seek secular office, and we can guess that he will be a professor some day rather than a parish priest. Parson or professor, the whole community was intended to benefit from his services; therefore, according to the medieval social contract, those who could afford to do so were obliged to support such poor students, who in turn were to pray for their souls. Surviving begging letters and responses to them give amusing evidence of the insolent demands of some of the college boys and of their unacademic expenses. But Chaucer's Clerk of Oxford spent all the money given by friends and patrons on books and learning, and "busily prayed" for the souls of the donors. "Gladly would he learn and gladly teach," is Chaucer's concluding note to the portrait of this scholar for all times.

On the other hand, the Host's treatment of the Clerk suggests Chaucer's awareness of the businessman's perennially ambivalent attitude to such scholars, even if they are priests. Remarking that the Clerk rides "quiet as a maid," the knowing Host advises him on company manners and literary techniques. Solomon says everything has its time, the Host admonishes, and now is the time not for study but for a tale. But, explains the Host, don't make us weep for our sins the way friars do in Lent, and don't put us to sleep. Keep your high style for another occasion, and speak plainly for us. The Clerk's response and tale fill out the portrait begun in the General Prologue. The Clerk agrees to "obey" the Host as director of the pilgrimage. And he tells a tale he learned in Padua from another clerk, one Petrarch, "now dead and nailed in his chest, may God rest his soul!" After a brief lecture, both pedagogical and moral, on Petrarch, the Clerk tells his moral tale of the patient Griselda.

The clerks in The Miller's Tale and The Reeve's Tale

are so different from this paragon that almost they ought not to be called clerics. Some translators do, in fact, prefer "student" to "clerk," a satisfactory substitution most of the time. And Nicholas and Absolon in The Miller's Tale and Alan and John in The Reeve's Tale are typical college boys in many ways, even in their scorn of the non-academic community. But although they do not behave like Christians, these students are clerics; in the Church for everything they can get, perhaps even the chance to save their ill-spent lives from the gallows with a neck-verse.

The Miller and the Reeve, as well as the characters in their tales, take for granted the sexual promiscuity, the lying and cheating of the clerks. But a word here and a phrase there suggest that even while telling a fabliau, Chaucer was contrasting these students with the virtuous Clerk. Clever Nicholas in The Miller's Tale, for example, is also a clerk of Oxford, and his room is described as is the Clerk's in the General Prologue. Instead of a study, however, Nicholas has a sweet-smelling room, suitable for an "expert" in "secret love affairs." Instead of Aristotle, Nicholas has textbooks of astrology. It is noted that the good Clerk has no musical instrument; Nicholas has a harp to which he sings all the time. Thus, says the narrator, Nicholas spent his time at "the expense of his friends" who provided the revenue for him. Unlike the modest Clerk, Nicholas exploits his clerkly standing: he calls the old carpenter "John," while referring to himself as "Master Nicholas," and he puts himself forth as an interpreter of God's will, in order to achieve his immoral ends.

Absolon in the same tale is a worldling who plays the guitar and the fiddle; he is a parish clerk who carries the censer on holy days and takes the collection. This is only one of his jobs, however, and it seems unlikely that he is in training for the priesthood. Not only is he a dandy who wears bright clothes, but he knows how to let blood, cut hair and shave, and draw up legal deeds. The quality of his spirituality is indicated not only by his pursuit of the carpenter's wife, but by his remark that he would sell his soul to the devil to be revenged.

Not to favor one university over the other, Chaucer sets The Reeve's Tale in Cambridge. Honorable young men these two students seem at first, anxious to keep their college from being cheated by the miller who grinds their corn. They hope to outwit the miller, who in turn thinks he can outsmart the greatest scholar. In the ensuing contest of immorality, the dishonors are about even. The miller robs them, they take revenge by getting into bed with his wife and daughter. Scholars that they are, one of them reasons that there is a law that says that if a man be grieved in one point, he should be relieved in another; the other thinks that the proverb that God helps those who help themselves suits his case.

No logic-chopping can save face for the two most shameful characters in *The Canterbury Tales*, the Summoner and the Pardoner, and Chaucer suggests no ideal type for them. Whatever Christian values were connected originally with their jobs apparently no longer seemed viable to Chaucer—or to anybody else we still read. Medieval summons-servers were petty officers (not priests) who were paid to summon sinners to trial before an ecclesiastical court, presumably to reform their morals. The Friar remarks in the prologue to his tale that everybody knows no good can be said of a summoner. The Friar's word, of course, cannot be trusted, but certainly no good can be said of the Summoner on the pilgrimage, and Chaucer implies only ill of the system in the portraits in the General Prologue and in The Friar's Tale.

The Friar says in his tale that there was no slyer fellow

FRIAR

in all of England than a certain summoner. This "Judas" made a great profit by blackmail. Without telling his superior, the archdeacon, without showing a warrant, he threatened with excommunication uneducated men who filled his purse to silence him. Prostitutes in his spy system told him who lay with them so that he could draw up false warrants for purposes of extortion. "To give him his due," the Friar says, "he was a thief, a summoner, and a pimp."

Like the summoner in The Friar's Tale, the Summoner in the General Prologue commits all the sins for which he cites others, and they are all written on his face. Children are afraid of his "fire-red face," with "whelks and knobs" no ointment can cure. For a quart of wine he would let a friend have his girl for a year, and he has in his power all the young people of the diocese.

Behind the hunting Monk is the saintly Benedict; behind the hypocritical Friar is the saintly Francis. As Chaucer shows it, behind the vicious Summoner is only a corrupt system, the archdeacon being only an educated version of the Summoner. It is with a sardonic account of the archdeacon's Christian justice that the Friar begins his tale. Naming the sins for which people could be summoned, the Friar concludes that they could not escape "pecuniary pain." The Friar is a prejudiced witness, but on this point Chaucer apparently agrees with him. In the Gen-

eral Prologue, Chaucer denounces not only the pecuniary
punishment imposed by the archdeacon but his abuse of the
power of excommunication. If the Summoner found
another rascal like himself, Chaucer says, he would teach
him to have no fear of excommunication, because "purse is
the archdeacon's hell." As naïve fellow-pilgrim, Chaucer
innocently thinks the Summoner lied since every guilty
man ought to dread excommunication; as creator, Chaucer
is making a bitter joke that would have pleased all the
reformers. And it should be observed by the way that the
good Parson does not avail himself of the system, being
reluctant to report those who do not pay tithes.

With the Summoner rides his friend the Pardoner.
These two minor functionaries of the Church have much in
common, especially love of money and indifference to morality. In a carefully drawn parallel, however, they are
shown to be not twins, but the opposite sides of a counterfeit coin. Singing a popular song together, the Summoner
carries the bass while the Pardoner sings the refrain. The
dark Summoner is "hot and lecherous as a sparrow," while
the blonde Pardoner is "a gelding" or "a mare." The Summoner is the incarnation of physical sin, the Pardoner
comes close to disembodied evil. Falsely cursing the innocent, the Summoner harms only the body; falsely pardon-
ing the guilty, the Pardoner injures the soul.

The irony of the Pardoner's autobiographical Prologue
is exceptionally bitter, bare of any pretence of decency.
The hypocritical Friar at least pays lip service to religion;
the honest Pardoner brags of how he exploits the religion of
others in his single-minded devotion to money. Less scru-
pulous than the fiend in The Friar's Tale, the Pardoner has
diabolical intelligence, and he delights in his skill, telling
the pilgrims that it is a joy to see him at work. When
Chaucer tells us that the Prioress imitates the manners of

court ladies, he does not imply that she has made a conscious choice of the world over Christ. But the Pardoner
judges himself. He explains how he stirs the ignorant to
devotion, and shames and defames skeptics so that they
offer money while he "spits out" his "venom under hue of
holiness." He preaches against avarice to make the people
free of their pence, and he doesn't care if their souls go
"blackberrying!" Even the moral tale he is about to tell the
pilgrims he usually preaches for gain.

At the end of his superlatively moral tale, he slips into
his customary sales talk and invites the Host to offer money
and kiss his relics. The Host's vulgar response expresses a
singularly accurate appraisal of the Pardoner's vocation:
You would make me kiss your old breeches and swear they
were the relic of a saint, he says, even if they "were painted
with your fundament." Instead of relics, the Host wishes he
had the Pardoner's testicles in his hand; he would carry
them "enshrined in a hog's turd." The insulting words of
the Host are a daring metaphor for the Pardoner's physical
and spiritual powers, the Pardoner having been called a
spiritual eunuch by more polite commentators.

The false pardons are a worse desecration of the holy
than the fake relics, relics being of the saints, the pardon of
Christ himself. The phrases are unfamiliar to the modern
ear, but many a medieval Lenten sermon elaborated on the
pardon of the New Law, "bought" by the Passion of Christ,
to use the medieval term. The practice of giving indulgences developed from the innocent-enough desire to extend the mercy of Christ while recognizing the claims of
justice by requiring penance or almsgiving. But Chaucer
presents only this Pardoner, in whom there is neither justice nor mercy, and who is the antithesis of Christ himself.
By his death on the Cross, Christ bought true pardon for
the mankind he loved. By his greed in the Church, the

Pardoner sells false pardons to the people he hates. And as the Church was founded on the great Pardon, it all but foundered on false pardons such as these.

Everybody knows that the selling of indulgences was one of the causes of the Reformation. Chaucer certainly hated the practice and may have wished to see the end of it. But apparently he did not desire the end of the orders of monks, friars, and nuns. The Monk, the Friar, and the Prioress are not urged to throw off the habit and join the Merchant, the Franklin, and the Wife of Bath, but to follow the example of the founders of their orders. And in The Canon's Yeoman's Tale, each order is warned to discipline itself.

As the pilgrims are riding along, two men make a dramatic entrance. Shabbily dressed, without baggage, they are obviously shady characters. When the subordinate begins to reveal their secrets, the master, a Canon of the Church, flees "in sorrow and shame." What manner of man is this, in hiding, on the run, and yet in ecclesiastical, if torn, garb? We learn from his angry assistant that the Canon is a swindling alchemist, who plays confidence games on others who want to get rich quick, but remains poor himself because he tries ever unsuccessfully to turn base metal into gold. And the Yeoman, who probably speaks here for Chaucer, not only explains the harm done by such villains when they are protected by the Church but states unequivocally the doctrine of reform from within.

Part Two of The Canon's Yeoman's Tale begins with a description of a certain canon who could infect a whole town; with his tricks and lies he befuddles many men. Yet, the Yeoman says, men travel many a mile to seek his acquaintance, not knowing his falseness. As the Yeoman sees it, as the orthodox reformers saw it, it was the responsibility of the authorities to expose the "falseness." The Yeoman protests that he is not slandering all canons, and that his intent is to correct not only them but others also. Everybody knows, he says, that among Christ's disciples there was only one traitor, Judas; the rest, who were guiltless, ought not to be blamed. The Yeoman's advice, then, is to expel rascals early, lest they cause shame and disgrace.

This direct address to the "reverend canons" is obviously inappropriate for the Yeoman riding along with the Canterbury pilgrims, among whom there is not one canon. The reasonable suggestion has been made that the Tale was originally composed to be read by Chaucer to an audience composed of, or at least including, canons. Whatever the circumstances of its composition, it serves in the *Tales* as an apologia for all Chaucer's attacks on the clergy. The "others" for whom the Yeoman says his story is intended may be the monks and friars and nuns whom Chaucer wishes not to slander but to correct.

God forbid, the Yeoman says, that the whole company should be judged by one man's wickedness; among Christ's apostles there was only one traitor. Among Chaucer's clerical characters, the percentage of traitors is much higher, and indeed, the whole medieval Church has been judged by them, perhaps unfairly. For example, one would never guess from the representatives in *The Canterbury Tales* that the great majority of monks stayed in the cloister, said their prayers, copied the manuscripts to which later scholars are so indebted, and went unnoticed. So goes the argument for silence against those ill-mannered people who write exposés. But while it is true that historians ought to distinguish satire from documentary, it may also be true that without the exposé, the cover-up corrupts the whole country. Chaucer, I think, was neither muckraker nor revolutionary, but a middle-of-the-road reformer who had good reason for washing dirty linen in public.

There was not much to be gained from writing polite letters to the bishops or archdeacons. Those who were not corrupt themselves had already outlined the standards and decreed the punishments, from reprimands to excommunication to prison terms, for everything from keeping pets in convents to selling false pardons. The problem was to implement the decrees in a society, as Chaucer shows it, in which on the one hand, the line between clergy and laity was often far from clear, while on the other, the institution was often an end in itself rather than a means to reach God. How could "the Church" control the clerks we see in *The Canterbury Tales?* Students who lived in colleges could be disciplined for flagrant misconduct, but the school was not considered to be *in loco parentis,* and nobody tucked the resident boys in, not to mention off-campus types, like Nicholas in The Miller's Tale. Besides, the laxity of the monasteries was hard to correct because of the solid tenure of monks, nuns, and friars. Prohibitions and penalties were often proclaimed, but visiting bishops were likely to be treated like policemen, and the brethren (rather like physicians, politicians, and professors) covered up for each other.

Chaucer, I believe, wished to change the institution by changing the people in it. Stories such as his were the communications media of the time through which minds and consciences could be awakened. Open your eyes, the Canon's Yeoman says, and see the harm this Canon does because men do not know his falseness. And in every clerical portrait, Chaucer reminds his audience, clerical and lay, of the good while condemning the bad.

His poetry is not, of course, the heavy-footed propaganda this analysis unwittingly conveys. He was not writing a handbook for contemporaries or a documentary for posterity, with charts of statistics of sanctity. But the Church played an important part in his interpretation of life, and on this score, there was no conflict between his spiritual and aesthetic values. The Truth he served required that he not minimize the evil which corroded the good. In that service he used all his literary skill; his wit here is least genial and most like a knife, perhaps because he hoped to cut out the cancer without killing the patient.

III

The Church and the Laity

e have all read old textbook accounts of the authoritarian Church which brain-washed generations of our ancestors into spending this life on their knees preparing for the next. When we read medieval fabliaux like The Miller's Tale, however, we think we have been misled. Most surprising in such cynical stories is their lack of surprise; men and women lie, cheat, drink, swear, fight, and fornicate with enormous gusto and no apparent sense of sin. There is such open enjoyment of the world and the flesh in some of the more popular *Canterbury Tales* that the secularly oriented reader may think that the framework of pilgrimage is just a literary device for bringing together diverse types and classes, and that a bus ride to Miami would really be more suitable. To secularize the journey, however, would diminish the humanity of the characters as well as the meaning of the author, and would require the elimination of a large block of material in which there is evidence that the Church's program of thought control was not wholly a failure. Indeed, Chaucer himself is proof of its success. Once we overcome our own rather narrow preconceptions of what is properly secular or improperly religious, we can see that Chaucer's lay characters illustrate the vices and virtues that trouble and bless a Christian household and a Christian commonweal; and that his own poems of personal piety confirm the basically moral impression of the body of his fiction.

It is not always easy to see what Chaucer's preconceptions were. Most pleasant of authors to read, he is not easiest to interpret; first of all, because of his complex ironies and secondly because, apart from a few short poems, he so rarely says in his own voice what he thinks. Since his contemporaries, such as the authors of *Piers Plowman* and *Sir Gawaine and the Green Knight*, often do say explicitly what is only implicit in *The Canterbury Tales*, they can serve as both background and commentary for Chaucer, if we are careful not to limit Chaucer to them. The fact seems to be that, with all due allowance for variations, there was broad agreement on the general moral principles that applied to laymen, and on the specific obligations entailed by vocation and class. Further, there were important links between the teaching of the Church and the way men thought about such lay concerns as social justice, chivalry, beauty, and war, to sample the most interesting.

The medieval laity, virtuous and sinful, in and out of fiction, do not seem to have challenged the general proposition that the Church was the teacher of morality. She was not the only teacher. As we shall see in a later chapter, Christian thinkers did not limit God to the Church but believed all men could understand justice, fortitude, prudence, and moderation, by the light of reason. Practically speaking, however, the medieval Christian learned even these pagan virtues from the Church, which called them "cardinal" from Latin "cardo"—the "hinges" on which all morality turns. So it is that in the description of the founding of the Church in *Piers Plowman,* Grace gives Piers seeds of corn called the cardinal virtues to sow in the souls of men; he then harrows the ground with the Old and the New Laws so that Love may grow among the virtues and destroy the vices.

The Old Law and the New—medieval literature is filled with references to their history and significance. Simplest in the education of the layman was the unadorned listing of the Ten Commandments of the Old. In the medieval play of *Moses* (the Hegge), for example, after the prophet receives the tables of the Law from God, he turns and teaches the Commandments to the audience. This was the basic knowledge needed for entrance into a quite nonelitist heaven. In *Piers Plowman* Langland's character "Dowel" did not need to know Aristotle or Augustine to understand Thou shalt not steal, or murder, or covet your neighbor's wife. Nor did he need to be a philosopher to comprehend the New Law which, as they said, "fulfilled" the Old as "Thou shalt love God and your neighbor." The Church Fathers and their medieval descendants were fond of quoting (as did Jimmy Carter in his inaugural address) the words of the Hebrew prophet Hosea, who said that the Lord requires men not to offer sacrifices, but to do justly, to love mercy, and to walk humbly. This is the unchanging law of God, the Church taught, fulfilled by Christ in his life and death.

There were also the man-made rules of the Church concerning sacraments and ceremonies, and including the obligations of almsgiving and support of the Church. Reformers complained that the people, encouraged by greedy or illiterate priests, emphasized these last items. Preachers and poets, including Chaucer, never tire of portraying

65

characters who hope to evade the moral law with the help of the institutionalized Church. Langland typically warns rich men not to make bold to break the Commandments because they count on Masses to be said after their death. Unless Do-wel speaks for them, he would not give a "peas-cod" for all their pardons and certificates!

Judging from the number of statements like Langland's, there must have been sermons that assured salvation to those who ignored the moral law while observing the ritual; I have yet to find one. Typical of those that have survived is insistence such as Langland's that baptism is not enough; Lady Scripture in *Piers* says that we must first have love and faith and fulfill the law of love. By love, Lady Church explains to the rather dull Dreamer, God created all his works; He taught Moses that Love was so heavy that heaven could not hold it, but let it fall to earth. Even if you are honest and chaste, she insists, unless you love men truly and share the goods God gave you, you will "have no more merit from your Masses" than "old Molly from her maidenhead that no man wants." Langland was not discarding Masses and sacraments any more than he was advising fornication for old Molly. But in his view, Holy Church herself establishes the priorities and teaches the laity that love and truth must come first for every class of society. (Kings and knights should be Truth's champions, he says, and not think fasting on Friday is enough.) And it is giving which is the key to unlock Love and Truth and show the direct way to heaven. Only after charity are the sacraments spiritually fruitful.

How far the laity followed the teaching of the Church is another matter. In a dark moment, good Bishop Brinton remarked that in all the years of his priesthood, he had not known any one in the congregation to give up vice as a result of his preaching. Fictional sinners, including Chaucer's, demonstrate a higher but still moderate rate of repentance. Langland's Dreamer dreams of a whole field full of folk repenting after a sermon by Reason on the seven deadly sins of pride, envy, anger, avarice, gluttony, sloth, and lechery. But on his way to confession, Gluttony drops into the local pub and gets drunk with Cissie the Shoemaker, Tim the Tinker, Clarice the Whore, and other low-life characters. Similarly, Langland's Brewer (who would be comfortable on Chaucer's Pilgrimage) feels sorry for his sins, but even when faced with the Last Judgment continues to water his beer.

The rich and the aristocratic were castigated not only for personal faults but for what we consider social, or anti-social, behavior. Many a sermon is extant in which those who live in luxury are called murderers of those who die of hunger. In this teaching, the Church was avowedly following the traditional Hebraic concern for the poor, the widowed, and the stranger. This concern went considerably beyond what "supply and demand" economists think suitable for the welfare of the state: in the logic of the Hebrew prophets, it is a "sin" not to feed the hungry. And since the obligation is to God, the worthiness of the recipient is irrelevant. What you do to the least of these, Jesus had said, you do to me. And in many a medieval legend, such as that of St. Martin, the recipient of the half of the giver's cloak turns out to be Jesus himself. It follows that the almsgiver must be courteous because the recipient is really God. Further, not only almsgiving but just wages, fair prices, honest workmanship, and even scholarships for needy students were moral obligations, and failure to perform them was matter for confession. Medieval social doctrine was based on this religious obligation, which proposes social justice as the fruit of love of God and neighbor. Judging from endowments and bequests, the resulting social system worked better than we might expect. But of course, it often didn't work at all, as the complaints of the poor bear witness.

What Dante, Langland, Gower, Chaucer, and all the other proponents of the doctrine meant was that the rich should give, not that the poor should take. But when occasionally the poor rebelled against the oppressions of the rich, they claimed only to be putting into practice this theoretic teaching which they, too, had heard from the pulpit. As they marched in the Peasants' Rebellion in 1381, they chanted a rhyme, probably composed by a priest named John Ball, which questioned the whole class structure as being out of line with the accepted doctrine that all are children of one Father, entitled to share in the heritage of the earth. "When Adam delved and Eve span," they demanded, "Who was then the gentleman?" Alas, those in power ruthlessly put down the rebellion with terrible slaughter of the diggers and spinners.

The medieval doctrine of the gentleman was, in fact, so revolutionary that each generation avoided its implications: the doctrine held that true nobility is derived not from caste or cash but from God, the source of all goodness. "Gentilesse," as Chaucer called it, was propounded by St. Thomas Aquinas and by Dante, to name just two of the great, was widely proclaimed from the pulpit, and was required of knights in romances and books of chivalry.

It is hard to take chivalry seriously. A substantial amount of Mark Twain's parody in *A Connecticut Yankee in King Arthur's Court* is true, and the jokes would probably have amused Chaucer. But Chaucer would also, I think, have suggested that life would have been even worse without the high line—whether of chivalry or of democracy, the two indeed being related historically and theoretically. It is possible that chivalry was a sincerely Christian attempt to soften the harsh brutalities of lay society by channeling men's violence, by sublimating their lusts, and by satisfying their need for dreams and ceremony.

The poet John Gower gave in his *Vox Clamantis* three rather prosy reasons for the origin of chivalry: to protect the Church, to foster the common good, and to defend the cause of orphans and widows. Knighthood was not, he said, for fame but for justice, and feats of arms performed for love or for fame were both in vain. Manuals of chivalry, however, such as the one by Geoffroi de Charny, made concessions to weakness: even foolish knights, sent out on quests by foolish ladies, gain merit if they perform good deeds. Through love, another author writes, knights restore charity and learning; through fear they restore truth and justice. A knight must develop strength and skill, justice, wisdom, charity, loyalty, humility, and above all, mercy.

The knight's ritual of initiation combined psychiatry, religion, and ritual. On the eve of the ceremony, the newly confessed initiate remained long in the bath, thinking of cleansing body and soul, before sleeping in a new bed with clean sheets. Fellow knights dressed him in a red tunic, signifying the obligation to shed blood to defend the faith; black shoes served as a reminder of the earth from which he came and to which all must return, and told him to put all pride underfoot; a white belt symbolized chastity, a red mantle, humility. At Mass, sponsors put golden spurs on his feet to remove from his heart the evil desire for possessions. The bishop gave him the kiss of peace, and his sword was blessed to serve not private power but the will of God, and to guard the honor of poor girls, widows, and orphans.

Did it work at all? Preachers editorialized about marauding knights who were seeking loot for themselves rather than glory for God, and in the cruder popular romances, challenges, fights to the death, and stripping of armor are all too common. Further, in the most famous romances, the exploits are performed to impress a woman. There is plenty of evidence to support the verdict of a sixteenth-century moralist named Ascham who characterized the romances as "open manslaughter and bold bawdry." But equal time should be given to Ascham's contemporary, Sir Philip Sidney, who wrote of the "love of honor and honor of love." The issue of bawdry/love we will leave to the next chapter; what is of interest to us here is the way the quasi-religious, quasi-military qualities are carried over into fiction.

One of the most profound examples is found in *Piers Plowman,* in which Jesus, when he becomes man, takes the "armor" of Piers. Thus armed, he "wins his spurs" in Jerusalem in his contest with the devil on Good Friday. In Langland's apocalyptic vision, the knighthood of Jesus entirely transcends social class, the Plowman whose arms he takes being "gentil" only in virtue. Similar little allegories of Jesus as knight appear even in medieval sermons.

Far narrower in concept is Sir Galahad, who is still familiar to the twentieth century as a result of many retellings of the Arthurian legends. Galahad was said to be descended from Joseph of Arimathea and Sir Lancelot, a most suitable combination of religious and romantic legends. So purified of sensuality and selfishness is Galahad that he is more monk than soldier: brave and bold, he refrains from killing; handsome and winning, he is not even tempted by women; untiring and singleminded, he spends his leisure time in prayer with visiting angels. His daily life is crowded with religious ritual and miracle, some of it hard to distinguish from magic, all of it phrased in a mixture of knightly and religious jargon.

Far more appealing, from the spiritual as well as the aesthetic view, is Sir Gawaine, in *Sir Gawaine and the Green*

Knight, by an unknown contemporary of Chaucer's. Nothing could be more brilliant than the knighthood that flowers at this court of King Arthur, nothing more worldly than the furred and jeweled ladies with their elegant games of wit and seduction. And yet here too is plainly traced the model of Christian chivalry. The hero is a good knight, even by Langland's strict formula. Combining courtesy, morality, bravery, and prayer, he keeps a tryst with death, courteously refuses a beautiful woman, and is not embarrassed to say his prayers, attend Mass, and invoke the saints. Even his partial failure is part of the endearing lesson. Like all pilgrims of all ranks, he must learn humility, confess, and be reconciled to God and men.

Chaucer's Knight, as we shall see later in this chapter, was kin to these knights, and the Wife and Shipman could have joined Langland's Shoemaker and Tinker in the tavern. All of his characters have to cope with the same virtues and vices, and the fact that Chaucer does not always draw the moral as do these writers does not mean that his ethics are markedly different from theirs. For all the horseplay that Chaucer apparently enjoyed, love and truth are not mocked in his ribald jests. For example, in The Miller's Tale it may even be that underlying the jest is the moral that without love and truth men and women do not rise above backstairs fornication. The marvel is that Chaucer comes to the same truths in numerous ways and is comfortable with a dozen different styles.

With his subtle and complex ways, Chaucer worked very comfortably within the medieval paradox. He could write The Miller's Tale at the same time that he was translating (to go a long step beyond The Knight's Tale) *Contempt of the World;* he could reconcile delight in every flower with asceticism, and laughter at the tricks of knaves with reverence for the miracles of saints, not in spite of but because of his religious culture. Saints and knaves are all in the same Church as the author, and it is a Church which admires both virginity and fecundity, gorgeous vestments on bishops and rags on saints.

The various parts of the paradox come together in *The Canterbury Tales,* and the outer frame expresses the multi-layered inner meaning. The pilgrimage is a literary device; it is a vacation, a frolic, an escape; it is a literal journey to the shrine of St. Thomas à Becket; it is a symbolic passage from this world to eternity. That Chaucer makes a pilgrimage sound natural is both a tribute to his art and a reflection of a world in which religion seemed as inevitable as the changing seasons. In the famous opening of the Prologue, we hardly notice the shift from the natural to the supernatural, so smoothly does it occur. In a few lines, Chaucer moves from the piercing of the drought of March by the showers of April to the birds that "sleep all night with open eyes," so moved are they by the new season, to the similarly responding humans who desire to go on a pilgrimage to the shrine of a saint. It is hard to believe that all the sundry folk described later are really taking the trip to seek "the holy blissful martyr" who answered their prayers when they were sick in the winter. But Chaucer does not analyze their individual motives, and it is just possible that he means that on some level of consciousness, even the worst of them have a spiritual dimension different from the birds.

This motley crew is not just a cross section of humanity but a microcosm of the Church. That Church was avowedly composed of sinners, whose ultimate destination was known only to God. All the Christians in Chaucer's works are members of that visible society, by baptism, by circumstance, sometimes by conviction. Like Mother Church herself, Chaucer lets good and bad ride together on the same pilgrimage; riding along himself, he shows the impact of the Church on the world. The rogues reject or ignore the teaching, committing all the sins described by the Parson; at the same time, name days and feast days, blessings and curses, weddings and funerals, are part of their daily life. The virtuous Christians, whatever their social class or occupation, make use of the teaching, prayers, and sacraments of the Church, pretty much as these are expounded in *Sir Gawaine,* in *Piers Plowman,* and by Chaucer's own Parson, as a way to God. Finally, in the short poems, in the epilogue to the *Troilus,* and in the Retraction, Chaucer reveals himself as a devout Catholic layman who loved this world but spent some time on his knees preparing for the next.

In spite of all their sins, the lay people are presented in a less harsh light than the clergy we looked at in the last chapter. The Miller, the Reeve, the Host, are funny, and we laugh with them as well as at them, perhaps because they are not in a position to do as much spiritual harm as the Friar and the Monk. And while the laity are, like the clergy, identified by their station—the Knight, Physician, Man of Law, Wife of Bath—and even judged accordingly, the identification of role and person is less absolute. A monk who prefers hunting to praying is a contradiction in terms: we wonder why he is a monk. A lecherous thieving miller—we wonder why he is on a pilgrimage, but he still qualifies to grind corn. While the Franklin eats too much and the Wife marries too often, the one is not expected to be abstemious, nor the other virginal. The Shipman is a thief and a murderer who throws overboard the prisoners he takes at sea, but he is a good sailor who knows his craft, tides and harbors, and navigation. The description of the Pardoner's preaching is tinged with bitterness because his skill is the instrument of his avarice, but the excellence of his style is praised nonetheless. Skills are admirable, and it is one of Chaucer's to portray them as such, even if their possessor is otherwise unworthy. The individual is more than the sum of his sins.

This Zen-like delight in the thing itself is often mistakenly thought to be incompatible with medieval religion. It is, on the contrary, a vital part of medieval Catholicism and is important in understanding Chaucer's religious spirit. Admittedly there were puritans, flagellants, and theologians who thought it dangerous to do anything but fast and pray, and who concentrated on the ugliness of mortality; for example, Pope Innocent III, whose *Contempt of the World* Chaucer translated, and for whose views he must have had some sympathy. But the asceticism Chaucer expresses in his own works consists rather in giving up something good for something better. Clearly he delighted in many kinds of beauty and worked for perfection of form in his own art. The jewel-like windows of a Gothic cathedral, the intricate detail of a sculpted flower barely visible under the pedestal of a column, these bespeak a similar joy in craft and beauty that was fostered by the Church herself.

In theory, of course, the Church was not advocating art for art's sake. St. Augustine, for example, warned that the mind ought not dwell on beauty to gain physical pleasure; he stressed the necessity of moving to the spiritual, to the perception of the "immutable beauty of God." It was in this vein that one of the great cathedral builders, Abbot Suger, explained the proper way to admire the bronze doors on the Church of St. Denis: Marvel not at the gold, he said, but at the workmanship, which in its luminousness will illuminate minds so that they will travel to the True Light, where Christ is the True Door. Elsewhere Suger wrote of his "delight in the beauty of the house of God," which calls him away from external cares, from the material to the immaterial. It should be observed that this art for

74

God's sake does not in fact diminish the pleasure; as Suger's words suggest, the association with the infinite raises the value of the object itself.

In Christian aesthetics, the universe is beautiful in parts and in the whole. Augustine talked of the beauty of order and number, of mathematics and music, of the processes of life and the revolutions of the heavens, all being reflections of the cosmic order. The beauties of Creation Augustine called "the gestures of Eternal wisdom." St. Thomas Aquinas discussed beauty in terms of radiance, harmony, and wholeness, terms fraught with philosophical meaning. In a homely image, itself suggestive of union between God and man, St. Bonaventure compared the world to a wedding ring. The Bride, he said, ought not to value the ring more than she does the Bridegroom; on the other hand, she cannot scorn the gift without insulting the Giver. Putting it another way, the Physician in *The Canterbury Tales* says, when he is praising Virginia's beauty, that Nature, the vice-regent of God, is in full accord with Him. In his "Hymn to the Sun," St. Francis sang the same theme, and the music was not a device to make the words palatable but an essential part of the religious expression.

That fourteenth-century pre-Puritan, Wycliffe, denounced music in church as a distraction, and later Puritans thought that singing, not to mention dancing, constituted a danger to morality. There is enough Puritanism left in our psyches to make the picture of the company of pilgrims riding out of town with the Miller at the head of the procession playing on his bagpipes seem irreligious to us. To many medieval thinkers, however, sighing was more of a sin than singing. Depression was considered a sin rather than a sickness, and Dante puts in hell a man who let himself be sad in God's glad world. In Chaucer, singing is a good thing in itself, whatever the disposition of the singer.

75

Singing, dancing, and playing the flute are part of the Christian education of the Squire. The boy martyr in The Prioress's Tale sings a Latin hymn to our Lady as he walks to school. The lecherous Nicholas in The Miller's Tale also sings, both the *Angelus ad virginem* and "King William's Note"; and the rascal sings so sweetly that the people bless his merry throat. The very chickens, Chanticleer and Pertelote, sing "My Love Has Gone Away," and even the stern Parson alludes to a popular song, the music of which may not have been different from "church music." Like David before the ark, Christians were supposed to make a glad noise in the presence of the Lord.

But "glad" does not mean drunk and disorderly. Chaucer's Parson puts the world and eternity into Christian perspective for the pilgrims and for the reader. Quite different in tone from apocalyptic Piers and courtly Gawaine, the prosy Parson also counsels not flight from the world but a proper use of it. Health, strength, beauty, agility, freedom, good wit, sharp understanding, skill, good memory, and natural power are all gifts, he says; but they can be the source of woe if, instead of using them in the service of God, men abuse them. This careful balance, which reflects the official teaching of the Church, is expressed also in the Parson's teaching of the way to lead a Christian life in the world. A parish priest well aware of the sins of the pilgrims, he calls his stern sermon a merry tale. The only joke in it is the mildly satirical reference to a "new French song": those who have never done good works, he says, may well sing at the end of their time, "Jay tout perdu mon temps et mon labour." But his is a tale with a merry ending, for it is intended to guide this company to the heavenly Jerusalem. In brief, the sermon gives a counsel of perfection, balanced by a realistic appraisal of mankind, and a belief in the mercy of God.

76

Categorized in the style of the professional moralist, and dealing with the effects of virtue and vice on the commonweal as well as the individual, the sermon offers a convenient guide to the vices and virtues of the characters on the pilgrimage, bearing in mind the difference between a preacher's definition of sin and an artist's portrait of a sinner. The Parson condemns murder, adultery, stealing, and blasphemy, and he describes at length the seven deadly sins with all their subdivisions. But the degree of seriousness of specific acts depends on the intention of the sinner, and it is their inner disposition that the Parson wants men to examine. Sins must be cured from the heart, he says, by loving God and neighbor. That is why he calls envy the worst sin: while other sins are directed against one virtue, envy is directed against all goodness.

It follows from this emphasis on intention that the distinction between mortal and venial sins is quite flexible, and must be made by the sinner. Since the Parson says that anything less than loving the Lord with whole heart, mind, and soul constitutes venial sin, the list is long. It includes: eating, drinking, sleeping, or speaking more than necessary; listening impatiently to complaints of the poor; refusing, without cause, to fast; coming late to Church or other work of charity; "using a wife" without "primary desire of engendering" or "intent to yield the debt of body"; loving wife or child or anybody more than is reasonable; withholding alms from the poor; scorning a neighbor; having wicked suspicions, etcetera.

The list is formidable, but the Parson has conceded that nobody is free from venial sin, and his "more than is reasonable" shifts the burden of judgment to the individual. For example, unlike the clergy, the laity are not bound by vows of poverty; they must decide what is reasonable for their means, their station, and their obligation to charity.

77

So the Parson does not condemn "reasonable" uses of cloth-ing, houses, and entertainment, but only superfluity which springs from pride and which harms the poor. He complains that the gowns of men as well as women trail in the mire and dung and are wasteful. The more cloth wasted, the higher the price; and if such fancy clothes are given to the poor, they are not even useful for protecting them from bad weather. Similarly, "pride of table" causes hosts to invite rich men to dinner and send away and rebuke the poor.

This last rebuke expresses the Parson's concurrence in the belief that charity would leaven the lump of social and economic injustice by making the rich assume responsibil-ity for the poor. The Parson's is not an egalitarian philoso-phy; he says that God ordains higher and lower stations for the peace of the commonwealth. But he thinks aristocrats need to be reminded of the accidental nature of their posi-tion. It is foolish, he says, to pride oneself on good birth, which is a gift of fortune. All are of one father and one mother, Adam and Eve, and true gentility, "gentilesse," comes from being virtuous, courteous, and merciful. With something of Langland's fervor, the preacher accuses unjust lords of extortion in their treatment of the poor, and re-minds them that they will die in the same way as their own servants, and will receive the mercy of Christ by the same measure they have measured to the poor. They should re-member that humble folk are Christ's friends, and that the pope calls himself servant of the servants of God. Strong language this, appropriate for the Parson who, we are told in the General Prologue, sharply "snibbed" those of high estate. But is it appropriate for any of the pilgrims he is addressing on the road to Canterbury? This particular tongue-lashing was probably intended to represent a typical sermon such as was often directed to the courtly audience who would hear or read the *Tales* of that humorous and courtly poet, Chaucer—who wrote the Parson's sermon for him.

While Chaucer probably meant the message, the very structure of the fiction reveals a distinction of roles that was also meaningful to Chaucer, as his own classification into occupations suggests. The Church, personified in the Parson, was to preach social justice based on love of God and neighbor; the Knight was to protect the Church; other members of the laity were to carry out the preaching in the world in whatever way was suitable to their station. As manipulator of words, all of which should be "written for our instruction," the poet is also a teacher; but his medium is the fable rejected by the Parson. Chaucer is no "divine," he repeatedly tells us, but a teller of tales. Even The Tale of Melibeus, which is as moral as The Parson's Tale, is told as a story, not preached as a sermon, for its tone and content must suit the lay pilgrim Chaucer. Preaching his sermon as the pilgrimage nears its end, the Parson says that one of the ways to come to God is by penitence. He does not have to tell us that many of the pilgrims have a lot to be penitent about; the poet Chaucer has already told us, without making a sermon of it. From the stories and conversations heard on the journey, we know that the wicked have been committing the vices, and the virtuous following the precepts outlined by the Parson.

We cannot examine all the characters in *The Canterbury Tales*, but certain patterns emerge which reveal the quality of Chaucer's commitment to the moral teaching of the Church. Looking at the wicked first, the most obvious, but not most typical, *exemplum* is The Pardoner's Tale, in which three blasphemous, drunken thieves murder each other for gold, thus proving that the wages of sin are death. It is an excellent story, contrived perfectly to illustrate the Pardoner's sermon against covetousness, drunkenness, and blasphemy. And the tavern scene, like Langland's, gives us a vivid picture of medieval low life. Most of the pilgrim rogues, however, and many of the characters in the tales told by them, are more complex than these three thieves, and are seemingly conceived in accordance with the Parson's rather than the Pardoner's way. The Parson says that there is no sin that was not conceived first in the mind, and that the inner disposition is as important as the outward act. When Chaucer brings the sinners before us, he opens their minds to show us how they adapt the teaching of the Church to fit their individual desires, usually without any crisis of conscience.

As Chaucer shows it, the teaching of religion is not at fault. He seems to have made a distinction between the lives of the clerics and the doctrine they preach. The corrupt Pardoner and the hypocritical Friar teach as sound doctrine as the good Parson; and they do not even tell pornographic stories. Why, then, didn't the people heed this good instruction? Reformers, including the Parson, put a substantial part of the blame on the poor example of the preachers. On the other hand, the good example of the Parson is lost on many of those present, on the Host, for instance, who is not impressed by the Parson's sanctity or learning and who objects to being rebuked for swearing. Most of the evil-doers are not making conscious intellectual or spiritual choices but are following the urges of the flesh, or the attractions of the world, or business as usual.

While they have thus resisted conditioning in faith and morals, a number of the characters have absorbed a considerable amount of Catholic cult and culture. Many of them are unthinking Christians who do not examine their lives, but who are baptized, married, and buried in the Church, who swear by Christ and the saints, and who go to Mass as they go to meals. This ironic combination of "churchiness" with disregard of the meaning of the faith is sometimes comical, sometimes blasphemous. Alison in The Miller's Tale, for example, having just agreed to commit adultery with Nicholas, goes off to "worship Christ." Worse, the scheming monk and the merchant's wife in The Shipman's Tale go to Mass together with the husband they are scheming to deceive. Mass is celebrated before dinner, and everybody goes, before and after adultery.

Less culpable than adultery, ignorance is not often excused by Chaucer as invincible. Assuredly the old Carpenter in The Miller's Tale must be excused for his folly in marrying a young wench since we are told that he didn't know "Cato's dictum" that men should wed "after their own estate." Anyhow, the fabliau plot requires an old fool, and the Carpenter's superstition serves a comic purpose; the scene in which he makes the sign of the cross over Nicholas and recites the night spell is funny. When we look closely, however, we see that his stupidity is not a virtue. When the Carpenter first hears that Nicholas is in a trance, he says he thought it would turn out this way. Men should not pry into God's secrets, he says; "yea, blessed is the ignorant man who knows only his Creed!" And he recalls the story of another clerk who, studying the stars, fell into a pit. The Carpenter may not deserve his fate, but his pride in ignorance is not Christian simplicity.

January in The Merchant's Tale is a much wickeder version of the Carpenter. A similarly doting old fool, January tries to outwit God with the help of the Church, in a way to arouse Do-wel's ire. Having broken the sixth commandment for years as a bachelor, January thinks that the rite of marriage will be his license for both lust and heaven. Blinded by lechery and selfishness, he goes through the forms of religion while corrupting its essence.

In a catalogue of sins, those of the Wife of Bath would

have to go in the same section as January's, but unlike January, the Wife is an amusing companion. Chaucer makes us laugh at the way she uses Church functions for secular purposes. For example, he tells us that she is such a prominent parishioner that she goes up to make her offering first; no other woman dares precede her. She has been on many pilgrimages, three to Jerusalem, others to Rome, Bologna, Compostella, and Cologne; she knows a lot about "wandering by the way." In the prologue to her tale, she explains that one Lent—a season she finds appropriate for strolling and gossiping because it's pleasant to walk in the springtime—when her fourth husband was in London, she prudently provided for her future. The better to see and be seen by available males, she made visitations, went to festivals, processions, sermons, pilgrimages, miracle plays, and marriages, wearing her scarlet dress. And sure enough, her husband died. She pretended to cry at his funeral, a cheap one because it would have been wasteful to bury him expensively, God rest his soul. It was an enjoyable funeral, though, because one of the pallbearers had such fine legs and feet that she gave him her whole heart.

These liturgical observances form a perfect exterior for the Wife's inner belief: her theology is to God as her play in the field is to Lent. As she reverses the meaning of Lent, so she reverses the teaching of Jesus himself, as well as of St. Paul and the Parson. Lecherous, deceitful, quarrelsome, her talk is as filled with Scripture as her days are filled with processions and funerals; she is a very Catholic joke. She has brazenly adapted God and the Church to her real religion, sex and marriage. As she remarks, she would have chided her husbands in bed even if the pope had been present. And at the end of her tale, with great consistency she prays to Jesus Christ for husbands meek, young, and fresh in bed, and for the grace to outlive them.

Some of the blasphemy in the *Tales* is thoughtless jargon, as suitable to medieval society as four-letter words are to ours. Drunk or sober, the rough characters like the Shipman, the Host, and the Cook, curse with a fluency to be envied by a secular society. Often, however, the blasphemy makes an ironic point for an audience that knows God should not be invoked in aid

WIFE OF BATH

of wickedness. In The Miller's Tale, Absolon, for example, courting the Carpenter's wife who is in bed with the clerk, begs for a kiss "for Jesus' love." A little nastier is the oath sworn by the merchant's wife in The Shipman's Tale, never to repeat the monk's words—by God and by the prayer book—though she go to hell for it. Entirely sincere is the Reeve's prayer that the Miller break his neck.

The sins range from swearing to murder, but the sinners share one quality: like Bishop Brinton's parishioners, they do not examine their own consciences. It is because they do not see their own faults that they do not fear hell. They are not innocent, sinless creatures of nature or even hapless products of a faulty environment. They have been well taught by the Church; indeed, the Wife, the Host, the Reeve, all have a certain theological expertise in Scripture, sermon, and commentary. Most revealing, they clearly and correctly evaluate the faults of others, whom they liberally send to hell. This most important point is epitomized in a comment of the Reeve's. A carpenter himself, the Reeve is bitterly angry with the Miller for telling a tale at the expense of a carpenter. Planning to retaliate with a tale about a miller, the Reeve complains in Scriptural phrase that the Miller sees the mote in the Reeve's eye but not the beam in his own. He is right; but he does not see the beam in his own, either. His revenge, he thinks, is justice.

Are they beyond hope? Not if they repent. That is why the widow in The Friar's Tale must qualify her gift of the Summoner to the devil; if the Summoner repents, the devil cannot take him. It is to give the pilgrims a last chance that The Parson's Tale was intended to be the last before Canterbury; his tale is the Church's message of penitence. The same message is heard in medieval sermons, romance, and visions, and is directed to all classes of society. In *The Canterbury Tales* nothing has been spared us of the vice, folly, and frivolity of the pilgrims. But pilgrims they are, and if only they will look into their hearts and be sorry for their sins, they can be saved. Remember the thief on the cross, the Parson says; no sin is so horrible that it cannot be "destroyed by penitence" and by the "virtue of the passion" of Jesus Christ.

The virtuous characters, however they differ in rank, wealth, or accomplishments, consciously follow the law of God as taught by the Church. They are well instructed in faith and morals, but not especially busy in church affairs. Engaged successfully in manifold worldly activities, they are basically unworldly; whether they have much or little, they are not attached to material possessions. They exemplify the Parson's teaching on both individual salvation and social welfare. Mercy, courage, humility, steadfastness, truth, all arise from an inner disposition for goodness and are manifested in diverse ways by the Plowman, Prudence, the Knight, Griselda, Constance, and Cecilia. These are idealized figures against whom we can measure other characters in Chaucer's works, and from whose stories we can deduce some of Chaucer's views on subjects such as war and chivalry.

The Plowman in the General Prologue is the secular counterpart of the Parson. The two are brothers, Chaucer tells us, and he probably means both physically and spiritually (they might almost be Piers Plowman cut in half). Both love God above all else, both follow Christ in their lives. The Plowman, however, is not a preacher; he threshes corn, digs ditches, and carts dung. An obedient son of the Church, he lives in perfect peace and charity, loving God and his neighbor.

Chaucer's Plowman is conceived in accordance with the medieval stereotype of the true, humble follower of Jesus, the good poor man contrasted with the wicked rich man castigated by the Parson. For the most part, however, Chaucer seems rather more conservative on questions of social justice than many of his contemporaries. He gives no picture of the suffering poor such as Langland's, in which the peasants are cold and hungry, burdened with children and overburdened by landlords. Chaucer's poor are not destitute. The poor Plowman has enough to pay tithes on, the widow in The Nun's Priest's Tale owns her farm; even the poor widow in The Friar's Tale has a new pan. And many of them, like Griselda and her father, lead a life of dignity and have a sense of their own worth. But Chaucer is neither sentimentalist nor Marxist; no class in his works forms a spiritual elite. All the vocations and ranks are necessary for the common good, and the public weal and woe are derived from private virtue and vice.

Private and public peace are united in The Tale of Melibeus, which is both a tract against personal revenge and an extraordinarily interesting document in the history of Christian pacifism. The fact that it is a translation of a

85

French translation of a Latin tract only adds to its historical significance. Of course, Chaucer is not Dame Prudence any more than he is Sir Thopas, but he certainly gives that lady's arguments against war a most favorable hearing. Melibeus in the story has a very good cause for war: three enemies have broken into his own house in his absence, beaten his wife and wounded his daughter, whom they left for dead. How should a Christian layman respond to such a situation? Rich and powerful Melibeus consults his friends and decides on war. His wife Prudence, however, says that vengeance is not cured by vengeance, or one wrong by another. Melibeus objects that if he does not take vengeance, the wicked will not be restrained. Prudence, quoting liberally from the Scriptures and the classics, insists that all must be judged by law, and that the best recourse is to the Judge of all.

No cause has been given for the attack on Melibeus's house, but apparently the storyteller thought that "unprovoked" and "surprise" attacks have some history of provocation. Avoiding political discussion, Prudence spiritualizes the argument, recommending that Melibeus examine his conscience to realize that his three enemies are really the world, the flesh, and the devil. Prudence's remedy is therefore to learn patience, follow the example of Christ and the saints, and make peace instead of war. When with her husband's consent she sends for his enemies, they are joyful over the sweetness of forgiveness and admit their faults. Finally, under her guidance, Melibeus pardons all without punishment, and his former enemies become his friends and allies. The tale ends with a line not in Chaucer's source: If we repent, God will forgive us and bring us to unending bliss. Amen.

There is no reason to doubt the sincerity of Chaucer's plea for a Christian peace in his Tale of Melibeus; nor is there reason to doubt the sincerity of his praise of the Knight in the General Prologue. It is, of course, possible that Chaucer hated war and yet admired the personal qualities of a good soldier. It is also possible that he was influenced by the Lollard view: one of the Twelve Conclusions strongly condemns war as contrary to the New Testament and hateful to Christ—unless there be "spiritual revelation." In fact, three of Chaucer's friends, Clifford, Clanvowe, and Latimer, were knights, and several others had joined a recently formed Order of the Passion, to "remedy all evils" and to expel the Turks. The Knight in the Prologue may have been modelled partially on one or all of these knights. Like them, he had fought in heathen and in Christian countries, in Morocco and Algiers, in France and Cyprus. He had fought with King Peter during the victorious battle of Alexandria, and had campaigned also in Lithuania and Russia in the service of the Teutonic order.

The difficulty in interpreting this part of the passage is that Chaucer simply lists the battles without the commentary, and nowhere else does he enlarge on knightly missionary exploits, or indeed, on the knightly role of defender of the Church. What Chaucer does enlarge on are the personal qualities that were traditionally required of the ideal knight. And there is something pure in the character of this soldier, as Chaucer has caught him. Courage is only one of his qualities; he is a "perfect knight" who loves chivalry because he loves "truth and honor, freedom and courtesy." For all his high rank, he is as "meek as a maid" in his bearing, and in all his life, Chaucer tells us, he has never been rude to anyone, regardless of rank. Finally, he is devout as well as gentle; still wearing his spattered coat of mail, he has gone on pilgrimage with his son, no doubt as an act of piety, possibly of thanksgiving for his return home from the wars. It is entirely fitting that later on in the pilgrimage, this man of war acts as peacemaker between the Host and the Pardoner.

The Knight's Tale celebrates the refinements of chivalry, without sacrificing the excitement of fighting. When Arcite and Palamon prepare to fight alone in a grove, they help each other arm before they attempt to kill each other. And before his death, Arcite, the "flower of chivalry," speaks of truth, honor, knighthood, wisdom, and humility. The Knight-narrator loves tournaments so much that he wishes he could join his characters in Athens. But he is neither cruel nor bloodthirsty, and he tells approvingly how the populace of Athens praised Theseus for making rules which all but eliminated death in the combat. In fact, this tournament seems to mark the triumph of law and order over private revenge. Theseus himself is the best of chivalric knights. He consoles and cares for widows and redresses their wrongs. The ladies have appealed to his "gentilesse"; and Theseus, with "piteous heart" like a "true knight," will attack a tyrant for them. All praise his mercy and goodness.

The only problem, and it may be a significant one, is that this model Christian knight is a pagan. We can shelve the problem by saying that he is the Knight's knight, rather than Chaucer's. But that leaves us a very limited supply of chivalry. Of the other knights in Chaucer's works, the most attractive is Arveragus, but The Franklin's Tale is also set in pagan times. The Knight in black in *The Book of the Duchess* is generally taken to be John of Gaunt, and it would be interesting to know more about what Chaucer thought of his knighthood. But the poem is really an elegy on the death of the knight's wife, the husband being pictured quite conventionally as a courteous lord.

The two knights who appear in romances set in Christian times are hardly paragons. One, in Chaucer's own Tale

of Sir Thopas, is a burlesque; the other, in The Wife of
Bath's Tale, is a convicted rapist. The hilarious doggerel of
Sir Thopas satirizes primarily the metrical romances; and
Thopas himself, hunting deer, wrestling, and climbing into
the saddle, satirizes bourgeois pretensions and perversions
rather than the real aristocratic thing. Still, the description
of Thopas's arming, of the elf-queen and the giant, of the
list of birds, can be taken as fairly broad parody of the whole
romantic genre which featured knighthood. And the other
literary effort of the pilgrim Chaucer, The Tale of
Melibeus, offered when the Host stops the "drasty rhyming"
of Sir Thopas, makes chivalry seem irrelevant. Further,
what saves the reputation of chivalry from the reprieved
rapist in The Wife of Bath's Tale is only the fact that he is
most unknightly by any standard. He fails in the simplest
courtesy to the hag he is indebted to, and he doesn't understand gentilesse. When he complains that his bride is not
only old and ugly but poor and low born, she explains why
his "arrogance" is not worth a hen, and she lectures him for
some sixty lines on the meaning of being a gentleman.
Quoting Dante and Boethius, she explains that gentilesse
comes not from riches and titles but from Christ and good
deeds, a concept he should have understood earlier on.
Looking at all of these knights, I would say that Chaucer
repeatedly praised the personal virtues inculcated in good
knights, but that unlike so many of his contemporaries, he
did not portray chivalry as a specifically Christian force in
society.

The gentilesse that later centuries came to associate
mainly with knighthood Chaucer advocates for every class.
In a verse-sermon entitled "Gentilesse," Chaucer explicitly
denies the union of rank and gentility. Like the hag in the
Wife's tale, Chaucer says that vice may well be heir to old
riches, and that the man who claims to be gentle must serve

virtue and flee vice. Parts of the same sermon are addressed to King Richard in the final stanza of a poem called "Lack of Steadfastness." And the virtues urged upon the King are exercised by that poorest of all subjects, Griselda, in The Clerk's Tale, two of the Clerk's themes being, in fact, steadfastness and gentilesse.

The Clerk-narrator tells us that everybody, whatever his rank, should be constant in adversity, as was Griselda. And the rich nobleman in the tale, Marquis Walter, does not judge by class when he is being reasonable. He observes that on the one hand, worthy parents often have children unlike themselves, and that on the other, God can send his grace into the humblest place; therefore Walter will not choose a wife for her family connections. He chooses Griselda because she is a virtuous and industrious beauty, who does all in charity. We see also in Griselda how private virtue leads to public good. When after her marriage, Griselda ruled the realm in the absence of her husband, there was no discord she could not appease. She made peace among angry nobles, so wise were her words, so equitable her judgment.

The interrelation of private and public peace that is implicit in The Clerk's Tale and explicit in The Tale of Melibeus is fundamental in Chaucer's view of a Christian society, as it is in Langland's. The Parson explains that from anger comes hate, discord, homicide, and war. Homicide is both bodily and spiritual; it includes striking a pregnant woman and disturbing conception by contraception, and it also includes failure to feed the hungry, who, if they die, are slain by the one who could have given them food.

The Man of Law's Tale offers a series of episodes which move from the personal, really from the person of Constance, to the general. Indeed, Constance is repeatedly the pawn in international affairs in which she has little voice or choice, but which she nonetheless influences, not through force of personality but through virtue. Perhaps it is her helplessness which helps teach the lesson of trust in God and goodness. Her beauty is a good in itself, but her virtues even more than her beauty lead first the Moslem Sultan and then the pagan King Alla to love her and to become Christian. A rather comfortable, housewifely person in spite of her extraordinary adventures, she is quite willing to marry King Alla. At the wedding feast, they eat, drink, sing and dance, and then go to bed like ordinary couples. She loves the child of this union dearly, and blames the heartless father for his ill treatment. When all is miraculously restored, she and Alla kiss a hundred times, and have "such bliss" that there is no greater "this side of heaven."

Constance's order of priorities is the same as the Parson's: all good things come from God and must be used in his service—and given up at his word. She is not anxious to die and she is far from fearless. She weeps when she must leave home, her face is pale with dread when she is falsely accused of murder, and always she prays for deliverance from her woes. But she bravely accepts the will of God, and when she expects to drown, she prays only that Christ will save her from the devil. An emperor's daughter, Constance is praised in terms similar to those used of Griselda: both are primarily daughters of the Church, untouched by pride or frivolity. Virtue, we are told, is the guide of all Constance's work, and humility "has slain all tyranny" in her; she is "the mirror of courtesy," her heart the "true chamber of holiness," her hand the "minister of generous alms." Humbly she converts the pagan Hermengild in Britain by her loving service; compassionate, she feels pity even for the man who falsely accuses her of murder.

King Alla is apparently well taught by Constance; he

becomes an articulate Christian and a loyal son of the Church. When his pagan mother falsifies the news of the birth of Constance's son in the expectation that Alla will renounce Constance, he surprises her by welcoming the visitation of the Lord. Now that he understands religion, he says, he puts his will in Christ's command; when Christ wishes, he may send him an heir. Later, having had his mother put to death, he is seized with remorse and goes on pilgrimage to Rome to seek penance from the pope. Finding Constance there, he begs her understanding, and they live in virtuous joy, with full confidence in the hereafter.

While legendary Constance might serve as a model for all Christians, historic St. Cecilia would suit only those with a taste for martyrdom and a flair for the dramatic. Indeed, she seems more like Galahad than Constance. Contemptuous of the world, confident of heaven, Cecilia courts martyrdom. Accepting her teaching on the truth of God, the Trinity, the Passion, and the joys of heaven, the newly converted also go cheerfully to their death. What is astonishing to the modern reader is that Cecilia's scorn of the world is portrayed as reasonable. While the sentiment can be attributed to the Nun-narrator, Chaucer does nothing to diminish the impression of respect.

The possibility that Chaucer thought unworldliness a desirable ingredient in the ordinary Christian's spirituality is strengthened by the Dantesque Invocation to Mary which forms part of the Prologue to this Second Nun's Tale, and is generally taken to be a prayer written earlier by Chaucer in his own voice. These lines combine a certain scorn of the world with devotion to Mary in a style that is typical of the piety of medieval laymen. Following the prayer of St. Bernard in Dante's *Paradise*, the lines praise Mary as the "well of mercy" and the cure for sinful souls. In choosing to dwell in her, the poet says, God "ennobled our

human nature," since within the "blissful cloister of he
sides," the "eternal love and peace took man's shape." In
other verses, the narrator expresses a sense of sin and a fear
of the devil and of hell, calling him/herself a "banished
wretch," and the earth a "desert of gall."

Chaucer is supposed by many commentators to have
outgrown this piety; the legend was early work, largely a
translation, they note, and Chaucer was young and green.
On the other hand, the Retraction at the end of *The Canterbury Tales* is dismissed as too late; Chaucer was old and
gray. Other explanations are found to explain away similar
passages written in his youth or maturity, in the hymn to
Mary, the "ABC;" the translation of Boethius; "Truth;" and
the Epilogue to the *Troilus*. The work that calls for most
explanation and is most frequently ignored is Chaucer's
now lost translation of Pope Innocent's *On the Contempt of
the World*, which Chaucer was working on at the same time
that he was writing *The Canterbury Tales*. *De Contemptu
Mundi*—the very title, translated by Chaucer as *The
Wretched Engendering of Mankind*, conjures up images of
cowled monks in dank cells, praying before a death's head.
However we explain it, the fact is that from beginning to
end, Chaucer apparently thought a certain amount of withdrawal from the world was beneficial to the faith and morals
of men and women living in the world.

"ABC," for example, was a translation, probably made
at the request of Blanche, Duchess of Lancaster, before
1369; earlier, that is, than the legend of St. Cecilia. Taken
by itself, this prayer to Our Lady signifies more about the
Duchess than about Chaucer. But taken as part of the
whole Chaucerian corpus, it is the first of many expressions
of devotion to Mary, and of a strong penitential spirit. The
poem (in which the first letter of each stanza follows the
alphabet) is a free rendering of a prayer in a long work of

DeGuilleville's, entitled A *Pilgrimage of the Life of Man*, a title which reminds us of Chaucer's own work twenty years later. Like the Invocation to Mary in the prologue of The Second Nun's Tale, the "ABC" stresses the mercy of Christ's mother and the unworthiness of the writer, worthy of damnation and afraid of hell. The note of forgiveness through Christ's Passion which is struck in so many later poems is heard here too: with "his precious blood" Jesus wrote "the bill of general forgiveness" on the cross. The penitent writer, however, fears that because of his bad behavior, unless Mary intercedes for him, God will exile his spirit to "eternal stink."

The *Consolation of Philosophy* which Chaucer translated in the 1380s united philosophy with this already rather ascetic Christianity. The "prison" of this work is both the cell in which Boethius is incarcerated and the body. The Lady who comes to enlighten the prisoner Boethius is Philosophy rather than Mary, but her scorn for what the world calls success and even for life itself, her insistence on the necessity of freeing the body from earthly affections, had already been expressed by Chaucer in the "ABC" and in the Invocation to Mary. I do not mean to belittle the Boethian synthesis, which was especially congenial to Chaucer at this time of his life, when he was so deeply interested in the religions of the pagan world. As we shall see in a later chapter, Boethius supplied him with the language to express his ponderings over the problem of evil in his stories set in classical times, such as the *Troilus*.

When at the end of the *Troilus*, however, Chaucer turned to his young Christian readers to draw a moral, he slipped smoothly back into the devotional language of the earlier poems. "Turn home from worldly vanity," he says, and "cast the visage of your heart" to that God who made you after his image. "Think all this world is but a fair" that

94

"passes soon as a flower," and love him who for love of us died upon a cross and is now in heaven. Apparently alluding to the unfaithfulness of Criseyde, Chaucer says that Christ will never betray anybody who puts his trust in him; what need then for these other loves? Again, at the very end of the poem, Chaucer prays to the Trinity for protection against "foes visible and invisible," and asks Jesus to make us worthy of his mercy, "for love of Mary."

The world Chaucer asks the young folks to give up is neither sad nor dreary; in Chaucer's imagery, it is as exciting as a carnival and beautiful as a flower—and as transitory as both. Is Chaucer recommending complete withdrawal from this world? Probably not, but he comes close to it in this passage. The balance taught by St. Bonaventure and by the Parson, life in the world with all loves subordinated to God, is hard to maintain in practice, and Chaucer occasionally tips a bit one way or the other. As we shall see in a later chapter, his warm and imaginative sexuality sometimes carried him too far to what he at other times considered the flesh and the devil. Sometimes, as in this passage in the *Troilus*, he sounds a strong note for a life of contemplation. Perhaps it is the tension between them that is partly responsible for the poignancy of the joyous, fresh world that Chaucer and so many of his contemporaries portrayed.

The balance is achieved in the poem called "Truth: the Ballade of Good Counsel" that we glanced at earlier. It is the courtly counterpart of The Parson's Tale, and the man who followed its advice would be the courtly counterpart of the Plowman. In part, it sets up a modest, practical goal: do not attempt to reform the whole world; accept what is sent and be satisfied with what you have; even if it is not great, it is free of envy and hate. There is also the strain of alienation from the world which, he says, is "not a home but a wilderness" through which pilgrim man merely passes on his way to heaven.

The dates of composition are very uncertain, but it is generally thought that somewhere between 1388 and 1395 Chaucer wrote this poem on "Truth;" that he was working on *The Canterbury Tales,* including those of the Miller, the Wife, the Pardoner, and the Man of Law; and that he made the now lost translation of *De Contemptu Mundi* by Pope Innocent III. Apparently his view of man and the universe was broad enough to accommodate all of these diverse works.

Innocent's tract of 1215 is grim in a style that was even then old-fashioned, yet it continued to appeal to devotional tastes at least through the sixteenth century. It begins with Job's lament over his birth—Why did I not end my days in my mother's womb—and ends many pages later with the poor soul being sent to hell forever on the Day of Judgment. In between there are sorrow and anguish for all, married and single, rich and poor, servants and masters, good and bad. The good are stoned, the wicked are worried, the world is a place of banishment and a prison, man a pilgrim and a foreigner unequally pitted against the devil, the world, and the flesh, and withal, afraid of death. The pains of hell are depicted, not the joys of heaven. Some of the descriptions of sin, such as gluttony, drunkenness, and avarice, are familiar to us from The Pardoner's Tale and The Parson's Tale, but the unrelieved gloom of Innocent is a far cry from the cautious optimism of the Parson, not to mention the exuberance of St. Francis and St. Bonaventure.

Why did Chaucer translate such a tome? It may be, as has been suggested, that he intended it for one of the pilgrims. My own guess is that his interest in the work was related in some way to his Lollard friends, that perhaps he was translating it for one of them. At least, it seems more than a coincidence that the extreme contempt of the body which characterizes Innocent's work also marks the writings of the Lollard Knights. Sir John Clanvowe, for example, wrote in his tract on heaven and hell of the "foul stinking muck of the false failing world." And Sir Lewis Clifford, father-in-law of that Vache to whom Chaucer dedicated "Truth," desired in his will that his "wretched carrion" be buried in the furthest corner of the churchyard, and that no cloth of gold be laid on his "stinking carrion." Such writers would have welcomed Innocent's book, which has so much the same tone. It is not the usual tone of Chaucer or, for that matter, of most fourteenth-century writers of tracts and wills.

The difference is of degree, however, not kind, and the intent of the work is often misunderstood in our time. To say that Chaucer approved the *Contempt of the World* is not to say that he wished he had never been born. Everything we know suggests the contrary, not only about Chaucer but about Innocent. The work is not an autobiography of a melancholy romantic but a sermon directed to the overconfident who thoughtlessly expect to live and prosper forever. It probably never had much of a vogue among the millers and others who needed it most. Its appeal was to sincere Christians who felt themselves in danger of worldliness and did such reading as an Ash-Wednesday style of remedy against sin. To Lady Anne, Countess of Pembroke, for example, was dedicated an English translation in the sixteenth century. The title page was adorned with a drawing of skeletons, and around the border were the words, "O Worms Meat Why Art Thou So Insolent." Stated more politely, that is the basic question behind Dame Prudence's prodding of her husband in The Tale of Melibeus; and she, too, had read Innocent.

But Prudence does not call Melibeus "Worms Meat," and Chaucer consistently moderates Innocent's style. The phrase in "Truth," "Here is no home, here is but wilderness" is positively cheery beside Innocent's stinking slough. And in the rest of the poem, the poet recalls the creation of man in God's image rather than the decay of his carrion.

While "Truth" thus shows the influence of Boethius rather than Innocent, Chaucer must have written the Prologue of The Man of Law's Tale with Innocent's work open in front of him. The first twenty-two lines are a paraphrase of part of the sixteenth chapter of the first book of the *De Contemptu Mundi,* the part describing the miseries of poverty. The Man of Law laments poverty's thirst, cold, and hunger, and the way it "shames your heart" and leads you to "beg, borrow, or steal." You even "blame Christ" and accuse your neighbor, angry that you have so little because he has all. The day of reckoning will come, you think, when "his tail will burn in the coals" because he did not help you. In fact, it is better to die than suffer indigence, because everybody despises you.

So far the Man of Law follows Innocent, but then he reverses Innocent's views on the rich. Innocent is quite as lengthy, if not as convincing, on the unhappiness of the rich as of the poor. He also most explicitly condemns the iniquity that judges a man by his possessions, saying that instead, each man ought rather to be thought rich as he is good and poor as he is evil. Further, he declares that the desire to keep riches is immoral, that it makes a man unthankful to God, unkind to his neighbor, and cruel to himself. To become rich, he says, men make their way over mountains, sound the depths of the sea, search the ends of the earth—all to scrape together wealth and honors, which are finally but troubles and afflictions of the mind.

The Man of Law sounds more like the president of General Motors than like Pope Innocent. "O rich merchants," apostrophizes the lawyer, "full of happiness are you, a noble, prudent folk!" Every line in the ensuing passage is parodic; unlike Innocent's merchants, these are wise and merry; the metaphor for their felicity is taken from the vice of gambling and juxtaposed with Christmas; and the travels considered so futile by Innocent are a source of satisfaction for all in the Prologue of The Man of Law's Tale.

The direction of the satire is not obvious, but one of the possibilities is that Chaucer was raising an eyebrow at the excesses of Innocent. Since Chaucer does not separate the two parts of the passage, the praise of riches could easily be mistaken as a continuation, rather than a parody, of the excerpt from Innocent. Indeed, the emended text is more convincing than the original, the obvious alternative to the misery of poverty being the satisfaction of riches. Who ever truly believed that riches are as great a hardship as destitution? Not Dame Prudence. She warns Melibeus of the dangers of misusing wealth, and she quotes Innocent on the sorrows of beggary, but she concludes that riches are good for those who use them well.

In The Man of Law's Tale there are four passages which correspond closely to passages in the *De Contemptu Mundi*. Two are moral commonplaces that we are familiar with from Chaucer's use of them elsewhere. One of these details the dreadful effects of drunkenness, the other decries the foul end of lust, which corrupts the mind and destroys the body. The two other passages seem out of place. It is not only that they interrupt joyful occasions (a wedding and a reunion) with reminders that joy is followed by woe, but that the tone is too negative for both Constance and the narrator of her legend. While there was enough woe in

99

Constance's life to justify her lamenting with Innocent and Job the day she was born, she does not so lament; she rejoices at every opportunity for life, as well as at the birth of her child. It does not occur to her that the world is a prison and man a nothing (by nature, just an upside down tree, says Innocent). In all of her trials, Constance makes the best of things, hoping in Christ; even on a good day, Innocent makes the worst of it, pointing out imperfections and predicting doom. Nor does the Man of Law share Innocent of riches, so in the last stanza of the tale, he repudiates the pessimism, saying that Jesus can send joy after sorrow. It is rather as though Chaucer was attempting to meditate in Innocent's style, but cheerfulness kept breaking in. At least, in spite of Innocent, the Man of Law's Tale presents a model of piety that is hopeful and loving.
and loving.

What makes this style of piety interesting is that it is very much like that displayed by Chaucer in his earlier works and in his Retraction. As she is set upon the ocean in a rudderless boat, Constance prays to the Cross, emphasizing the pity that has "washed the world from its old iniquity." She is optimistic because the "victorious tree," the "cross that bore the King of Heaven" protects "those who are true." "Protect me," she prays, and "give me power to amend my life." In his Retraction at the end of *The Canterbury Tales*, Chaucer, thinking about death, sounds like Constance. He asks Jesus and his Mother and all the saints to send him grace to be sorry for his sins, and to give him the grace of a good confession. "Through the grace of him who is king of kings," and who "bought us with the precious blood of his heart," Chaucer hopes to be one of those who will be saved at the Day of Judgment.

Many readers who are startled by Chaucer's retraction of many of his works speculate that he was subject to some dramatic conversion, as was Boccaccio. But there is no dramatic break in Chaucer's poetry. If we were to print together all the devotional poems and pieces of poems, the Retraction would logically conclude the series begun with the "ABC." What makes the Retraction different from the rest of the series is not the quality of its piety but its adaptation to the circumstances of *The Canterbury Tales*. In the course of the work, Chaucer has judged the pilgrims on how faithfully they have carried out their vocations, whether as knight, wife, martyr, etcetera; in the end he judges himself by the standards of faith and morality proper for storytellers. So he rejects the "worldly vanities" of the love stories and the tales conducive to sin, and thanks Jesus for giving him the grace to write the legends and books of morality and devotion.

Most readers would exchange all of Chaucer's saints for the Wife of Bath. Was Chaucer really wishing her into oblivion in the Retraction? I think not. The fact that he was writing the fabliaux at the same time he was translating Innocent suggests that at no time did he consider the fabliaux serious sin. By the Parson's definition (edited by Geoffrey Chaucer), the poet had committed venial sins whenever in his works his slyness or wit went so far as to give approval to sin; it is possible that looking back he could remember lines that could have been amended and still been funny. As for the notion that the Wife of Bath's manners and morals should be imitated by young women, that may be a mortal sin, but it is the reader's not the writer's.

It is possible, of course, that in choosing absolutes, Chaucer wished he had avoided venial sin, and written only homilies. It is also possible that he would have defended his enjoyment of the Wife, the Miller, and the Host as not irreconcilable with his moral stance. The fact that

Chaucer has caught with consummate skill the vitality and humor of the vulgar does not mean that his was the vulgar outlook. Neither parson nor professor, Chaucer the story-teller can laugh at the human comedy without sharing the theology of the Host or the marital customs of the Wife of Bath. We sometimes mistake good spirits and even charity for agreement. In fact, it may have been Chaucer's piety as much as his temperament that kept him from condemning his characters. In all of Chaucer's prayers, he judges only himself; it may have been one of his rules to condemn the sin without destroying the sinner. In the Middle Ages, everybody said that God is love, and the Parson's remedy for sin is love of God and neighbor. The Parson also points out that penances ought not to make the penitent bitter or angry but should bring him to the sweetness of Christ.

As fellow Christian listening to the Parson, the pilgrim Geoffrey takes his companions at their own evaluation. The poet Chaucer knows that aesthetically it is most effective to let the rogues unwittingly condemn themselves. It is indeed part of the Christian comedy that the sinners condemn each other but not themselves. They live for the pleasures of the moment, they are greedy for goods regardless of the laws of God and man. Yet they are pilgrims who may still repent before they reach Canterbury.

The good lay people are portrayed as accepting the doctrine, moral code, and pious practices taught by the Church. In varying degrees they partake of the world's goods, its beauty, knowledge, and love, always remembering these are gifts of God and that they pass in time. All, including Chaucer, examine their consciences and are concerned about the hereafter; they pray for deliverance from hell, but do not send others there. Pilgrims, characters in tales told by them, and the author of all, are all on the same pilgrimage.

IV

Sex, Marriage, and Love

A s both early and late proponents of clerical celibacy remarked, the chains of matrimony may be golden but they are chains nonetheless. In the Middle Ages as in our own time, men and women experimented with ways other than celibacy to evade this golden rule. One perennial way was to slip off the chain by simple adultery; in literature, this is a crude sport, mainly of the lower classes. The upper classes toyed with an alternative which later generations have called courtly love, which was sometimes only complex adultery. The Church, of course, condemned adultery, and many priests considered procreation the primary purpose of matrimony; but there was considerable diversity of opinion even among churchmen over the function of sex in marriage, and the meaning of love, human and divine. Chaucer was famous as a love poet, and indeed he seems to have aired the whole subject in various literary forms: in the dream frame of *The Parliament of Fowls*; in the romance of *Troilus and Criseyde*; and in the assorted *Canterbury*

Tales, which themselves cover the whole spectrum from the infrared of the Wife of Bath to the ultraviolet of St. Cecilia.

On this, more than on any other subject, readers would like to have Chaucer think as they do. The sex-is-fun school considers the Wife of Bath Chaucer's contribution to the sexual revolution. The exegetical critics, scorning relevance, make Chaucer more straitlaced than his Parson. Moderates find Chaucer both as romantic and as sexy as the times require. Trying to put all the diverse pieces together, I have come to think that the articulately Christian Chaucer described in the previous chapters was certainly not an advocate of adultery; but neither was he a simple-minded defender of grim old-fashioned marriage. He was, I believe, a Christian who preferred sex, marriage, and love to go together but who saw that they usually did not. With humor, affection, anger, detachment—with skill and art—he described what he saw: sex, bold and unadorned, fun, funny, and anti-social; marriage, with or without love, the accepted base of society; love, with or without marriage, the greatest joy the world offers to mortals. And all of these transitory, only the love of God enduring to confer immortality on the poor confused creatures who have spent so many of Chaucer's lines discussing their own views.

While Chaucer's style was unique, his range was typical of his time. Everybody had a theory about love, from St. Bernard of Clairvaux to the Wife of Bath. Some acquaintance with these theories is therefore important in evaluating Chaucer's religion, because without it we are likely to misread a conventional attitude as radical or heretical.

Chaucer's free talk about sex, for example, and his descriptions of the sexual act as mirthful and joyous do not mean that he was liberated from the Commandments. Crude talk was frowned on as impolite and inelegant, but in itself it was not considered morally shocking. Preachers and moralists were most explicit in their description of sin, and so were the illustrators who adorned their tracts. The lesson warned of eternal punishment for a moment's pleasure, but nobody denied the pleasure, and neither of the partners is portrayed as drawing away in disgust. Some of the celibate writers drew away, but from what they call the "foul delight of wanton lust," as Innocent put it in his *De Contemptu Mundi*. Fabliaux descriptions of the delights were widely circulated in all classes of society throughout medieval Europe. In most of these, including those told by the elegant ladies in Boccaccio's *Decameron*, the joke lies in the way the adulterous woman succeeds in outwitting her stupid husband. The situation is avowedly immoral, but an immoral lesson need not be drawn from it; often there seems to be no lesson at all.

In medieval, as in most societies, marriage was an attempt to domesticate sex and reproduction. The Church, in turn, attempted to sacramentalize the social institution. What is binding is the promise and the union; the priest only blesses the legal and the natural, the exchange of vows and the bed. How far the blessing takes the sin out of the sex seems to depend, for most ecclesiastical writers, on the social usefulness of the act. The subject was so much discussed that authorities can be found in defense of almost every view, but we need not go beyond The Parson's Tale in search of a typical manual. Chaucer compiled the sermon from several sources and probably intended it to be representative of the usual clerical view.

The Parson's attitude toward the pleasures of sex is very different from that modern view which considers gratification the goal or basis of matrimony. When, however, the Parson's remarks are translated out of ecclesiastical jargon, their substance is more substantial than the hasty reader thinks. For example, marriage is recommended as a remedy for lechery. How, practically speaking, can that be? The answer is, by yielding the debt of one's body to one's partner. The Wife of Bath was quite within her rights in demanding payment of this debt from her spouses, and if they refused, they were committing a sin. This being so, nobody could have said (as some modern books say they did) that the only time a husband and wife should come together was when they hoped to produce offspring.

If the only purpose of marriage were procreation, the medieval saint of matrimony would have been Zenobia, who, we are told in The Monk's Tale, would never consent to her husband except to conceive a child, for, she said, otherwise it was lechery and shame. If, however, Zenobia had been a Catholic instead of a pagan, she would have been committing serious sin in refusing her husband, who might be driven into adultery as a result. Paying the marriage debt was not sinful; on the other hand, the Parson complains that married people think all good enough because they are married. They do not want to know that a man may slay himself with his own knife, that coming together only for burning delight is a sin. The devil has power with such folk, he says, because they put Jesus Christ out of their hearts. Although the Parson's ruler can obviously be flexibly used by the individual measuring his marital motives, the general message is one of restraint.

In the midst of the general ambivalence, Chaucer has the Parson reveal his particular bias. Among the Canterbury pilgrims, only the Parson would complain that the pants worn by the young men are so tight that they don't cover their members but show off swollen protuberances in front and behind, their buttocks resembling the hind part of a she-ape in the full of the moon. This is preacher-talk; true celibate that he is, the Parson's real preference is for

106

virginity. There is no grudging in his brief description of the dedicated virgin as the spouse of Jesus and the equal of the martyrs. And he says succinctly that a virgin bore our Lord Jesus Christ, and a virgin He was himself. But the Parson is not recommending virginity to the group of pilgrims. He knows that the power of sex had been recognized and accepted since the days of St. Paul, who had said it was better to marry than burn; and in recognition of the importance of sex in marriage, the Church had ruled that vows of abstinence had to be taken by both or neither spouse. Further, the Parson agreed with the medieval doctrine that while lust is the most popular sin, it is not the worst. Lechery is the seventh of the deadly sins. The first six are all hateful in themselves—envy, anger, covetousness, etcetera—but sprinkled with a little holy water, lust can be transformed into love. And it is the loving part of the lust that the preachers considered the basis of happiness in marriage. A man should love his wife by discretion, patiently, and temperately, says the Parson, as though she were his sister.

With these qualifications, marriage is considered the state of life in which most people, pagan as well as Christian, work out their salvation, and it is a good state. The reason adultery is so horrible a sin, says the Parson, is that it breaks the commandment of God and befouls the author of matrimony, who is Christ; the nobler the sacrament, the greater the sin in breaking it. God established marriage in Paradise, before sin; the "natural law" which operated then meant that one man was united with one woman, and that thus mankind was to be multiplied. Further, Jesus showed his belief in marriage by being born in marriage and by going to a wedding where he turned water into wine. Finally, as St. Paul says, a man shall love his wife as Christ loved the Church, who loved it so well that he died for it.

So should a man for his wife if necessary. For her part, a woman should be obedient to her husband, who should use his authority with reason. Above all worldly things, says the Parson, for a perfect marriage husband and wife should be true to each other, body and soul.

This concept of marriage, which is in the background of many of Chaucer's stories (those about Prudence, Constance, and Griselda), is not ignoble, but neither is it romantic. It elevates responsibility, duty, children—in brief, it gilds the chains without hiding them. It plays down passion; sex is contractual, and love can be achieved rather than fallen into.

There were also current extremely romantic views that subsequent centuries have called courtly love, or *fine amour*, and which demanded devotion transcending all other ties. In life and literature, such devotion was frequently expressed in marriage. A historical couple famous for their mutual devotion, the Black Prince and Joan of Kent, travelled even to war together, and to the day of his death he addressed her as "fair sweet friend." Similar fictional lovers, like William and Melior in *William of Palerne*, can be described as married lovers. And sober-minded John Gower, in his *Tract for Married Lovers*, advised husband and wife to be "loyal friend with loyal friend," and not to measure their love but to give all.

Still, it is not really surprising that the desire to liberate lovers from measure and moderation led to questioning of the bonds of matrimony. A most famous and puzzling book called *The Art of Love*, written in the twelfth century by Andreas Capellanus (that is, Andrew the Chaplain), raises the question of whether "pure" love can survive the contract of marriage. In one dialogue, for example, Countess Marie, a real personage, is reported to have said that love is impossible in marriage; other aristocratic persons say that if one is *obliged* to satisfy a partner's needs, one is no longer free. Fidelity is a virtue—to a lover who has no legal claim. Whether Andreas was satiric or serious, his book reflects a highly sophisticated society which was discussing, if not living, meaningful relationships which scorned legal bonds and the sixth commandment.

Did Countess Marie really mean what Andreas says she said? It is possible that he fictionalized her; or perhaps the real lady followed the custom of arguing either side in a debate just for the fun of sharpening wits. The debate was perhaps the most popular intellectual genre of the Middle Ages, a good part of the University system was based on it, and the most famous theological works (Abelard's and Aquinas's, for example) took that form. Nothing seems to have been out of bounds in the school debates, the authorities complaining occasionally of the number of arguments assembled (in order to be rebutted) against such basic doctrines as the Trinity and the immortality of the soul. In similar style, debates over love, which casually undermine Christian marriage, appear in romances. There is some evidence that ladies held "courts" where they disputed much as Andreas portrays them, and even judged "heretics" and offenders against the rules of the game.

Something of the spirit of the game was derived from the lyrical theology of the Middle Ages. "The reason for loving God is God Himself," wrote St. Bernard of Clairvaux in a work called *On the Love of God;* and the "measure of loving God is to love Him beyond measure." Love, he says, is a "matter of affection, not a contract; it neither gains nor is gained by a compact. It exerts its influence freely and makes me free." In one of his many commentaries on the Canticle of Canticles, Bernard, while warning that the book is not about sex, nonetheless compares the relation between God and the soul to that between men and women. Such a marriage is not a contract, he says, but an embrace beyond all law. Pure love, he insists, is not mercenary; it gives all without counting the cost.

It is always difficult to judge the interrelations of life and literature, but a number of stories offer dramatic proof of the force of these ideas. The most intriguing is that of Heloise, a remarkable twelfth-century woman, who wrote about her life, whose story was told by Jean de Meun in *The Romance of the Rose* and was known to all of Europe, and who is still remembered. Theoretical and articulate, Heloise rejected what she considered legalism in her love of Abelard as Bernard had in his love of God. "I wanted simply you," she wrote to the already famous philosopher, "nothing of yours. I looked for no marriage-bond, no marriage portion." Even after she became pregnant, eighteen-year-old Heloise refused to marry her thirty-four-year-old lover. Learned, eloquent, passionate, she insisted that she preferred "love to wedlock" and "freedom to chains." She said that she would rather be Abelard's whore than the Emperor's wife, and she scorned as prostitutes women who married for money.

Although some of this sounds like the youthful rebellion that one outgrows, some of it is based on a philosophy of intention that both Heloise and Abelard continued to hold later in life. Believing that deeds are not good or bad in themselves but must be judged by the spirit in which they are performed, she wrote, "guilty though I am, I am also wholly innocent." The deed was fornication, but the intention was pure love. When she entered the convent after Abelard was castrated by her uncle's servants, she was consistent in judging her new life by her intentions. Not only did she expect no reward from God since she had done nothing for love of him, but she condemned herself as a hypocrite. Men praise her chastity, she says bitterly, but they do not know the unrepentant hypocrite she is, chaste in body but not in soul.

Another intellectual and passionate, but far less spiritual, twelfth-century woman was one Beatrix de Dia. This Countess Beatrice was a *trobairitz*, that is, a woman troubadour, who wrote poems to a lover she wished to have in "her husband's stead." She would like to hold him naked in her arms at night, she wrote, so "enraptured" that he wouldn't leave. And being a writer, she alluded to a fictional pair, saying that her love was greater than that Floris had for Blancheflor.

So familiar are some lovers' names that the line between fact and fiction seems blurred. Paolo and Francesca—real lovers, immortalized by Dante, who in turn partly blames the romances for the real adultery which led them to his fictional hell. Francesca really was married against her wishes to an ugly old man, and fell in love with his handsome younger brother, Paolo, who loved her. As Dante tells it, one day the warm and sensuous young things were in the garden reading the Book of Lancelot. When they came to the lines in which Lancelot kisses Guenevere for the first time, "that day they read no more." The pilgrim Dante swoons with pity for the lovers spending eternity whirling around in each other's arms; the author Dante is making the point that for all the extenuating circumstances, adultery is adultery.

In a great deal of medieval fiction, the moral question is bypassed one way or another. There is no adultery in the charming twelfth-century French tale of Aucassin and Nicolette, but these young lovers never consider obeying their families' wishes for "suitable" marriages. Threatened with hell, Aucassin asserts cheerfully that that's where he wants to go, with all the great knights and beautiful ladies with their lovers. Morally more startling, the Fair Maid of

Astolat is portrayed by Malory (in the fifteenth century) as defending on her death bed, after Confession, her desire to have Lancelot as her paramour. There is no sin, she asserts, in loving as she was created by God to love. And since Sir Lancelot is a noble knight, "also the work of the Creator," does she not honor God in loving Lancelot? For his part, Lancelot, always faithful to Guenevere, has refused the maid, not on moral grounds but because "the heart must be free; it cannot be ordained whom we shall love."

The lovers we still remember, the most "romantic," are those extra-marital pairs, Lancelot and Guenevere, Tristan and Isolt, and Troilus and Criseyde. And the writers who told one or another story or compiled the vast collections of romances loved their lovers. Beginning the story of Lancelot and the Cart, Malory says it was the month of May, when "buds ripen and blossoms appear in their fragrance and loveliness. And the month when lovers, subject to the same force which reawakens the plants, feel their hearts open again, recall past trysts and past vows and moments of tenderness, and yearn for a renewal of the magical awareness which is love." "First," Malory goes on, "a man must love God his Creator, and then, if he is to be ennobled, he must love a woman, for God has created him thus." Less charmed with Guenevere than with Lancelot, Malory nonetheless says that "because of her unfaltering love for Sir Lancelot" she would "end her days honorably and with sweetness."

The *Tristan and Isolt* of Gottfried von Strassburg goes furthest in transforming what the Parson would have called adultery into a religion of love. It is not the Christian religion, but it uses the mystical language of Christianity. God, who is invoked frequently, so loves lovers that he protects Isolt when she tricks her husband in words as well as deeds. The lovers never feel guilt before God or before

King Mark. Indeed, magic obviates morality; they can't help falling in love because they accidentally drink a potion. In a famous grotto of love, God is supplanted by the Goddess of Love. Gottfried knew what he was doing, for he tells us that this same cave had been used in the old days of heathendom for love dalliance. And then he carefully describes the grotto in symbolic terms used by commentators for a Christian church; in the center, where the altar would be in the sanctuary of a church, is a bed, carved of crystal stone, where the sacred union is consummated.

Gottfried's allegory is long and elaborate, and a considerable part of it parallels St. Bernard's commentaries on the Canticle of Canticles. Whether the borrowing from Bernard makes *Tristan* more or less blasphemous is hard to say. Bernard applies the heavily sensuous imagery of the biblical Bride and Bridegroom to the Church and Christ; Gottfried applies it to Isolt and Tristan. Perhaps the mystic and the poet would not have shocked each other with their interchange of religious and erotic images and symbols. Or perhaps the conflict is inherent in a Christianity which adores both incarnation and virginity.

The scope of these romances seems a bit narrow by comparison with the work most important to us because Chaucer translated it, borrowed from it, and modified it in dozens of ways. Indeed, anyone who wants to know what everybody read from the twelfth to the fifteenth centuries might well peruse *The Romance of the Rose,* the two hundred surviving manuscripts giving testimony of its enormous popularity. Called the book most characteristic of the Middle Ages, it includes two extreme views of love: at one extreme, sex is more or less transformed into a religion; at the other, it is considered an amoral natural function like digestion.

The first part of *The Romance,* begun about 1235 by

Guillaume de Lorris who died before finishing it, is often considered a perfect example of romantic love. But this allegory in which the lover is called the Lover and the beloved the Rose seems to me a most shrewd and "realistic" portrayal of the psychology of seduction; it offers a prototype for certain chapters in the courtly love stories, but not for *Romeo and Juliet*. Dalliance divorced from responsibility is most attractively and unsentimentally portrayed in the garden, itself the prototype for so many later gardens of delight. Here are Sir Mirth with his mistress, Gladness, who has given him all her love; beautiful and perfectly matched, they are always laughing and kissing. The God of Love, who is there with Sweet Looks, gives the Lover advice borrowed from Ovid's *Art of Love:* dress well; clean your nails and teeth; spend freely; if you look good on a horse, ride around to be seen, etcetera. All of this advice is calculated to help the elegant and courteous Lover achieve his goal of plucking the rose. Helping him also are Beauty, Fair Welcome, Idleness, and Youth; protecting the rose against him are Evil Tongue, Jealousy, and Shame. For his own reasons, the Lover is glad these enemies have been guarding the Rose. When he has the opportunity for a close look, he is pleased that "the unfolding flower had not yet spread so as to show the seed, which still was by the petals well concealed." Similar erotic language is used in the brief conclusion added by an unknown writer, who wrote that Beauty secretly gave the Lover the bud, the tender grass provided a bed, the petals made a cover—and the blossom was never again closed against him.

The mood of the lengthy continuation by Jean de Meun is quite different; sardonic and sharp, Jean looks at romance with a jaundiced eye, and is not taken in by the Lover's rhetoric for a minute. A character named Lady Reason, who may well be Jean's spokesperson, calls love an "imaginary illness" originating from "disordered sight." The purpose of sex, she says, is procreation, and Nature has made the task pleasant only so that laborers will like the work. Some men ignore this goal and pretend to be in love, but only until their lust is fulfilled. Lady Reason's point is that while sex is necessary for the race, sensible men who conform to the law of reason will prize friendship rather than carnal love. Jean, however, does not expect young men to be persuaded by reason; he shows the Lover finding his own kind of Friend who counsels deceptive tactics to get the Rose. Flatter, Friend says, cajole, bribe, weep, kneel. Be a big spender: money opens all doors, and "cuts castle walls like cake." Further, don't let the guardians know your design is to deflower the Rose. Pretend to be Platonic, but when the time comes, prove yourself a man and pluck the Rose. The Lover is shocked at first, but his scruples are easily overcome. In the final action, the flaming fire of Venus sets the castle ablaze and the Lover plucks the Rose in a long erotic, not to say obscene, passage.

The Friend's cynical advice to men is more than matched in a long speech to women by an old bawd, La Vieille. Don't give away your heart, she says, but sell at the highest price; take with an open hand, but close your fist when it's your turn to give. Attract men: dye your hair, use makeup, dress to show off good points, don't spill when you drink, go to church to be seen, etcetera. And her speech on the sexual urges of women outdoes the Friend's on lustful males. She says that all women love to play the game, that every female, like every horse, longs for every male she sees. According to her philosophy (quite different from the Parson's), the free interchange of all women and men was intended originally by Nature, but has been frustrated by the law of marriage; women are only trying to get back their natural liberty.

It is not surprising that medieval feminists and moralists found plenty to object to in Jean de Meun and that the argument was still going on in Chaucer's day. One complaint was that Jean identified Paradise with sensual pleasure and that he made female genitals sacred. On the other hand, one of the defenders of the book, a French humanist and Ciceronian named Jean de Montreuil, said that the most enlightened men would "rather do without their shirt" than without this book, so profound did they find it.

The diverse and contradictory views sampled here were all part of Chaucer's education, assimilated and transformed into his own complex vision of human sexuality and divine love. Chaucer refers to the characters and stories we have looked at, but his path is not the same as Jean's or Gottfried's or Heloise's or even Dante's. Chaucer does not glorify adulterous love, although he sees its attractions. *The Parliament of Fowls, Troilus*, and portions of *The Canterbury Tales* reflect the view that while sex and love are great joys, the worship of Venus leads to disaster. Further, in Chaucer's works, the relationship between a man and a woman is finally not an isolated act in a grotto or a garden, but part of the social and even of the universal fabric.

The Parliament of Fowls seems to me, for all its discursiveness, a morally unified poem, and the laughter which fills it is suitably innocent as befits the moral ending. Apparently written in celebration of St. Valentine's Day, the poem circles the problems of human love before settling them, for the moment, in a mass marriage under the auspices of Nature herself.

The first setting for love in this dream poem is a garden which resembles that in *The Romance of the Rose* and is devoted to Cupid and Venus. Chaucer does not minimize the charms of unclothed Beauty, Youth, and Pleasure present here. But within the temple Venus is the bitter goddess

116

of jealousy; Priapus is also there, and in a corner Venus is disporting with her porter Riches as she rests half-naked on a bed of gold. Painted on the walls are those who died for love. Unlike Gottfried's *Tristan*, there is no confusion here between the goddess of love and the God of Scripture. And the point seems to be that sensuous lust leads not to life but to death; the only remedy being, as the words on the entrance gate warn, to run away.

When the dreamer emerges from this closed-in temple of private delights and sighs, he sees the "noble goddess Nature" in her open-air bower on a hill of flowers. It is St. Valentine's Day and all the birds are assembled publicly to choose their mates before engendering the species. In this Parliament the birds debate questions of love; their speeches satirize the attitudes of the social classes they represent. The upper-class birds, exemplifying courtly love, speechify for so long that the lower-class birds become impatient. "Kek kek! Have done, come off!" they cry. Amid much laughter, a parody of a love debate ensues, in which each speaker reasons as is natural to him, from the true turtle dove ("let him serve her till he die") to the churlish duck ("there's more stars than a pair"), with the tercelet remarking that those who "come from a dunghill" can't guess what love really is. Finally, Nature settles the central problem, the competition of the three tercels for the love of the formel, by letting the lady eagle decide to wait a year before choosing among her three suitors. Then Nature gives all the birds their mates, and with "bliss and joy" each takes the other in his wings, thanking always the "noble goddess of nature."

The conflict in this poem is not between the courtly and the common. The styles of the birds are different, but all are agreed at the end, and all will end in matrimony. Indeed, Chaucer seems to be taking the anti-romantic view that there is *not* a separate law for courtly lovers. There are a number of difficulties in this poem, but the main conflict seems to be between the Venus of lustful, illicit passion, and Nature, or natural law, which blesses sex and makes it serve the common good. *The Parliament of Fowls* is not a Christian poem; it assumes that marriage and law exist without revelation and that such natural knowledge is available not only to philosophers like Cicero (whom Chaucer introduces in the beginning of the poem), but to the ignorant as well—to seed fowls and falcons alike.

Troilus and Criseyde is a far more ambitious poem than *The Parliament* and, of course, a far greater study of love; yet, it is narrower in one way than the allegory of the birds. The crucial action of the *Troilus* takes place in and around the golden bed of Venus, and in this study of secret, indoor love, the lovers never take a walk up the hill to the goddess Nature, and nothing seems further from their thoughts than a public ceremony. Why? Unlike Isolt and Guenevere, whose husbands are legal if not moral barriers, Criseyde is a widow, rich, well-born, independent. Chaucer could not change the plot so drastically as to marry the lovers, but he could easily have shown them yearning for matrimony but, say, fearing the king, if that was what he meant. On the contrary, Chaucer seems to have gone out of his way to make the situation more like that of those lovers whose romance was held together only by mutual fidelity, and protected by secrecy.

In Chaucer's source, Boccaccio's *Il Filostrato*, when Pandarus first approaches Criseyde on behalf of Troilus, she says, "Have you lost your senses? Who should have his pleasure of me unless he first became my husband?" In Chaucer's version, the possibility of marriage is never suggested, and indeed, "marriage" seems to be a dirty word. Troilus uses the word only when he fears that when

Criseyde goes to the Greek camp, her father will marry her to some Greek. Criseyde refers to husbands in general as jealous or masterful impediments to freedom; in particular, she mentions her own husband only in a lie, when she denies to the Greek Diomede that she has loved any Trojan since her widowing. What is contemplated from first to last is an extra-marital affair. And it is one of the assumptions of Troilus, Criseyde, and Pandarus that such an affair might be indulged in by elegant people.

That Chaucer was thinking about a situation current in his own time is suggested by the Introduction to Book II, in which he points out that while customs of love change in various times and places, yet "they made love as we do." Anyhow, there are "many roads leading to Rome," and some lovers carve on trees, others on stone walls. The light tone of "carving on trees" is maintained in part of the poem, and apparently the road to Rome taken by Troilus and Criseyde was one well travelled by polite people. But although the lovers are portrayed with understanding and tenderness, the seamy side of the intrigue and the frailty of the relationship are also repeatedly exposed. And at each stage of the journey, Chaucer raises serious questions that lead to the religious answer at the end of the book.

The complexity of the characterization matches the "dreadful joy" of the affair. Troilus is both hero and anti-hero. Like Lancelot and Tristan, he is brave and handsome and faithful, qualities Chaucer never belittles. Further, true love educates him, and he dies a hero. On the other hand, there is something parodic about him from the first. An exaggeration of the knightly knight of the romances, he weeps so much, Chaucer tells us, that he almost drowns in his tears. So timid is he before his "sovereign lady," that he is speechless and faint. On a more serious level, his uncritical acceptance of the lies and plots of Pandarus are at least

119

unheroic, if not immoral and insensitive; this, of course, is what a noble man descends to in pursuit of a lady.

All that is ugly in a secret affair is personified in Pandarus, who establishes his role for all time in his opening lines. He would help Troilus, he says, even if the desired woman were Helen, the wife of Troilus's brother. What a good friend, say some of his latter-day admirers; and indeed, he is very like the Friend in *The Romance of the Rose* who plans the deceptions to be used by the Lover in pursuit of the Rose. It may be for the benefit of those not disturbed by the seduction of a brother's wife that Chaucer shows Pandarus taking the kinship closer. "Were it my sister," Pandarus exclaims, "by my will she would be all yours tomorrow!" And when in fact the lady is revealed as his niece, whom Pandarus is expected to protect, he feels no conflict of interest. But I think the reader is supposed to feel the conflict, and to see that this pleasantly immoral Friend is a bawd and liar who has less concept of honor than the duck in *The Parliament of Fowls*.

Criseyde is a weak sister whose infidelity, Chaucer says, he wishes to excuse as far as possible. He does so by showing her beauty, elegance, and "sliding" character. Fearful of losing the proffered love of Troilus, unwilling to say the definite no that is the only way to keep from yes, fearful of gossip and rumor, unprotected by family or moral code, she is always in an ambiguous position. Feeling that she is falling in love with Troilus, she debates with herself in arguments that were current in the Middle Ages and are still convincing in the twentieth century. She is "her own woman," she thinks, well-off and young, and has no husband to be jealous. Shall she not love if she wants? She is "not a nun," and so long as she keeps her good name. . . . On the other hand, once in love, she won't be free, and she sees in others the "dreadful joy" and pain of "stormy love."

And who knows, she broods, how it will all end! The reader knows that it will all end, alas, when Criseyde, in the Greek camp through no choice of her own, will easily argue herself into the arms of Diomede.

It is in Book III that the love of Troilus and Criseyde is consummated. This book is a tour de force in which romantic love is both satirized and glorified, and the carnal and spiritual are juxtaposed in a paradox that can be reduced to either term only by omitting half the scenes. The Proem to Book III is a Hymn to Venus which comes close to identifying the goddess of love with the love of God; sexual love with the love that created the universe. And the poet addresses Venus in terms he uses elsewhere for the Blessed Virgin Mary. Recalling the lush imagery of both St. Bernard and Gottfried von Strassburg, the passage gives promise of a glorified sex like that of Tristan and Isolt.

In his manner of including the sordid details of the intrigue which precedes the gladness, however, Chaucer seems to be satirizing rather than following the romantic poets. At one point, for example, Pandarus is worried about possible scandal. Troilus swears he would never tell, but to prove that there is nothing "bawdy" about the affair, he protests too much. For one thing, he makes a point of the fact that Pandarus's part in the affair is not for money. Further, he offers to "do the same" for Pandarus with one of his own sisters. Morally we are with that "good fellow" in *The Canterbury Tales*, the Summoner, if we leave out the quart of wine for which he would lend his girl to a friend.

Further, only the most determined romanticist can refrain from laughing at the beginning of the famous bedroom scene. First, Pandarus manipulates Criseyde, confusing her, lying to her, providing her with face-saving lines. Then, when all is ready, when the time is ripe to pluck the rose, Troilus swoons, and it takes the pandar himself to

121

undress him and throw him into bed with Criseyde. So far, the scene is a burlesque of all knight and lady encounters, a striptease which bit by bit strips the courtly disguise from the lustful creatures.

But then the naked body is so beautiful, the carnal union so ecstatic that only the language of religion can begin to describe it. The experience is not one of simple sensuality but of ecstasy touched with reverence and humility. Troilus's hymn to Venus, like the narrator's in the Proem, addresses love as the holy bond of all things, and in doing so very smoothly borrows phrases from Christianity. All were lost, Troilus says, unless "Love's grace" surpassed our deserving. And in a passion of gratitude to Criseyde, Troilus says that since God made him to serve her, she will find "truth and diligence" in him all his life. "Welcome," cries Criseyde, "my knight, my peace, my all!"

The high line is maintained by Troilus but not by Criseyde and Pandarus. The cold light of the morning after reveals a backstairs scene, with Pandarus leering at Criseyde, still in bed. The vulgar tone of the conversation in the secret room from which Troilus fled at dawn reminds us of Boccaccio. Troilus, however, is still on the heights with Boethius. Troilus's song of rejoicing, based on the spiritual love described in the *Consolation of Philosophy*, praises the love that "governs the earth and sea," "joins peoples," and "brings couples to dwell in virtue." So God, author of nature, binds hearts with his "bond of love."

This modified Boethius may be a key to an interpretation of human and divine love. Troilus obviously considers his love true and lasting. The dirty parts of the intrigue, that were not of his devising anyhow, have been left behind; and although the carnal has not been left, it has been linked with the spiritual. His song implies that his passionately fulfilled love has lifted him to a partial understanding of the love that moves the universe. I wonder if Chaucer meant us to see this and the following passage as steps on a ladder on which Troilus will ascend to heaven, leaving the carnal steps behind. Even on this rung, when he cannot imagine love without a body, he does not talk, however mystically, of sexual union, as does Gottfried's Tristan. There is no reference to bed in Troilus's song, no use of the Bride and Bridegroom imagery of Gottfried or St. Bernard. Both language and sentiment are pure, stressing virtue and stability, perhaps in preparation for the last act in the drama. At least, we are told at the end of Book III how love had altered his spirit. Now his speech was "most of love and virtue," now he scorned all wickedness, honored the worthy, and aided the distressed. Like the model Knight of *The Canterbury Tales*, now he treated no one proudly, but was kind to all. We are told that he began to flee from "Pride, Envy, Ire, and Avarice."

From Lechery? Not yet. Not until he dies in battle and is transported to the eighth sphere. Before that, he learns that bliss does not last and that Criseyde has forsaken him. His limited perception of the God of the universe has not given him fortitude, but he remains faithful to Criseyde, scorns Pandarus's advice to take another love, and dies not in bed but in battle. And as soon as Troilus is transported to the heavens, he sees the "brittleness" of earthly joys. When he leans over the bar of heaven, Troilus does not wish he had settled down in a garden apartment with Criseyde. Instead, he despises the wretched world and condemns blind lust.

Readers who think that the message of the poem is that romantic love is the highest good are irked with Chaucer for, as they say, changing his mind in this ending. They are as annoyed with Chaucer for sending Troilus to heaven as they are with Dante for sending Paolo and

123

Francesca to hell. But the point of both authors is that romantic love is not the summum bonum, and that the lovers who thought so were mistaken. The love of Troilus and Criseyde is the best this world can offer—only to those who know only this world. There is considerable Dantean influence here, in the way Troilus looks down on earth, in the final prayers, and, I think, in the basic conception. In *The Divine Comedy*, Dante shows a progression from carnal to spiritual love, from the earthly to the divine Beatrice, from paganism to Christianity, from Virgil to St. Bernard. This pattern may have been in Chaucer's mind when he was writing the conclusion of the *Troilus*. Not only does he echo many of Dante's lines, but he moves from pagan gods and pagan love to Christ and Christian love. Like Dante, Chaucer uses paganism as a metaphor for one of the perennial choices of mankind, that is, romantic love. When he turns to young Christians, Chaucer builds on Troilus's knowledge in the light of the Christian revelation. As Troilus looks down, the young folks are asked to look up, to go beyond Troilus's lesson that the world passes as a flower, to the specifically Christian substitution of Christ for worldly lovers.

This ending is Chaucer's own, very different from Boccaccio's. Boccaccio ends the *Filostrato* with a pragmatic warning: O youths in whom "amorous desires spring," check your steps; do not easily "put your trust in woman." Choose very carefully, "lest in the end you die for a worthless woman." The conclusion of the *Troilus* tells the young of both sexes to choose the love of God, who will always be faithful.

Of course that is not to say that Chaucer did not value human love, or even that he valued it less than those who deify it. The quarrelsome tone is ours, not Chaucer's, but he seems to have been weighing priorities, too. In *The Canterbury Tales* his characters argue among themselves—

the Wife of Bath, the Clerk, the Merchant, and the Franklin answering each other in tales and comments, in what
has been called the Marriage Group. But Chaucer does not
take sides openly enough to keep the critics from debating
over his views, and any simple conclusion can be dis-
proved. Since few of the stories neatly illustrate only one
point, any interpretation of his views on love and marriage
must be derived from his handling of plot and character,
and from his irony or lack of it. In such an interpretation,
many of the tales not in the so-called Marriage Group must
be included, even if there is no articulate argument in the
narrative. Whether by accident or design, the narratives
themselves range from the grossest adultery to celibacy in
marriage, with pagan romance and Christian matrimony
well mixed in between.

Gross as is the adultery in the fabliaux, youthful lust is
not portrayed as repulsive. Chaucer tells us about sex in the
same tone he uses to tell us it was a joy to see the Canon
sweat: it is an act of nature that gives pleasure when well
performed. Chaucer neither minimizes nor moralizes the
fun, nor does he show any later revulsion; none of his
characters would have understood Shakespeare's 129th
Sonnet.

It would be hard to imagine a grosser situation than
that in The Reeve's Tale. It is pitch dark, the ladies do not
know who has climbed into bed with them, there is no
preliminary talk, no pretence of affection. And yet it
doesn't sound like rape; the miller's wife enjoys the expertise of one clerk, and the daughter and the other clerk part
on terms of tenderness. Another fabliau, The Shipman's
Tale, is distasteful because of the deceitfulness of the monk
and the woman. In fact, the bedroom scene between husband and wife seems more immoral than that between wife
and monk because the woman appears more hypocritical

125

and whorish. The sex is sordid because money is at stake; still, there is "mirth" all night on both nights.

The Miller's Tale is more complex. The "kiss my ass" antics at the climax indicate that the affair is bestial at bottom, so to speak. And certainly when Nicholas grabs Alison by the haunches and protests that he may die for love of her, we recognize the old dance. The pair are only in lust and only her husband, the old carpenter, stands between them and instant gratification. But Chaucer does not dehumanize his characters to prove a point. The young people are most attractive physically, the husband is old and stupid, and their lovemaking is not mechanized. For all their crudity, Alison and Nicholas are not satisfied with behind-the-stairs fornication; the whole elaborate plot is contrived to give them a whole night together, a night of "revel and melody," of "mirth and solace."

The Merchant's Tale is also a fabliau in part, the part in which the young wife has sex with her lover in a pear tree her blind, old husband helped her climb. It is also a bitterly ironical portrait of marriage à la mode, told from the point of view of the Merchant, who says he has known more care and sorrow in two months of marriage than in his whole previous life.

In the fabliaux we have glanced at, the adultery is avowedly illicit, mutual pleasure. In The Merchant's Tale, legalized concubinage masquerades as Christian marriage. In a characteristic stylistic device, Chaucer lets us hear January mouthing the Christian principles he is perverting. Sixty-year-old January, having followed his appetites for many years, says he must marry for the good of his soul. But it is perverted pleasure not piety that leads him to choose a twenty-year-old girl. With a nod at the Church's acknowledgement of the difficulties of chastity, he protests his virility; in fact, on his wedding night, he drinks aphrodisiacs.

126

Chaucer portrays the old man's conduct as revolting, and his sympathy at this point is with May, who must put up with the old lecher's night labors and afternoon "play," be she "lief or loth."

We do not know much about May's thoughts, since January does most of the talking, but we know enough to judge that she fits the role of concubine. Just before she climbs the pear tree, she assures blind January he has no need to be jealous, and she swears by her religion and "her honor as a lady." As January perverts the ideal of marriage to lechery, so May and Damian reduce the romantic ideal to adultery. Their affair sounds like a fabliau version of *Troilus and Criseyde*. Damian falls in lust with May at first sight. Like Troilus, he takes to his bed; like Criseyde, May visits his bedside and promises not to "commit homicide" by denying him. The mood of romance requires leisure, but there is no time here for anything more than ingenuity. The climax on the pear tree, viewed by the miraculously restored January and defended as therapeutic by May, could hardly be more cynical.

The Wife of Bath is the counterpart of January in a number of ways. As he does not like "old beef," she does not like "old bacon"; ironically, he is like her first three old husbands whom she scorned, and she is the old wife he would not consider marrying. And both use land and money in the battle of the sexes. But while she is vulgar, she is not monstrous as he is. While both quote St. Paul, her use of Scripture seems less hypocritical than his; he pretends his practice fits Christian theory; she reworks the theory to suit her practice.

The Wife is a theorist, a forerunner of modern secularism in her exaltation of sex and marriage over virginity, and even of one kind of feminism in her advocacy of the sovereignty of women. The Wife is too funny and too vulgar: her arguments are too obviously molded by her appetites, and her portrait is too much like the old bawd in *The Romance of the Rose* for us to identify her views as Chaucer's. Still, Chaucer has modified his sources; the Wife is not just a bawd, and her views, as Chaucer lets her present them, are worthy of being heard and answered not only by the other pilgrims but by generations of their descendants.

The Wife is popular as a spokesperson for a traditional brand of anti-clericalism that sneers at the marital theorizing of celibates. Not "authority" but "experience" is enough for her, says the Wife. It is not so; the Wife is as "textual" as the Parson, but her choice of texts and her interpretations all lean to the practical and earthy as opposed to the theoretical and celestial. Her favorite text is "wax and multiply," and she defies the clergy to find a text defining the number of husbands lawfully permitted. Her connection of theory and practice is amusingly clear: "Blessed be God," she says, "that I have wedded five!" "Welcome the sixth," whenever he comes.

What really irks the Wife is the lavish praise bestowed on virginity with its consequent belittling of marriage. As she reads Scripture, God specifically commanded matrimony, not virginity. St. Paul, she remarks, admits he had "no precept" for virginity, and he "dared not command a thing which his Master did not." God left the choice to us, and certainly, "if there were no seed sown, whereof should virginity grow?" Lest the reader forget whence comes the argument, Chaucer lets the Wife go sly, her theology lapsing into a leer. She unnecessarily glosses "It is good not to touch a woman" as meaning "in bed" or "on a couch." It is as perilous as "bringing together fire and tow," she says, and "you know" what this example resembles.

Everybody knew. Everybody also knew that her next argument was sound. She concedes that maidenhood is to

128

multiple marriage as gold is to wood; still, wood does good service. Virginity, she says, is a counsel of perfection, like the counsel to give all to the poor and follow Christ. (This is a palpable hit at the clergy, who had chosen to be perfect, but who were notorious for not giving all to the poor.) She is not one who wishes to be perfect, but will "bestow the flower of her age" in the "acts and fruit of marriage."

Her discussion of the marriage debt is sheer comedy. To prove God intended engendering, she makes liberal use of the clerical precept that in marriage sex becomes an obligation to one's mate. Whenever her husband wishes to pay his debt, she says, she is willing to collect, for he is "her debtor and slave," and she has the "power over his body." That's what St. Paul meant, she explains, when he bade husbands love their wives well. Her three old husbands, she confesses, could only with difficulty "fulfill the statute by which they were bound." You know what I mean! she leers. And then she laughs when she remembers how pitifully she worked her old husbands at night. No contractual obligation was necessary with her fifth husband who was twenty when she was forty, and who could always win her over because he was so fresh in bed.

Not always an end in itself, sex is also a weapon in the marital battle. The Wife says she attacked first and ended the war. On the one hand, she accused her old husbands of wenching when they could barely stand, and the old fools were tickled in their hearts at the idea. On the other, she demanded a present at bedtime, before she feigned appetite which she did not feel for "old bacon." The battle was over when she "governed" them in accordance with her law. Hers was a benevolent dictatorship, and under it they were "blissful." Her fifth husband was difficult at first. In a reversal of the situation with her first three husbands, she had given him the land, and he had greater youth and sexual charm than she; further, he wished to be the master of a wife who stayed at home and practiced obedience. But after a fight in which he feared he had killed her, he "gave the bridle into her hand," the "governance" of house and land, and of his tongue. Whereupon they had a perfect marriage according to the Wife's formula: subordination plus sex equals peace.

The same moral is to be drawn from the tale which the Wife tells after her long prologue. Professedly a romance, the characters in it are no more romantic than May and Damian in the The Merchant's Tale, the hero being a knight who has been convicted of rape, the heroine an old hag with magical powers. Of interest in the history of courtly romances, however, is an incidental detail: a "court" of ladies who apparently discuss questions of love. To satisfy this court, the Knight must find the answer to the question of what it is that women most desire. When the knight finally applies the correct answer to his own plight, and gives the governance to the loathly lady, the story ends happily, by the Wife's standard.

Partly in answer to the Wife, the Clerk tells a tale which exalts the patient Griselda, who was entirely subordinate to her husband. But the Clerk realizes that the joy of this couple was something less than perfect, and he does not hold up Griselda as a model to wives, nor is her obedience his answer to the Wife. He says that his point is that as Griselda obeyed her husband, Walter, so all should obey God. Presumably "all" includes both Walter and the Wife of Bath, and the Clerk's condemnation, in the course of the story, of Walter's absolute sovereignty may glance at the Wife. More than an answer to the Wife, this old folktale also expresses (at some cost to the principle of a well-made story) both the attitude of the man-about-town to matrimony, and the Christian way to choose a wife.

Unlike the Wife, the Marquis Walter does not wish to marry; but his reasons against, are as selfish as hers for, marrying. Walter wants not to be boss but to be free: he never thought "to constrain himself," he says, in the bondage of matrimony. This traditional male reluctance to enter the blissful state described by the Wife is finally overcome by Walter's sense of social obligation.

It is in his description of Walter's motives in choosing Griselda that the Clerk poses a real alternative to the concepts of marriage held by the Wife and January. The Wife picked husbands by the amount of their wealth or the shape of their legs. Old January's preparation for matrimony was to fantasize over the delectable and submissive body of young May. Walter has a higher concept. First of all, he agrees to the "bondage" in order to engender an heir. And once having accepted the obligation of the common good, he insists on the highest good: he rejects social and economic qualifications for his bride in favor of the excellence that comes from God.

His procedure is also quite different from the Wife's or January's. While hunting, Walter often watches Griselda, not with wanton looks but with serious consideration. The physical is not ignored in Walter's evaluation, but linked with moral qualities: Griselda is a virtuous beauty. Commending her "womanliness," virtue, and goodness, Walter decides he shall wed only her. This is not a romance and there is no pretence that Walter has fallen in love or is panting with passion. Through reason alone he has chosen a bride who is both fair and faithful. He quite properly asks her father's consent and then sets the terms to her, terms which she is presumably free to refuse.

The narrator is not free to change the basic story of the exaction of an unreasonable promise; Walter requires absolute obedience in word and deed and Griselda accepts.

Before the story is continued, however, their early wedded life is described as an example of the happiness conferred by virtue. The peace between husband and wife extends to others and their marriage bears good fruit not only for them but for the kingdom which Griselda rules most justly in Walter's absence.

Walter's decision to test Griselda's fidelity to her promise, a test that lasts for sixteen years and includes a pretense of slaying their two children, divorcing Griselda, and taking a new wife, is obviously unrealistic. We are in a never-never world in which there are no laws against murder, and time is of no consequence, but a promise must be kept to the letter. Such a märchen could be interpreted in a number of ways; the Clerk imposes a Christian meaning. His view opposes that of the Wife, but not by exalting the sovereignty of the husband. The Clerk consistently voices disapproval of Walter's conduct, and he generalizes his view by saying that it is evil to test a wife and put her in "anguish and dread." His is the accepted Christian view, expressed by the Parson, that the authority of the husband must be used in accordance with reason and bound by love. Some men, the clerk reflects, "know no measure" when they find a patient creature, and he points out approvingly that the common people hated Walter as a murderer. When he says near the end that the story is not told so that wives should follow Griselda, we can believe him. His view is that only God has absolute sovereignty; neither Walter nor Griselda is his model for the Wife, but the Christian marriage he describes early in the story.

As befits his station, the Franklin's manner of speaking about marriage is quite different from that of the Clerk. According to the General Prologue, the Franklin is "Epicurus's own son," a worldly man who seeks pleasure and in whose house it "snowed" meat and drink. The Franklin also believes, however, that possessions are useless if the owner is not virtuous. His tale is of worldly, courtly lovers of equal rank, quite different from Griselda and Walter; but his ideal of marriage does not conflict with the Clerk's but is rather a romantic adoption of the same principles. As unrealistic a story as the Wife's and the Clerk's, with similar magic and binding promises and marriage talk, the point of The Franklin's Tale is that ladies and gentlemen need not imitate the Wife or Griselda or Walter; beautiful people can have a beautiful marriage if they truly love each other and work at being civilized.

This romantic fairy tale is set in remote Brittany, where a knight "served in many a great enterprise" for his lady and long feared to speak of his love. At last she decides to take him for her husband because of his "worthiness and obedience." He swears of "his free will" that "never in his whole life" will he "take mastery or be jealous," but obey as lover to his lady," except that he would like the "name of sovereignty" in public, for appearances. She thanks him and says that since of "gentilesse" he offers her so large a rein, God grant there will never be strife between them that is her fault. She will be "his humble, true wife." "Take my truth," she says, "till my heart breaks."

Some recent commentators shake the head over this exchange and say that the husband's words are responsible for the later trouble: he should have assumed the headship in matrimony, in accordance with the teaching of the Church. It is true that the Parson says the husband should be boss, albeit a reasonable and loving one, but his emphasis is not necessarily Chaucer's nor is it *de fide*. Even St. Augustine had said that the ideal marriage is based on mutual love and companionship, although the husband leads and protects the wife. Further, St. Bonaventure insisted that headship in matrimony must not be confused

FRANKLIN

with "mastery," and that the husband must love his wife as himself. It is "mastery" that Arveragus in the tale abjures; he loves Dorigen as himself, and it is he who makes the final, controversial decision.

Certainly the Franklin's view is presented without irony, and certainly the Franklin thinks he is describing an ideal, Christian, romantic marriage, rather like that described in Gower's *Tract for Married Lovers*. Presumably answering the Wife and Walter, the Franklin remarks that love will not be "constrained by mastery; when mastery comes in, the god of love beats his wings and farewell, he is gone!" He argues that women by nature desire liberty, and adds, "so do men." Liberty for what? Not just the Wife of Bath and La Vieille in the *Romance of the Rose*, but such real and fictional pairs as Heloise and Abelard, and Guenevere and Lancelot, meant, as we have seen, extra-marital sexual freedom. But for married lovers it meant liberty from jealousy and tyranny, with consequent increase in mutual fidelity, of "loyal friend with loyal friend."

The Franklin's little homily is carefully Christian. Starting with the loving attraction that is the natural basis of matrimony, the Franklin supernaturalizes it by relating it to that "high virtue" that vanquishes, "as the clergy say," things that "rigor" could never achieve. The way to nurture love without constraining liberty, he says, is by patience. We have seen patience personified in the wife Griselda; in the Franklin's view, husbands are also bound to practice this most Christian virtue. Learn to endure, the Franklin says in a paraphrase of the Christian marriage service, in sickness and in health.

The application of the teaching to the tale that follows is tricky, because like The Clerk's Tale, The Franklin's Tale is an old märchen that must not be taken literally. Here a civilized doctrine of an ethics of intention is superimposed on a primitive story of bondage to the literal words of a promise never intended to be kept.

The setting and characters are highly sophisticated. The garden in which the rash promise is made is like that in *The Romance of the Rose, The Merchant's Tale, The Parliament of Fowls,* and dozens of other medieval stories, and is only too well suited to dalliance. We see the temptations inherent in a courtly life of ease and idleness, in which the very customs of courtesy may trap a lady who does not carefully guard her words. Surely this is a reflection not of ancient Brittany but of the elegantly immoral court of Richard the Second. But the Franklin's point is that elegance need not be immoral. Dorigen is not flirting with adultery, nor is she ambiguous like Criseyde. Once she understands Aurelius's drift, she tells him plainly, as "a final answer," that she will never be an "untrue wife." It is by way of courteous dismissal that she adds lightly that she will be his only when the rocks are all removed from the coast; and he knows her meaning, for he asks, "Is there no other hope?" No, she replies, and preaches a little sermon which emphasizes the purity of her intention. "Shut such follies" from your heart, she urges. "What pleasure should a man have" in loving the wife of another man "who has her body whenever he likes?"

When the rocks do seem to have moved and Aurelius

claims his promise, Dorigen does not consider a secret meeting which she might conceal from her husband. It is a vindication of their relationship of trust that she tells him the whole story, and like "a true and humble wife" asks him what she should do.

Keeping to the letter of a promise is the motif of many an old tale. Even in The Summoner's Tale, the friar is obliged to divide the fart equally because he had so promised before the present was named or given! In various tales about King Arthur and King Mark, Guenevere and Isolt respectively are literally given away to minstrels by their husbands who had carelessly promised "anything" for another song. No mention is made in any of these tales of the sixth commandment, because in fairy tale logic only one difficult choice is propounded at a time.

On this level, then, Dorigen's is a fairy tale promise like those in the Wife's and the Clerk's tales, which must be kept in the story but is not to be taken literally by the audience. But the very nature of the choice makes us speculate about what a real husband would do. Many readers want Arveragus to take the mastery, to kill Aurelius or send Dorigen away on a trip. To this noble husband, however, his wife's word is as important as his own, and she must keep her promise for "Troth is the highest thing that men may keep." The Franklin, knowing that many of his hearers will criticize both knight and storyteller, asks all to withhold judgment until they hear the end. His plea misses the point that the knight's choice must be made without that foreknowledge. But the ending helps the reader evaluate Chaucer's view, because in this kind of exemplum, the conclusion of the plot makes a point, a happy ending proving that the characters made the correct decision. Chaucer may not have believed that a knight, a squire, and a clerk would "really" forego their privileges, but he apparently

136

liked the notion that gentilesse breeds gentilesse; he may even have thought that the perils of a high civilized style are worth risking in matrimony, as well as in religion and poetry.

Of all the tales in the Canterbury collection, the Franklin's comes closest to portraying a balance of carnal and spiritual love. While the presence of sex is felt strongly, there are no bedroom scenes as there are in the fabliaux and the *Troilus,* and sex is subordinated to love in marriage. With The Knight's Tale, the balance shifts far enough away from the carnal to give us a picture of love so romantic that it includes no physical contact at all. The Knight's concept may be said to be the opposite of the Miller's, the high line versus the low line; Emily and her two knights form amusing counter and contra parts to Alison and her two clerks.

As The Miller's Tale satirizes low-life adultery, The Knight's Tale incidentally satirizes high-life romance, or at least, its extravagant conventions. When Palamon first sees Emily from his prison window, he thinks her a goddess, and worships accordingly. He and Arcite think only of Emily, day and night, for years. Deprived of the hope of seeing Emily, Arcite is "always solitary" and "sleepless," "lean and dry," "hollow-eyed and pale," "melancholy and fantastic." Worst of all, the sworn friends are ready to fight to the death for the love of this lady to whom they have never spoken a word.

It is one of the characters in the tale, the great Theseus, who remarks on the "high folly" of this behavior. The "best game of all," he says is that she for whom they bleed knows nothing about it. The Knight-narrator himself describes the Temple of Venus in most unromantic terms. On the wall of this piteous temple are depicted all the woes love's servants endure: broken sleep, sighs, tears, and the fire of desire. On the other hand, the constructive side of romantic love is expressed by Arcite on his deathbed. He speaks, in much the vein of Troilus, of the wisdom, humility, honor, and truth that result from the service of love.

There is no basic contradiction between these passages, however. The Knight is primarily a soldier who loves chivalry, truth, and honor. Love fits into this pattern by giving a knight something to fight for and by improving his manners. Considered in itself, it is really a bit comical and unreasonable, but the Knight only occasionally considers it in itself. The high chivalric romance told from this exclusively masculine view is sexless, not primarily because the Knight has an exalted view of marriage but because he has not thought about it at all.

Marriage is an important consideration in the stories of those Christian heroines, Constance, Griselda, and Prudence, but sex and romantic love play only a small part in their dramas. The limitations are in part a matter of literary genre. We do not expect romantic love in homilies starring characters who are largely personifications of virtues. But why not? The fact that Chaucer's performance matches our expectation is significant in the moral as well as the literary realms. Behind the generally accepted reticence is the feeling that sex may be beautiful, but it's not quite holy; as the Parson put it, "carnal delight" and "excessive adoration" are tinged with venial sin because the actors are not thinking about God. Saints have to be as singleminded about God as Palamon and Arcite are about Emily. Such a state of mind seems easiest to achieve in a life of virginal contemplation, but our ladies are married, active saints. Hagiographers are likely to follow such saints into church, kitchen, council chamber, and almshouse, but not into the bedroom, although the physical bond of their marriages is never in doubt.

The Man of Law's Tale, which features constancy,

belongs in some ways to the same literary type as the Knight's and Franklin's stories, being part romance as well as legend. As in some of the most extreme troubadour stories, the exotically pagan Sultan of Syria falls desperately in love with Constance, the daughter of the Emperor of Rome, just by hearing reports of her beauty, goodness, and courtesy. The marriage arrangements, however, in which Constance's feelings are of small concern, realistically reflect many a political alliance. And when after many improbable adventures, Constance marries King Alla of Britain, the Man of Law's brief comment reflects his view of contemporary Christian marriage. After the feast, he says, they go to bed as is right and reasonable. For though "wives be very holy things," they must "take in patience at night such necessities as are pleasing to folk wedded with rings," and "lay their holiness aside a little." The smirk may not be Chaucer's, but the view could be. We need not think Constance cold or unwilling; she is an affectionate woman who loves her husband. If we may be so rude as to imagine the bedroom scene, we can guess that she did not call Alla her "peace and her all," as Criseyde called Troilus; but neither did she preach him a little sermon on the four last things.

In the marriages of Constance, Griselda, and Prudence, the bond of union is physical, and the marriages are fruitful; unlike Criseyde and the Wife of Bath, these women all bear children. They are, as the wedding service puts it, joined with their husbands as one flesh, but two souls under God. Griselda tells Walter plainly that since when she came to him she brought her maidenhead, he should not send her away naked. Her request, the first she has made, is a reminder of that least-remembered virtue, modesty.

But it is not only modesty that makes the romantic irrelevant here. The love that is associated with this kind of union is not ecstatic or dangerous but sober and stable, constant and prudent. The bedroom is not, in fact, the most important room in such a marriage; the women are competent in every other room, and they advise their husbands on religious, political, and social affairs. For all the extravagance of the fictions, we get convincing glimpses of domestic life in which the partners talk over daily problems. And the marriages go wrong only when the husbands do not follow the injunction of the wedding service to love and trust their wives.

Happy or unhappy, all of these loves are passing. When Constance and Alla are finally reunited, the Man of Law reminds us that joy does not last but is followed by pain and loss. Only the spiritual is not subject to decay, only the divine endures. That is the message at the end of the *Troilus,* and that is the theme of The Second Nun's Tale; and there is no reason to think that Chaucer was shocked by St. Cecilia's early and absolute rejection of the usual compromises of marriage.

Twentieth-century readers *are* shocked by Cecilia's confident advocacy of celibacy in marriage. The very phrase is an affront to our proprieties; but to medieval man, celibacy in marriage was only the extreme to which respect for chastity might be carried. Cecilia's case was unusual, but the treasuring of virginity did not seem odd. Chaucer's devotional poems to Mary praise her virginity most sincerely; and in the extreme case of The Physician's Tale of Virginius, there is no hint of criticism or astonishment at the attitude of the pagan father who kills his daughter rather than have her "dishonored." Of course, celibacy in marriage was not one of the options offered by the Goddess of Nature in *The Parliament of Fowls* to ordinary birds, but saints were extraordinary—not freakish, but supernaturally heroic. And the devout husband and wife who, usually after years of matrimony, chose to live as brother and sister (as praised by the Parson and rejected by January), were still husband and wife, bound in faith to Christ and to each other. A medieval audience would not therefore have been horrified at Cecilia's proposal of celibacy to her pagan groom on their wedding night. They would have been impressed by her bravery and faith; but that's what made her a saint, and anyhow, she had an angel at hand for all emergencies.

The Second Nun's Tale was apparently not written for *The Canterbury Tales,* but when Chaucer assigned it to the Second Nun, he may well have seen that it presented yet another view in the running argument of the pilgrims on marriage. Not at all a formal debate, the argument includes stories, allusions, and asides, and most important, the characters themselves. The Second Nun and St. Cecilia incarnate a point of view as much as does the Wife of Bath. And when we listen, we hear a Cecilia who is quite as outspoken as the Wife, and at least as vigorous a proponent of her own views on matrimony. Like the loathly lady in The Wife of Bath's Tale, on her wedding night she presents her husband with a hard choice: respect her vow or be slain by the angel who guards her virginity. Without any doubt of the rightness of her theory of celibacy in marriage, she calls Valerian her "sweet and well beloved spouse dear"—as she tells him he must not touch her "in villainy."

Now both her theory and her practice are applauded in words which might be construed as an answer to the Wife of Bath. The Wife had asked in her Prologue, if there were no seed sown, whence would virginity grow? Pope Urban in The Second Nun's Tale says that the "seed" of chastity had been sown in Cecilia by Jesus, and that the "fruit" is Valerian's conversion. But this process of reasoning is dangerously circular. If, as is likely, the Wife's Prologue was written later than the legend, the Wife may have been answering Cecilia. No doubt she was answering all the Cecilias she had impatiently heard about all her life. The use of identical phrases may prove only how conventional seed and fruit images were in medieval table talk about sex.

In any event, there is nothing in the text to make us think that Chaucer found Cecilia's view on marriage preposterous. The praise accorded Valerian for quickly assenting to her good advice is quite straight-faced. And while it was a joke that the Wife's love sent her husband to heaven by providing his purgatory on earth, Cecilia's chaste love is seriously acclaimed for bringing her husband to "bliss above." Further, Cecilia's conduct would seem to follow in some ways the advice Chaucer gave in the *Envoi* to *Troilus*. There he advises not just old ladies and professional celibates, but "young, fresh folks, he or she," to refrain from worldly vanity, and to think "all the world but a fair that passes as a flower." This is exactly the counsel of young and fresh Cecilia to Valerian who, by the way, receives miraculous out-of-season flowers that do not fade.

Chaucer, of course, was not so naïve as to take his own stories literally. In The Second Nun's Tale he was not advising maidens to refuse to consummate their marriages any more than in The Clerk's Tale he was advising wives to hand their children over to the executioner. Nor in The Franklin's Tale was he advising lonely wives to avoid excessive melancholy and rash promises. There is, however, a common denominator in all of these stories, a rather modest, medieval moral that Chaucer probably accepted: it is that honorable people keep their promises under duress. The märchen told by the Franklin, the exemplum told by the Clerk, the legend told by the Nun, all illustrate the virtue of fidelity to one's vows, whether they be taken in celibacy or matrimony, to God or to man.

While on the one hand, the words of promises are binding, on the other, intentions are more important than deeds, the spirit than the letter. Not many people went as far as Heloise in discounting the act entirely, but almost every serious writer or thinker went as far as the Parson and Dante in thinking the moral value of both virtues and vices depended on motives. In Chaucer's stories, when the motives are wrong, the marriages fail. He presents as hateful or contemptible legally impeccable marriages between old men and young women, the use of sex as a weapon in the war for power, and hypocritical speeches of love.

The evidence of his life and works suggests that Chaucer shared the admiration of his time for virginity, holy matrimony, and satires of marriage, not necessarily in that order. He never denies the attraction of lust, and he sees the power of romantic love to educate and civilize. He does not denigrate the human qualities of beauty, courage, knowledge, and the striving for love and honor; but he sees the peril of exalting human love as an end in itself. In effect, Chaucer seems to have believed what the Parson taught, that all loves should be subordinated to the love of Christ. Not a parson himself, however, he laughed at the sexual antics of the race, and he knew also that the Parson's description of sex as the payment of the marriage debt was woefully inadequate.

It all comes together in Chaucer's works, without any chronological line of developing skepticism or piety. The poem "Envoy to Bukton" written in 1396 on the occasion of Bukton's approaching marriage, conveys the spirit of a bachelor party. The poem echoes not only the Canterbury characters but Juvenal, Valerius, and Jean de Meun, who so grieved for friends planning matrimony that they asked if there were no halters for sale or bridges to jump from. The best joke is that in the Envoy, Chaucer advises his friend to read the "Wife of Bath," as though she were an authority on the woes of marriage like St. Jerome. Within a few years of this cheerful chaffing (Chaucer died in 1400), he wrote the Retraction. In this farewell, the author asked God's mercy for whatever sin there was in *Troilus* and the other love poems, and thanked Jesus and his Mother for his legends of saints and homilies—no doubt including the tales of those good married women Constance, Griselda, and Prudence.

Superb artist and deep Christian, Chaucer was famous in his own time as a painter of the whole range of human loves; nowhere are the passing joys more joyful than in Chaucer's work, but often he reminds us that they are passing, from Troilus in the eighth sphere to the Man of Law on the pilgrimage quoting Innocent III's *Contempt of the World.*

V

Faith and Feminism

t is not stretching the modern instance to refer to the feminism of the fourteenth century; there was at least as much talk then as now about the position of women, and even the jokes that are current now were old then. As they are reflected in Chaucer's work, the terms and focus of the argument were somewhat different, but the tendency to stereotype was the same. There was plenty of room for argument. According to Christian doctrine, the sexes are equal before God, and the same moral criteria apply to both. Nothing beyond that is *de fide*, there being nothing in the Creed about the position of women. That means that this enormously controversial subject was wide open, with all sides claiming divine sanction, both in the actual controversy in Chaucer's time and in the fictional arguments he portrayed. Chaucer faithfully recorded all the clichés with his usual humorous detachment: the accusations of the satirists and the answers of the feminists, the unconscious chauvinism of the Parson, the militancy of the Wife, and

145

the misogyny of the Merchant. And typically, we must deduce Chaucer's views not from the speeches of any one character but from the cumulative weight of story and character. In fact, we can gather some of his feeling about the role of women from the romances and homilies in which feminism is not an issue.

There was very little chauvinism in Chaucer's character, but just as little militancy, and as he would not please the extremists now, he did not please them then. According to his own account in the Prologue to *The Legend of Good Women*, Chaucer was reprimanded by the extreme faction of "liberated" women at court. In their complaint that Chaucer had portrayed the unfaithful Criseyde and had translated the anti-feminist *Romance of the Rose*, and in their insistence that only a particular type of good woman be portrayed in literature, we hear the voices of a coterie of determined propagandists. What is confusing to twentieth-century readers of *The Legend* is that the anti-feminist stereotype was quite different from the Victorian one fought by their latter-day sisters. To understand Chaucer's works, we must know that the contention of the satirists of the fourth to the fourteenth centuries was that women were sexually insatiable, and that they thus robbed a man of his health as well as his wealth. The Wife of Bath's pride in her sexual prowess, sometimes read as liberation today, was, in fact, derived from the misogynists. Defenders of women, like Chaucer in *The Legend*, insisted that women were not like the Wife, but were modest and faithful unto death. Chaucer's compliance was only partial, however; he provided the required type without rejecting *The Romance* or Criseyde, not to mention the Wife.

In twentieth-century social and literary histories, the anti-feminist literature of the Middle Ages is described in solemnly indignant terms, and to be sure, some of it is very nasty. If solemn indignation is the only proper response, we should, therefore, be very angry with Geoffrey Chaucer, who mined the field for comedy. If one may say so, there was often something ridiculous about the whole controversy, and some of the disputants knew it. Most of what we call anti-feminism originated as anti-matrimony; some of the ensuing low comedy thus stemmed from the ancient obscenities that surrounded the marriage bed and led to that traditionally ludicrous figure, the cuckold. Whether the author was Juvenal, St. Jerome, Theophrastus, Walter Map, or Matheolus, to name the ones most cited, the message from one man to another was: Don't marry. There is no possibility of happiness in marriage, says Roman Juvenal, because all women are evil, a remark which (wherever he got it) echoes King Solomon's Proverbs.

Perhaps the extravagance and vehemence of the arguments submitted should be taken as testimony to the enduring attractions of the female and state attacked. After all, there is little evidence that anybody ever refrained from marriage as a result of reading one of these tracts. And the "just between us boys" tone is pathetic as well as provoking, because it implies the necessity of conspiracy and silence, lest the formidable female (like the Wife of Bath) hear and punish. Only on his deathbed, for example, did the much-quoted King Phoroneus dare whisper to his brother that he could die happy if he knew his brother would never wed.

What these desperate men were apparently most threatened by was a combination of female sexuality and dominance. True, they cite such presumably feminine vices as vanity and gossip, and they speculate that a servant would be cheaper around the house, but the real excitement and most of the venom arise from the fear of being cuckolded or dominated or both. Tract after tract warns the would-be husband that nothing he can do will ensure the

147

fidelity of his wife, whether she be beautiful or ugly, rich or poor, young or old. Even if she is technically virtuous, she will be dreaming of someone else. And at the same time, in spite of the intentions of God himself (manifest to every male reader of the Bible), the wife will manage to gain the upper hand. To prove the point, the writers begin with Eve and cite from Scripture, myth, and history examples of women who brought disaster on their husbands by disobedience and infidelity. The comedy implicit on every level of this literature was made explicit by Chaucer in his male as well as female characters, in January and the Host as well as the Wife and Alison. Nor was he above using the jokes directly; in the "Envoy to Bukton" he borrowed from Juvenal the notion that it is better to commit suicide than be enslaved by marriage.

Defenders of women also sought a share of the media, and were apparently successful towards the end of the fourteenth century. A measure of their success we have already observed in Chaucer's public penitence in *The Legend of Good Women* for having translated *The Romance of the Rose*, a book which was the center of an interesting chapter in the history of feminism.

According to a thirteenth-century French source, which may not be true, a number of court ladies wanted to whip Jean de Meun because of his scurrilous attacks on women in *The Romance*. They had cause; and perhaps they wanted a stick because they despaired of matching him in the manipulation of words. In the "Apology" for his book, for example, Jean says righteously that his satire on womankind was not written in hatred or drunkenness but with the desire to instruct. If any honorable ladies think he lies, let them search the "authorities"—who couldn't all be lying too, and who all agree with him—since they knew the ways of women. Even more unanswerable are his supremely clever dramatizations of anti-feminist arguments in the persons of female characters or their presumed friends. La Vieille, the bawd whom we have already discussed in chapter four, gives instructions on how to be a successful prostitute and remarks that all women long for every male they see. Genius, a character closely allied with lady Nature, outlines the proper treatment of a wife: provide clothes; let her buy and sell, even pursue a craft if she has ability; but don't give her too much power, because sovereignty makes a woman oppose her spouse in everything.

Even what should be construed as an indictment of men comes out of Jean's pen as a degradation of women. The Lover's Friend (who learned from Ovid) explains cynically that since women don't like to be restrained or scolded, don't reproach them even if you catch them in the act; smile and pretend to be blind. Even more cynical is the Friend's advice to the Lover to use a little force when the time comes to pluck the Rose. "They all" like a little force, he explains, and are only pretending not to yield. Worst of all from the feminist point of view, that Rose is not even a woman, no less a person, but a symbol of sex. All of this and more the feminists saw.

But there are other things in *The Romance,* and, I think, another way of reading it, and perhaps this was Chaucer's way. Jean de Meun was an anti-romantic moralist who, like Chaucer, had translated *The Consolation of Philosophy* of Boethius as well as many other serious works. Romantic love, not to mention the worship of woman portrayed in popular fiction, seems to him a delusion, a pretense to satisfy lust without disturbing the amenities. The whole apparatus of sighs and swoons and sweet words he sees as allies of fornication and prostitution. The purpose of sex, he believes, is biological; the rest is humbug. And this humbug is nurtured especially by women, who are too

149

frivolous to admit that the end of the Romance—yes, of the elegant *Romance* by Guillaume de Lorris, with all its fine words—is blind orgasm. Jean has been called, with some justice, the Voltaire of the thirteenth century.

On the other hand, or perhaps on the opposite side of the coin, Jean shows a grudging respect for unfrivolous women. Having advised seduction to the Lover, the Friend advises "innocent" men not to be too impressed with face and form, but to heed character "founded on art and science." Beauty doesn't last, he says, but a woman who has an education "will make a fitting helpmeet" as long as she lives, and "will be better at the end than at the beginning." Further, such a woman delights in a man of intelligence who proves to be wise and good. In the Golden Age, he continues, all were equals, and true companionship was united with love, not separated by the battle over supremacy.

Jean comes close to saying that Heloise was such a superior woman, but he manages to make the compliment left-handed. It comes in the midst of a discussion of jealousy, in the course of which the Jealous Husband gives a little summary of anti-feminist works, referring to Theophrastus who regretted having wed, and to Valerius who grieved when he saw that his friend Rufinus would take a wife. In the midst of this traditional diatribe, he inserts the story of Heloise. Anti-feminism hits a new low here: praising Heloise for arguing against marriage with Abelard, he turns the praise into an attack on the rest of womankind by attributing Heloise's superiority to her unusual control of her feminine tendencies. Sad to say, Heloise herself (if her letters are authentic) accepted the anti-feminist line. When she attempted to argue Abelard out of marriage, she used the same anti-matrimonial texts they had studied together. But Jean's interest in her goes beyond polemics. What his spokesman admires in her is not the romantic young girl of the love story but the independent, educated woman, who, in fact, had many of the same views as Jean. Emphasizing her wisdom and learning, he tells us that Heloise demanded that Abelard love her without claim, "without supremacy or mastership," so that both might pursue their studies freely. Conceding that some say her letters show insanity, he admits to finding them "marvellous."

The Romance was the work Chaucer translated early in his career and made amends for later. The translation was his own idea; *The Legend* was, as he says in the Prologue, put upon him by the ladies. If the Prologue was written in 1394, as it may have been, the controversy over *The Romance* was becoming very warm; and it is quite possible that Chaucer had met, certainly he had heard about, the lady at the center, Christine de Pisan.

Christine was a remarkably successful feminist. Born in Italy in 1363, Christine at fifteen married a French gentleman, and at twenty-five was widowed with three small children. She decided to earn her livelihood as a writer, and in the course of the years, she wrote lyrical, sacred, and scientific poems and moral, political, and educational prose. Like several other medieval women authors (Hroswitha and Marie de France, for example), Christine did not run into chauvinistic hurdles in her literary career, kings and nobles all approving her plans. It was not primarily out of self-interest, then, that she took upon herself the defense of women, especially against Jean de Meun, still a widely read author. She called on all honorable men to support her against *The Romance of the Rose*, and many did, notably Jean Gerson, the Chancellor of the University. Many also defended *The Romance* in a war of tracts and epistles and poems. As a result of Christine's efforts, two societies were formed, one in 1399, another in 1402, the members of which bound themselves by a vow to defend the honor of women. There is no evidence, however, that the circulation of *The Romance* decreased.

The title of Christine's first published work on the subject, *An Epistle to the God of Love,* reminds us of the God of Love who reprimands Chaucer in the Prologue to *The Legend of Good Women.* Any literary indebtedness would have to be on Christine's part, since her work was not published until 1399; but the same controversy is reflected in both. Relations were very close between the French and English courts. Chaucer himself had been to the French court more than once on different missions; and one of the Lollard Knights with whom he was friendly, Sir John Montague, third Earl of Salisbury, was a friend of Christine's. Indeed, when Salisbury was in Paris in 1396 for the marriage of Richard II to Isabella of France, he took Christine's elder son back to England, to be reared as his own son. It may well be that the English ladies Chaucer portrays in the Prologue had got their feminist inspiration and direction from their French sisters.

From the point of view of faith as well as feminism, Christine's *Epistle* is more interesting than Chaucer's *Legend of Good Women.* Ignoring the usual commentaries, Christine cites the most ignored passage of Scripture, Gen 1:27, "God created man in his image; in the divine image he created him; male and female he created them," to show that God created woman as well as man in his own image. Taking the offensive, she says further that God made woman of finer material than man—Adam of dust, Eve of bone; and Eve is nobler than Adam because she was created in Paradise and he was not. (Perhaps the Wife of Bath would have made these points if Christine had written earlier!)

Most of Christine's heroines, like Chaucer's, are proving not theology but a special kind of morality. In these and similar works, "good" and "bad" are entirely relative terms, referring only to the adversary point of view. The same stories are therefore not always told in the same way, but are modified in accordance with the point of view of the author. The most borrowed-from list of both bad and good women can be found in one work, a tract by St. Jerome. In his *Answer to Jovinian,* a monk who had apparently turned against asceticism, virginity, and celibacy, Jerome formulates his list of bad women as an argument against marriage. In another section of the same epistle, he cites virtuous women from Scripture, myth, and history to prove the universality of Christian moral teaching. To prove the misogynists wrong, Christine and Chaucer celebrate the virtue of female fidelity.

In Chaucer's *Legend,* the ladies appear not just as good women, but as "Cupid's saints," martyrs who suffered or died in devotion to their lovers. Only the pro-feminist motive explained in the Prologue makes it possible to imagine Cleopatra and Medea wearing halos; all is forgotten here except their enthusiasm for Mark Antony and Jason. The legends not only omit anything unfavorable about the ladies but are also biased against the men. As a result of deletions and additions to the classic stories, Dido, for example, is not only innocent and trusting, but Aeneas has promised to marry her; the vengeances of Medea and Philomela are omitted; and the constant refrain in this legend of bad men is, Don't trust men, unfaithful, fickle, seducers all.

It's hard to believe Chaucer was entirely serious about these "saints"; it's impossible to believe he was sorry he had written *Troilus and Criseyde* and had translated *The Romance of the Rose.* For one thing, either-or is not Chaucer's style. Unlike Jean de Meun, he probably did not want to offend the ladies unnecessarily. His placating nature is seen

153

near the end of *Troilus,* where he begs the ladies not to be angry with him for portraying the guilt of Criseyde. Similarly, in *The House of Fame* he warns women of the wiles of men who wish to seduce them; and there is no reason to doubt his sympathy for all the women like Dido who were abandoned by their lovers. On the other hand, he is careful in the Prologue to *The Legend* to avoid renunciation of the two works; he remains silent while the Queen answers the God of Love for him. She excuses him on the grounds that he is a kind of professional translator who translates anything he's asked to translate, without necessarily knowing what he's saying! When the poet finally speaks I think we can take what he says as broadly true of his work. He says that true lovers ought not to blame him for "speaking shame" of false lovers; and that whatever his sources meant, it was his intent "to further truth in love" and warn of vice and falsehood. For all his pleasant manner, Chaucer is asserting his independence of both Jean and the feminists.

From the long-range feminist, as well as the literary, point of view, Chaucer was far more successful when he did not follow the party line depicted in *The Legend.* In other portraits of women, good and bad, the stereotype is evident enough, but as Chaucer's and the reader's interest increases, the characters become complex and overshadow the clichés. Chaucer describes with the artist's verve all the shades and colors; he enjoys the jokes on both sides; he looks at women through a man's eyes, and does not find revolting a voluptuous Venus floating naked on the sea. While he was thus not necessarily thinking about religion when describing a woman, his judgments of women were shaped in part by his Christianity. In his portrayal of society, the women who achieve respect, equality, or superiority are persons who in one way or another transcend the battle of the sexes.

If we measure feminism by attitudes toward the double standard, by interests and influence outside the home, and by qualities of leadership, independence, and courage, it is not the Wife of Bath but St. Cecilia who is the radical feminist. Was Chaucer using these measures? I do not think he wrote to prove a list or fill a formula, but it does seem that his creative imagination was at work on the connections between faith and what we call feminism, and that in his fictional world, one strengthens the other. Certainly the Wife and Cecilia both embody and articulate extreme views, while the other females, pilgrims or characters in tales, fall somewhere in between in both feminism and sanctity. The men, meanwhile, are expressing their opinions, and they're usually wrong.

The Wife is certainly an outspoken defender of the rights and privileges of women. She might well serve as the patron saint of those latter day feminists who proudly proclaim female concupiscence and edit *Playgirl.* In her own time she was a composite of anti-feminist stereotypes that by some aesthetic miracle came alive so that she became one of the "authorities" against marriage as though she were a real person; she is cited along with Seneca and the Bible by Justinus in The Merchant's Tale, and by Chaucer himself in the Envoy to The Clerk's Tale and the "Envoy to Bukton." Derived in part from the old Bawd in *The Romance of the Rose,* she is a visible and audible argument against women in her insatiable lust, her incessant talk, her craze for clothes, and her lies and tricks. Besides incarnating the arguments, she answers them, and her answers reveal a very limited feminism which depends entirely on sex.

The complexity of Chaucer's serio-comical satire can be seen in the Wife's long speech in which she accuses her husbands of speaking the anti-feminist line. To do so, she herself pours out Jean de Meun's invective. "You say," she

155

says she said to her husbands, that if a woman is poor, she costs too much, if rich, it is a "torment to endure her pride." If she is fair, the Wife continues, you say that every man is after her and a "castle wall can be kept against assault" only so long; if she be ugly, you say that she desires every man she sees and "leaps on them like a spaniel." You say that "oxen, asses, horses, and hounds" are all tried out before men buy them, but men make no trial of wives until they are wedded, and then the wives show their vices. You say you must always "praise my beauty" and make a "feast on my name day" and be kind to my relatives, you "old barrelful of lies!" All this and much more the Wife pretends her husbands said when drunk, and the husbands would apologize although they hadn't said a word. Is Chaucer suggesting that the feminist movement was so strong that a husband, drunk or sober, dared not make such remarks to his wife? That he apologized for what he hadn't said?

And alas! the remarks are all true of the Wife, who not only brags of her misconduct but generalizes it by asserting, for example, that no man can swear and lie as boldly as a woman. Similarly, women's desire for freedom, considered natural and even noble by defenders of women, is demonstrated to be, as the satirists said, a blind for immorality. We love no man, she says, who "keeps check" on where we go. We want to be free. But then, misinterpreting a proverb she says, "If husbands have enough, why should they care how others fare?" A man who won't let another "light a candle at his lantern is a miser."

The battle for sovereignty that was discussed in the last chapter was, of course, also part of the feminist controversy. The book read by the Wife's fifth husband that precipitates the battle was an anthology of all those tracts mentioned in this chapter, including Jerome and Theophrastus. The twist here is that it is from these very legends of bad women, from Eve to Xantippe, that the Wife herself has been quoting and copying. Still, there is truth to her assertion that if women had written the stories, they would have written of the wickedness of men. The Wife cannot rewrite history, but her victory over one man, if not over the legend, is symbolized by her tearing the book. Her victory, however, is only symbolic. Having won supremacy, what does the Wife do with it but give her husband all the things he thought he needed the mastery to get! Similarly, in her tale, once the hag is given the mastery, she gives the knight a bargain he could not have arranged himself. Happy with the appearance of mastery, these women cannot imagine a reality in which their position is not in Adam's bed. The Wife, we are told, is a cloth maker, but that occupation is only peripheral to the central business of her life, which is men.

Chaucer saw as well as his characters that if women had written them, the history books would be different. So, too, with Scripture. Had the crucial opening chapters of Genesis, for example, been subject for centuries to an army of feminine interpreters like the Wife of Bath—the mind boggles at the possibilities. Chaucer offers a few, and they suggest the extensive latitude of contemporary interpretation. When the Wife argues against St. Paul, for example, she is quite within her rights; indeed, she is demonstrating an orthodox freedom that critics sometimes deny her creator. This, and her other arguments, are correctly culled from Scripture. The interest to the feminist is that the florilegium concerns only one subject, and that her exegesis is suited finally not to a Biblical scholar but to a bawd.

The comedy depends in part on audience recognition of allusions because the Wife is answering the usual clerical interpretation, which we can sometimes check with the Parson. With a high manner, for example, the Wife reports

157

that she would tell her spouse to imitate the patience of their sheep Wilkin. You preach Job's patience, she would say; practice it. Since man is the more "reasonable" creature, she continued, he should be the one to give in, in a family argument. Now this is no doubt a twist of the clerical interpretation of the Fall. Chaucer's Parson conventionally explains the eating of the apple in terms of current behavioral psychology. Eve, the perennial female, represents the flesh, he says, and the "flesh delighted in the beauty of the forbidden fruit." But until reason, that is to say, Adam, perennial male, consented, mankind remained in a state of innocence. It is from Adam's consent that the human race took original sin, Eve being the "less rational creature." The Wife is ironically exploiting her less rational position.

Chaucer saw also that the way the commentaries were written was influenced by the chauvinism of the male writers; the exegetical comments of his male characters, including the Parson, reveal their personal bias as well as traditional views. When, for example, the Parson relates the story of the creation of Eve to the position of women, he includes a couple of little digs at women that reveal his mind rather than that of the universal Church. He echoes the usual gloss when he says a man should bear himself with his wife in "patience and respect" as Christ showed when he made the first woman. He made her "not from Adam's head," lest she claim too great authority. He made her "not from Adam's foot," lest she be held too low. God made woman of Adam's rib so that she should be his companion. So the husband should love his wife "as Christ loved the Church," and die for her if necessary. So far, this is entirely conventional exegesis. But the Parson's personal bias is expressed in his remark that when the woman has the "mastery," she makes too much confusion. No examples of this are necessary, he says, "everyday experience suffices." As for the contrary argument, he remarks that one reason women must not be looked down on is that they cannot suffer patiently!

Attitudes toward Eve as Woman tended to be ambivalent. The medieval cliché was: Since Eve was mother of us all and Mary was mother of Christ, what was lost through a woman was regained through a woman. Further, Mary's response to the angel, "Be it done to me according to thy word," was considered a model for men as well as women. Still, Eden was lost through a woman, and it was Eve's weakness that brought about all our woe. It may be this emphasis that leads men in trouble to remember Eve rather than Mary. Sir Gawaine, for example, is a paragon of courtesy toward woman throughout almost all of the story of the Green Knight. A devotee of Mary as well as of court ladies, he finds himself in the difficult position of having to refuse the seductive wiles of his hostess without offending her. He manages this problem, but fails the test by accepting a supposedly magical girdle which will save his life. When Gawaine discovers all this was a trick planned by the Green Knight, he does not blame the Knight. Instead, he says it is no wonder a man goes astray in his wits through the wiles of women, and he recites the litany of the misogynists: Adam was deceived by Eve, Solomon by many women, and Samson by Delilah. Gawaine even makes Bathsheba guilty of David's sin, saying he was "overcome" by her beauty.

Gawaine's chastity test suggests that the double standard was not as all-pervasive as we sometimes think. Certainly in the most famous romances: Lancelot and Guenevere, and Tristan and Isolt, it is the lady who is adulterous, both her husband and her lover being strictly faithful to her. Guenevere discharges Lancelot from "her service" at the slightest, always unwarranted, suspicion of philandering. So far from retaliating, the great warrior submissively waits until she needs him, whereupon he performs some spectacular deed and they are reunited in bed. The power of Guenevere and Isolt over men is of particular interest to the twentieth century for it suggests management roles for women. Such ladies, however, were not officially a source of pride to "good" women, who valued chastity highly, and considered its lack more shameful in the female. As we have already noted, Dorigen in The Franklin's Tale scorns the adulterous heroines and does not see why any man would wish to love a married woman whose husband has her body at will; but at the same time she is not shocked by the immorality of the seducer.

In the teaching of the Church, expressed by the Parson, fidelity is required of both husband and wife, the sixth commandment binding both sexes equally. It seems to me that Chaucer never sanctions an adulterous relationship. But his low-life characters do. The broad-minded Miller, in a view shared by the Wife of Bath, advises husbands not to be inquisitive; so long as they "find God's plenty there," he says, "no need to inquire of the remnant." In the fabliaux like The Miller's Tale and The Shipman's Tale, the promiscuity of the female is taken for granted, but the double standard is also implied. Most of the husbands to not accept their cuckolding quietly, and the tricks are intended to deceive them into believing their wives virtuous. The Wife of Bath denies with some show of indignation that her gadding about makes her guilty; her husbands are rather pleased to be accused of wenching.

Some of the same patterns are traced in The Merchant's Tale, in which Chaucer shows with some asperity that the buying of a virginal young bride by an old lecher is socially acceptable. The misogynist narrator of this multi-level satire sees the unsuitability of the match, but his concern is only for the husband. Even the priest in the traditional wedding service bids May follow Sara and Rebecca, without recommending Abraham and Isaac to January. But while the priest blesses the bed, Chaucer's irony damns the whole arrangement.

Like so many Chaucerian characters, the Pilgrim-Merchant is apparently familiar with traditional invective against women. He portrays January as a fool for praising wives and for disbelieving the arguments of Theophrastus against women. At one step further removed, however, the reader rejects January's praise of wives not for its folly, but for the selfishness not observed by the narrator. Old January daydreams about the perfect wife who will love and serve him unwearyingly and unquestioningly. He has heard Theophrastus's arguments against marriage, and in typical medieval style, he relates them to deny them. He cites Theophrastus as saying that a servant is cheaper and more industrious than a wife, and more faithful in caring for a sick husband, since the wife is really waiting for his property and may make him a cuckold. "God curse his bones!" cries January; but his answer to Theophrastus assumes the same male-centered standard for wives. Interpreting Genesis for his own comfort, January recalls the story of Eve's creation as Adam's helper. Elaborating on this blissful prospect, January envisages a wife who will never say "nay" when he says "yea." "Do this," he will say; "All ready, sir," will be her response.

The narrator's joke is that this isn't the way it is; the author's earnest is that this isn't the way it is meant to be.

One of January's friends, Justinus, who is much admired by the narrator for his shrewdness, does not really differ from January in his concept of the wifely role. Taking a wife, he asserts, is no child's play. Following the old books, he says a man should inquire whether she drinks too much, or is proud or shrewish, or wasteful or wild. At least she should have more good points than bad. And a man of your age, he warns January, should beware of a young wife; the youngest man is busy enough to keep his wife to himself.

Justinus turns out to be right, and the story turns into a low-level duel between the sexes, generalized for all mankind by Pluto and Proserpina, the King and Queen of Fairyland, who happen to be present. "Wife," says Pluto to Proserpina in what he doubtless considers a reasoning tone of voice, "daily experience" proves the "treasons" of women; he knows "ten hundred thousand tales" of their fickleness. Wise, rich, and glorious Solomon, he adds, knew their wickedness, and never found a good one. This little harangue is a prelude to Pluto's indignation over January's imminent cuckolding in the same garden which the invisible King and Queen are enjoying. Calling January a worthy knight whose only fault is that he is old and blind, Pluto decides to foil the adultery by opening January's eyes at the critical moment. Proserpina replies in the spirit of the Wife of Bath, reinterpreting the Scriptures to serve her view. Calling Solomon "idolater" and "lecher," she unwittingly proves his view of women correct by defending May, and she promises to give May, and all women for her sake, the knack of giving a bold excuse when caught in the act. And sure enough, May does convince January that her "struggling" in the tree with the young man was responsible for the old man's strategically timed cure, thus taking the credit and the victory from Pluto.

The comedy is continued in the Epilogue to the tale, in which the Host, that paragon of male virtues, remarks that women like May are busy as bees to deceive simple men with their tricks. Meanwhile he reveals himself as so henpecked that he is afraid anything he says will be repeated to his wife.

162

Bad May, like good Dido in *The Legend,* serves mainly as a prop in the feminist controversy. In the romances, *Troilus and Criseyde,* The Knight's Tale, *The Book of the Duchess,* and The Franklin's Tale, the controversy is not in the foreground, but besides allusions to it, part of the central interest of the romances is in the character and role of the heroines. Unlike Jean de Meun, Chaucer does not think a rose is a rose is a rose. The moralist may condemn their sins equally, but the poet distinguishes between such sinners as May and Criseyde. From Chaucer's portraits of Criseyde, Emily, Blanche, and Dorigen, we can deduce Chaucer's prescription for a courtly lady. Not a martyr as in *The Legend,* not a slut as in the fabliaux, she is beautiful, elegant, aristocratic, intelligent, well bred, well spoken, educated, warm, and loving. Knowing her is an education for a man; but she is always in danger of being enslaved by her response to men.

Criseyde is officially a "bad" woman who comes to a bad end, but Chaucer does not let her infidelity obscure her charms. The result is that she pleases neither the feminists nor the satirists. The extremists think Criseyde should quickly say yes or no to Troilus's suit, either jump into bed like Alison or slam the door like Constance. But Criseyde is not harlot or martyr or feminist; Chaucer shows her both drawn and fearful, both with good reason. She mentions feminist arguments in passing: in her first debate with herself, she notes that consent will mean she will no longer be free, but will be bound to please Troilus; and in Book III, she says that even if Troilus is a king's son, he will not have "sovereignty" over her. But these are only the slogans of the moment, and they are swallowed up in the passionate love which, for the moment, wipes out distinctions of superior and inferior. It is only for the moment, however, and what Chaucer feels for her is affectionate compassion, not respect. He will not condemn her, he says, more than she is already condemned.

Most striking for us here, Chaucer does not generalize her infidelity as did his sources. Boccaccio's moral at the end of *Il Filostrato* is a warning to young men. Choose carefully, Boccaccio says, lest in the end you die for a worthless woman. Far worse is the opinion of Guido della Colonne, one of Chaucer's acknowledged sources, who remarks that Troilus was credulous to trust Criseyde's tears. Woman is by nature inconstant, he says, and if one eye weeps, the other smiles out of the corner. If the seducer doesn't seek them, Guido winds up, they seek him in shops and public squares. Chaucer goes so far in avoiding this kind of conclusion that he ends illogically by grieving over all the women who are betrayed by men.

Colorless Emily in The Knight's Tale represents the Knight-narrator's ideal lady. We can assume that she has the required accomplishments, because otherwise the ideal young men would not have fallen in love with her. Only for a moment does Emily come alive when, in her prayer to Diana, she says that she loves hunting and walking in the wild woods, and does not want to be a wife and be with child. When Arcite wins the battle fought over her, however, she casts a friendly eye on him, for in the narrator's simplistic view, "women follow the favor of Fortune." When Arcite dies, Emily goes through the motions of mourning and after a suitable interval is given willingly enough to Palamon. In this most romantic of tales, the marriage is arranged most unromantically, and Emily plays her ornamental role with barely a murmur.

Most beautifully idealized is Blanche in *The Book of the Duchess;* she combines the charm of the well-born aristocrat with the virtue of the Christian laywoman. Beautiful and noble, she sings and dances, laughs and plays so sweetly that "dullness" is afraid of her. She does all "in measure." Intelligent, eloquent, reasonable, she doesn't flatter or flirt or send knights on foolish quests. She loves everybody as a man does his brother, and she is so truthful that "Truth himself chose her as his resting place." As good as "Penelope" or "Lucrece," she would have been loved by her knight if he were as great as "Hercules, Achilles, or Alexander."

Dorigen in the later Franklin's Tale follows this model, but she falls short of Blanche's perfection. Although she finds—or puts—herself in a position trickier than Penelope's, she thinks of herself as a Penelope type, and is a feminist only in the way of the ladies in *The Legend of Good Women*. As was observed earlier, she does not question the double standard. The conventionality of her role is suggested further by her response to the dreadful news that the squire has met the seemingly impossible terms of her love. Contemplating suicide as an alternative to adultery, she tells St. Jerome's much-quoted stories of faithful wives who preferred death to dishonor. It is her husband, Arveragus, who is the feminist. "Troth is the highest thing that men may keep," he says, and by men he means men and women. In order to prove that his wife's word of honor is as sacred to him as his own, the poor man sacrifices the male's customary sexual dominance and discards the whole notion of the wife as owned sex object—to the dismay of many a twentieth-century commentator.

Blanche and Dorigen have a much narrower scope than their knights; they are not warriors or politicians; but they are not dolls in doll houses either. "Womanly" they are, a great comfort to their men. They are also persons, in some ways superior, in reason and in truth equal. Unlike May, they would not have married January; they choose their mates. In a polite way, they are honest, and they try not to play love-sex games. They are respected as human

165

beings by their men, who (unlike January) see that if they want Penelope, they should try to be Ulysses. In brief, both men and women are liberated by this civilized love.

The three women whose unromantic road seems thorniest to a modern feminist are Constance, Prudence, and Griselda. Virtuous and married, they obey, without much question, tyrannical fathers, husbands, and God. Obviously they are largely personified virtues which men as well as women are supposed to practice. But why didn't Chaucer show men personifying them? One reason, to judge from all of Chaucer's works, is that he thought women less vicious than men. At least, there are no female horrors to compare with the Pardoner and the Summoner. Further, many of Chaucer's good men behave well under the tutelage of a woman. Finally, what distinguishes Constance, Prudence, and Griselda is that they personify virtues traditionally represented as female.

It has indeed been said by such enemies of Christianity as Hitler that the Christian virtues of humility, patience, and obedience are in essence "feminine," because they are opposed to manly violence and machismo. For their own reasons, some modern feminists likewise throw out both the virtues and the Christianity. Their complaint is that the very inferiority of woman's position was conducive to this kind of sanctity, and if they must choose between sanctity and equality, militants choose equality. The abolition of the double standard, for example, means not chastity for men but promiscuity for women. Chaucer, on the other hand, chose both Christianity and equality; he asks young folks, "both he and she," to practice chastity. And he would probably have defended the embodiment of the virtues as "she" as a compliment to woman, never dreaming that the twentieth-century legend would prefer the insult of the Wife of Bath.

There are a number of asides and allusions in the stories of Constance, Prudence, and Griselda that suggest that Chaucer was aware of their position as women. The Man of Law, for example, is portrayed as ambivalent. When a woman is evil, she is so because she is a woman. When the Sultaness in his story plans to kill the wedding guests, the narrator is reminded of the way the Serpent made an instrument of Eve and "brought us all in bondage." Well does Satan "know the old way to women!" On the other hand, he feels for Constance when she must go far from home to wed a man she does not know and who may not be a good husband; for, after all, the constancy and courage of a woman are the theme of his tale.

Virtuous as she is, Constance is not a doormat like Griselda, perhaps because she is the daughter of an emperor rather than a peasant. At the beginning, she complains that women are born to thralldom, and she weeps bitterly at parting from her family and friends to travel across the sea to a strange marriage. In the course of her adventures, she puts up a fight against a rapist; and she is an articulate Christian who converts King Alla and other pagans. Nonetheless, the dominant impression is of a woman who is manipulated: her father puts her on one boat, her mothers-in-law put her on two more, and Constance accepts all as the will of God. Her submissiveness, of course, does not extend to sin.

Prudence in the pilgrim-Chaucer's Tale of Melibeus seems to be acting a servile wifely role, but all the while she is manipulating her spouse, not, like the Wife of Bath, for her own sovereignty, but for God's. And in passing, we get God's prudent view of the feminist controversy: the traditional male invective is false. When Prudence first attempts to dissuade Melibeus from going to war as his flattering friends had advised, he retorts with anti-feminism. He

167

asserts that all women are wicked, and that he would be shamed if it appeared as though he had given Prudence the "mastery" over him. Patiently she explains that our Lord Jesus would never have been born of a woman if all were wicked, and that when Jesus rose from the dead, he appeared first to a woman. Prudence also defends herself, protesting that she is no "jangler," and she adds that if a wife counsels wisely she should be praised, not blamed. Listing good women in the Old Testament, she adds that if women were not good, God would not have created them and called them helpers of men, but rather their confusion. (This last phrase was apparently familiar enough to be satirized. In The Nun's Priest's Tale Chanticleer slyly reverses the adage: he uses the Latin word for "confusion" but translates it as "joy and bliss.") When Melibeus is finally persuaded that Prudence will restore his daughter Sophia, that is, wisdom, to him, he agrees to be governed by her. Like the Wife of Bath, and like the loathsome lady in the Wife's tale, Prudence has won the mastery, but her use of it is different from theirs. First, she tells Melibeus, he should ask God to be his counselor; he must give up anger, vengeance, and greed. Learn patience, she says, and follow the example of Christ and the saints. At the end, Melibeus thanks God for sending him a wife of such discretion.

At the end of this sober homily extolling a woman, we have a bit of comic relief at the expense of a woman. The Host wishes his wife Goodleaf had heard this tale. When he punishes the servants, he says, she brings him clubs, crying, "Slay the dogs, break their bones!" If a neighbor fails to bow to her in church, she wants her spouse to fight for her. She calls him "milksop," and threatens to take his knife and give him her distaff. And although the Host fears that some day when she sends him out to fight he will kill somebody, he is so afraid of her "with her big arms" that he obeys.

As in so many of the Host's comments, the comedy and the irony work on more than one level. The Host's wife is obviously, as he says, the opposite of Prudence; she counsels war and uses violence herself. More comical is the incongruity of the reversal of roles, symbolized by the exchange of the knife and the distaff. Taken as a whole, the passage is the Host's unconsciously ironic comment on the running discussion of women's rights. In the vulgar view, whatever the talk of church and court, men like the Host are henpecked by brawling wives quite unlike Prudence.

The old jokes are laughed at again at the end of The Clerk's Tale of the patient Griselda. The mood of satiric raillery is set by a reference to the well-known Chichevache, the cow who ate patient wives and was correspondingly lean. In this mood, the Wife of Bath is invoked, and a song sung for love of her and "all her sect." Women are advised to follow the advice of the Wife, not the example of Griselda, to "endure nothing," to "fight back" however they can. Show the husband "no respect," "bind him in jealousy," "let him weep and wail!"

This satiric Envoy may be a tacit acknowledgement that The Clerk's Tale holds an ambiguous position in the feminist controversy. Which side is Griselda really on? She is certainly a "good" woman who disproves the nasty generalizations of the satirists. But one does not have to be a militant to feel the urge to strangle Griselda. The difficulty is that she is "good" according to the prescription of January in The Merchant's Tale; to whatever her husband asks, she responds "Yes, sir," when even Prudence would have argued. It is easy to see her as every male chauvinist's dream wife.

But the Clerk-narrator says, and we can believe him, that this is not what he means. For his part, he is pro-women and anti-sexism. He says that clerks speak of Job's humility but rarely praise women, whereas the truth is that "no man equals women in humility or faithfulness." Taken this way, The Clerk's Tale is a lesson for men as well as women, and Griselda is modelled not on January's sensual dream but on Christ himself. As Prudence is the prudent woman worthier than rubies of the Old Testament, Griselda is the crucified Christ of the New.

The parallels are drawn lightly, but there are a number of allusions to sacrifice and submission, to Gospel and liturgy in The Clerk's Tale. When, for example, Walter defends his choice of a poor girl, he says that God can send his grace into an ox's stall, the reference, of course, being to the Incarnation. So wise and just was this Griselda that the people thought she was "sent from heaven." The promise she makes before her marriage to Walter (on this level, her union with God) never to disobey "willingly in word or deed" paraphrases the Confiteor. Her change of clothes is clearly a symbolic rite, like that of a novice in a convent. So that none of her old things be brought into the new life, the court ladies remove her rags and array her in new, queenly garments. She later says of herself that when she left her clothes at home, she left "her will" and "liberty." Finally, her acceptance of Walter's order to hand over her children to what she believes will be their death is an obvious parallel with Abraham's sacrifice of Isaac, itself a prefiguration of the Passion of Christ. Like a Christian Abraham, she blesses the boy with the sign of the cross before handing him over.

And yet, the overwhelming impression Griselda makes on the twentieth-century woman is not that of Abraham or Christ. A prisoner of the story, she is not really like, to take a striking female Christ figure, Dante's Beatrice. The fact that Dante (male sinner) is obedient to Beatrice (female image of God) is satisfying not only on feminist but

170

on aesthetic and religious grounds. More important, neither Beatrice nor Dante endures the undeserved miseries of Griselda, inflicted by a capricious and unjust lord. Griselda's absolute silence and submission to injustice are hard for us, especially those of us brought up on the cult of Will and Self Expression, to admire. One has to have a taste for Gandhi or Uncle Tom to appreciate Griselda's notion of conquering by submitting. It is a notion not popular among militants in the causes of nationalism, civil rights, or women's rights.

Nor is it the whole way of female Christian militants. Certainly neither silence nor submission characterized St. Cecilia. The popularity of the story of this Roman Christian—a story known widely through the telling in the *Golden Legend*—suggests the admiration of medieval men for this most uncompromising woman. She is not much admired in the twentieth century, both her faith and her morals being out of style. Her militant methods, however, deserve our attention.

Cecilia forces the action at every stage, accompanying it with theory and plan. No shy virgin forced into matrimony against her will, she goes gladly to her wedding, dressed in gold, but with a hairshirt underneath, and a detailed plan of action under that. It does not occur to her that her projected marital celibacy is deceitful; she considers it a true marriage, and she does not offer the bridegroom the option of flight. Valerian does everything she tells him to, going promptly to Pope Urban for baptism, and soon after to his death as a martyr. As Urban says admiringly, this man, a fierce lion when Cecilia took him, has been transformed by her to a meek lamb.

Cecilia was in fact running a most dangerous underground operation, as we can see in the story of Valerian's brother, Tiburtius. Albeit convinced of the truth of

171

Christianity, Tiburtius is afraid of martyrdom. It is Cecilia who overcomes his fear of death by a sermon on the better life of heaven. And when he questions her about the Trinity, she is entirely qualified to "preach." Only then does he go to the pope, who apparently has no bias against women preachers. When the persecution begins, the young men go so nobly to their deaths that they convert others. Cecilia preaches to these pagans, brings priests to them at night to baptize them—and buries them herself.

Finally she is arrested and questioned by the prefect Almachius in a courtroom scene rather reminiscent of the 1960s. Deliberately disruptive, Cecilia tells the judge that he has begun his questioning foolishly and ignorantly. Almachius asks whence come her rude answers; whence, she replies, but from "conscience and good faith." His power, she says, is like a "bladder of wind" that will blow away when pricked by a needle. And the higher authorities he represents are all "mad" to consider Christians guilty. When Almachius tries to make her foreswear her religion, she begins to laugh. Lo, she says, apparently turning to the audience and pointing at the judge, he "stares and raves" in uttering his judgment. When Almachius tells her to put aside her boldness and sacrifice to the gods, she responds with an attack on idolatry and on Almachius's blindness in believing in "stones." The people will "scorn and laugh" at you, she concludes, because men know your idols are worthless.

Finally, Almachius condemns her to death. First they attempt to burn her, but she remains cool. Then the executioner attempts to cut her throat, but the three strokes allowed by law do not kill her, and for three days she lies with carved neck, never ceasing to teach the faith. She explains before her death that she had asked God for respite of three days to save these many souls; and she asks Urban

SECOND NUN

for only one favor, to have her house turned into a church. Hers is a grim end, with plenty of blood, but Cecilia is not pictured as grim, morbid, or hysterical. Besides debating, teaching, and working miracles, she sings, laughs, and kisses. Her hairshirt does not irritate her disposition.

The interpretation of Cecilia's name in the Prologue to The Second Nun's Tale emphasizes spiritual qualities in a quite non-sexist way. Cecilia, we are told, was a path for the blind, and a union of heaven and the active life; her name also means lack of blindness because of her great light of wisdom. Just as men see the sun, moon, and stars in the heavens, so men "see spiritually" in this maiden the "magnanimity of faith and the clarity" of her wisdom in works bright with excellence. And just as philosophers write that heaven is "swift and round and burning," so was Cecilia swift and "ever burning bright with charity." Cecilia's name suggested no softness to the original hagiographer, to Chaucer, or to the Second Nun telling her tale because Cecilia was in fact a most aggressive maiden, a leader of men, more fearless than they in facing the Roman prefect, and in suffering torture and death. And no Christian man resented her dominance.

If what I have called Cecilia's feminism had collided with her religion, the feminism would have had to go. What goes instead is the chauvinism of the men, in direct proportion to the coming on of their Christianity. And while Cecilia's

173

feminism is subordinated to her Christianity, it is none-theless real. A literal follower of Pauline doctrine, she believes implicitly in a single standard for the sexes in every aspect of life. And while miracles such as hers were extraordinary, her feminism was not unique. Christian doctrine and Church organization had combined to change radically the social and economic realities of a certain number of women. The same St. Paul who had said that the husband should be the head of the family as Christ is of the Church, had also said that in Christ Jesus there is neither male nor female. The long history of Christianity offers many examples of Christians who tried seriously to follow the latter as well as the former precept.

That same St. Jerome who was famous for his lists of both good and bad women regarded intellect and spirit as neither male nor female. He encouraged his independent women friends, often in the teeth of family criticism, to make time and place for the same study, prayer, and works of mercy that occupied his men friends. It was in the house of one Marcella in fourth century Rome that a group of widows and maidens met to study the Scriptures with Jerome, who taught them Hebrew as well as celibacy. With a group of these ladies, the widow Paula and her daughter Eustochium started a nunnery in Palestine. At Bethlehem, Paula built four monasteries, three for nuns, one for monks, with herself at the head of the nuns, Jerome at the head of the monks. It was there that Jerome translated the Bible from the Hebrew with the aid of Jewish scholars.

Occasionally, in such a double monastery, a woman was head of both monks and nuns, but most often, the highest office went to a priest, an office not then open to women. By and large, however, nuns and priests were not competing for the same jobs. The segregation of the sexes gave women in convents a whole realm in which to exercise their administrative, intellectual, and spiritual talents, subject mainly to their own tastes and limitations. Obviously, the elimination of men from their lives eliminated such time-consuming occupations as child-bearing and rearing.

Sociologically speaking, St. Cecilia's married celibacy gave her this freedom from domesticity while leaving her active in the world, but ordinary girls had to choose. Most of the advertisements for the convent dwelt on the joys of heaven, but Jean Gerson (who as was noted earlier, sided with Christine in the battle against Jean de Meun) put forth many worldly reasons to keep his sisters from marrying. In a *Discourse on the Excellence of Virginity*, he described the evils of wedlock from the wife's point of view: the husband may turn out to be a drunkard, a spendthrift, or a miser; even if he is honest and good, he may be unfortunate and suffer from bad harvests and the death of his cattle. Jean warns also of the miseries of pregnancy and the danger of death in childbirth. All of these and many more ills, he said, can be avoided in the convent.

Celibate himself, Gerson saw only the advantages of monastic avoidance of natural disasters. The anti-celibate Lollards, however, condemned vows of continence for women on the ground that women are too frail and imperfect in nature to keep them. Even, or especially, widows, "being delicately fed," should be given in marriage, the Lollard Conclusions read, to keep them from secret sins. Orthodox manuals for nuns conceded the fact of temptation, but were perforce more optimistic about the possibility of resistance. In the orthodox view, the conventual elimination of sex and marriage was also supposed to remove nuns from the psychological battle. Concealing the curves of her body, the nun's habit signalled that she was not a sex object; the uniformity and plainness of the garb

175

announced also that in the community of Christ all were sisters, that there were neither rich nor poor.

The symbolism of the habit was apparently lost on the Prioress, who had instead taken advantage of the system to rise to a position of importance. As the successful head of a convent, she commands respect from the men on the pilgrimage; and the Host, by calling on her after the Knight, shows that he considers her to outrank the rest of the company. Nobody finds it remarkable that the "Nun's Priest" is her underling and is rather afraid of her, but the anti-feminist remarks he drops in his tale of Pertelote and Chanticleer suggest that he is unhappy in his subservient role. Most interesting, Chaucer's criticism of her is levelled not at her "masculine" authority but at her clinging to the silliest part of the feminine stereotype, love of jewelry and expensive clothes. A woman who chose the religious life was expected to put away such nonsense.

The Second Nun is so far liberated from female role playing that Chaucer could assign verses to her that he probably wrote as an expression of his own thoughts. It has been suggested that the words "I, unworthy son of Eve" in the Second Nun's Prologue were given to her because the phrase appears in the liturgy sung daily by nuns in the convent. While the possibility is interesting in itself, the case for it seems unconvincing. It is more likely that the Dantesque Invocation to Mary that forms part of the Prologue was an earlier, personal poem of Chaucer's, and that in it the poet referred to himself as an unworthy son of Eve. When he incorporated the poem in the Nun's Prologue, he either neglected to delete the phrase or let it stand as not inappropriate for the nun. In any event, the tone of the whole passage is quite ungirlish. The Invocation is also a reminder of Chaucer's devotion to Mary, whom, however, he keeps out of arguments over the position of women.

Chaucer, of course, was promoting neither celibacy nor feminism. But it seems that in his portrayal of the human comedy, men become increasingly capable of recognizing ability in a woman as they cease regarding her as a sex object. By the same logic, the further Chaucer's women move into the battle of the sexes, the less real equality they have. The comical or vicious women in Chaucer's stories use their varying degrees of social and economic freedom to fit themselves more securely into the slavery of sexual stereotypes. In varying degrees the virtuous married women exercise a certain amount of independence and disprove the charges of the misogynists. On balance it seems to me that in Chaucer's view feminism and Christianity are not in conflict. This is a medieval rather than a modern view, and I think it can be illustrated by a comparison of Chaucer's Prudence with Jean de Meun's Heloise. Radical, "modern" Heloise accepted the slurs against women because they served as arguments against matrimony. Having received the same education as men, Heloise joined them in finding marriage and children an impediment to self-fulfillment. And the independence which seems so attractive to us was divorced from religion. The success she wanted for Abelard was in the Church but not in Christ. Conservative, medieval Prudence, on the other hand, answers the anti-feminist arguments both by text and by act. And she converts her husband from his anti-feminism at the same time that she converts him to Christ.

Looking more broadly at Chaucer's view of women, I would venture to say that in his own way he was pro- rather than anti-women. He does not blame the world's or men's woes on women; neither does he pretend to think they are all faithful, chaste, and honorable. He pays them the ultimate compliment of describing them as individual human beings, possibly a little more complex and interesting than men, some of whom treat them as equals. His final judgments of women, as of men, are based on Christian values, and sometimes these conflict with secular ideas of liberation.

In the Christian view, human beings are liberated not by indulgence but by virtue. In philosophical terms, *Lady Philosophy* explains to Boethius in the *Consolation of Philosophy* that true freedom means liberation from the prison of desires for clothes, for sex, for money, for power. In religious terms, Christ is the Truth that sets both men and women free. In Chaucer's works, more women than men are liberated in this way; most of his saints are women. Teaching, preaching, cajoling, suffering, dying, they become saints by imitating Christ. They do not imitate their husbands; indeed, Melibeus and Walter become liberated men only when they recognize the wisdom and goodness of Prudence and Griselda.

VI

The Old Testament and the Jews

Inside Chaucer's House of Fame, in the poem of that name, are pillars on which stand famous historians of various peoples. Among them are Josephus, Statius, Homer, Geoffrey of Monmouth, Virgil, Ovid, Lucan, and Claudian. On the first pillar, Chaucer tells us, stands the Hebrew Josephus, who told the history of the Jews. He bore high on his shoulders "the fame of Jewry," and seven others, "wise and worthy," stood by him to help him bear the heavy weight; they wrote of "battles as well as other marvels." Probably Josephus is first, the scholars say, because the Jewish religion was considered the root of all others; and his pillar is made partly of lead, the metal of Saturn, because Saturn was considered the father of the planets.

We may take this tribute as Chaucer's considered view of the prominent position of Hebraism among world religions. The list as a whole, however, suggests Chaucer's relatively slight intellectual and imaginative indebtedness to the Hebrews. Had Chaucer's contemporary, Langland, devised such a hall of fame, he would not have left the "seven others" unnamed while he went on to describe the pagans at length. Nor does Chaucer seem to have thought of the Bible as great literature; at least, he did not mine it for stories and heroes as other medieval writers did. Abraham and Moses, for example, are conspicuous by their absence from his pages.

Chaucer's choices, as well as his omissions, are rather unusual, and I believe they are also crucial in understanding his attitude to both Biblical and contemporary Jews. Most of the brief Scriptural references of Chaucer's characters echo contemporary comments as we know them from other works; but the long passages which reveal thought and care are parodic to an unusual degree. The medieval descendants of Moses are also viewed in a very limited way. They appear in only one tale, but that one, the Prioress's, is important in a study of Chaucer's religion, not only because the tale is anti-Semitic but because the narrator is a respected holder of Church office. Chaucer, I hope to show later, did not approve her views, probably not because he was especially concerned about the Jews (there were none in fourteenth-century England) but because he was disturbed by the quality of the Nun's Christianity.

Chaucer's lack of serious interest in Old Testament heroes is most striking when compared with the extreme reverence displayed by his contemporaries. However hostile they were towards contemporary Jews, however intrigued they were by the Greeks and Romans, medieval Christians believed that "salvation is of the Jews." Emphasis on the Judaic origin of Christianity can be traced in an unbroken tradition from the beginning to the Renaissance; and even philosophers whom we call Platonists or Aristotelians never doubted that the primary teacher of the word of God was Moses. St. Augustine, for example, tireless allegorizer of Scripture as he was, had no patience with allegories of pagan gods. "What is it to me," he asked, "that Neptune represents the sea? Anyone you like to name is as much god to me as the sea." He believed that unlike the fables of the pagans, what the pagans called "the fables of the Jews" contained the core of Truth.

Of most longlasting importance was the use of the Old Testament in apologetics. In controversy with the pagans, Christians of the early centuries defended "the law" of the Hebrews as a "preparation for the Gospel." In controversy with the Jews, they had to "prove" their doctrine exclusively out of the Old Testament because the Jews accepted no other authority. The authority of the Old Testament was thus established, and throughout the Middle Ages it was invoked routinely in explanations of doctrine addressed to Christians of all ages. And as Christians claimed the Old Testament, so they proclaimed the doctrine that the New Testament and the New Law "fulfilled" the Old Testament and the Old Law, and that the Church was the "fulfillment" of the Synagogue. The relation of the two laws and the two religions was the subject of many tomes in the first fifteen centuries of our era; and every aspect of the subject was portrayed in the plastic arts, from the sculpted figures of the apostles standing on the shoulders of the prophets to the minutely detailed medallions on stained-glass windows portraying parallels of Old and New Testament stories and persons. Every point was described in pious fiction and histories of the world, allegorized in visions, and dramatized in plays.

Not only is this theology of the Old Law missing in Chaucer's works but his Scriptural references seem to me to reflect popular notions rather than private meditation. Chaucer frequently shows the degree to which the names of Old Testament heroes were household words with all classes of society. When, for example, the Pardoner in *The Canterbury Tales* cites "Lamuel," he adds, "not Samuel, but Lamuel." Fearing that his hearers might not recognize the obscure Lemuel, the Pardoner could assume that they knew Samuel well enough to make the substitution. Apparently they also knew Samson so well that the sound of his name could be used to imitate the noise made through the nose by a drunken man as "Sampsoun Sampsoun." The Pardoner correctly adds that Samson never drank wine. Exploiting the common reverence for all things ancient Hebraic, the Pardoner calls the prize of his bogus collection of relics a "holy Jew's sheep's shoulder bone." It has been suggested that the holy Jew who, according to the Pardoner, taught our ancestors how to work cures, was Jacob, but apparently any holy Jew would do.

It is doubtful whether the Pardoner spent his evenings reading the Scriptures, and many of his references to the Bible (like those to Seneca and to the medical treatise of the Arabic Avicenna) could have been picked up second-hand. Twice, however, he admonishes his audience to read the Bible themselves to find clear confirmation of his points. With the notable exception of the Parson, Chaucer's characters do not sound as though they had taken the Pardoner's advice. The Biblical stories, phrases, and precepts they know were part of the common culture, readily accessible in sermons, liturgy, and plays. For example, the allusion to the death of Isaac as a figure of the death of Christ, in Chaucer's "ABC," could be understood from looking at the stained-glass windows without even listening to the sermon.

Many of the references to Old Testament persons which appear in Chaucer's works follow standard patterns of good and bad types. Virtuous wives such as Rebecca, Sarah, Judith, and Abigail are recalled by January in The

Merchant's Tale, as part of his dream of the consolations of marriage. In the quite different context of The Tale of Melibeus, Dame Prudence cites almost the same list: Rebecca, Judith, Abigail, and Esther. The Wife of Bath's fifth husband has an equally well-known list of wicked women, which includes Eve and Delilah. The comparisons are not, however, essentially sexist. The Clerk compares the patient Griselda to Job, and the Man of Law links his heroine to a number of Old Testament heroes.

The Man of Law's parallel cases are unusually extensive, but they too reflect an ancient tradition rather than a study of Scripture. The parallels occur in sets of questions and answers in connection with Constance's miraculous deliverances. Men might ask, remarks the Man of Law, why Constance was not slain at the feast. He answers with another question: Who saved Daniel in the "horrible cave where every wight save him was devoured by the lion?" Again he asks, "Who kept Constance from drowning in the sea?" The answer is, Who kept Jonah in "the fish's stomach until he was spouted up in Nineveh?" Each exploit of Constance raises the question of the source of her strength, and is answered by an Old Testament parallel. The final answer is that the same God who led the Hebrews across the Red Sea, who gave strength to David and to Jonathan, now sent the "spirit of vigor" to Constance.

We might ask another question. How is it that the Man of Law expected his fellow Christians to believe the story of Jonah more readily than that of Constance? The Man of Law probably did not know himself, but there is reason to think that neither Chaucer nor Trivet (Chaucer's source) had gone to the Bible for his material. The Lawyer is using a literary-moralistic tradition, the roots of which went back to the earliest days of Christianity, to controversy between converted and unconverted Jews, who accepted no authority other than the Old Testament. Since the Jews did accept literally the most unlikely miracles of the Old Testament, they could not logically reject the possibility of equally unlikely Christian miracles. And the point of the concordance was that the same God who had performed miracles for the Jews now worked similar ones for the Christians. Later Christians, not necessarily concerned with the Jews, inherited both the authority of the Old Testament and a set of miracles ready for parallels. The most popular, in Apocryphal Gospels and other pious fiction, were the deliverances of Daniel, Jonah, Judith, and Susannah. The Man of Law has compared Constance to three of these; Constance herself draws the parallel with the fourth. Herself a Roman Christian, she prays for a miraculous deliverance such as God had vouchsafed to the Hebrew Susannah, whose plight was similar to her own.

Even the argumentative tone of the Man of Law is derivative, a survival of the ancient controversy, modified by circumstances to answer skeptics instead of Jews. One of the most popular books in which this convention appears is the sixth-century *Dialogues* of Pope Gregory, and this book Chaucer did know. When in the *Dialogues*, a number of Christian miracles have been compared to Old Testament miracles, a skeptic questions the extraordinary similarity. Gregory assures him that the similarity proves the truth of the miracles, because Christians call on the same God who helped the Hebrews.

The Man of Law's Tale, which is largely a translation, thus adopts a popular exegetical tradition as a rhetorical device in the service of simple piety. On the other hand, several of Chaucer's most original stories, The Wife of Bath's Tale, The Miller's Tale, and The Merchant's Tale include parodies of other exegetical traditions as well as of Scripture itself. Medieval parody does not necessarily imply

184

disrespect. In the well-known *Second Shepherds' Play*, for example, the parodic episode of the shepherds' visit to a newborn baby that is really a stolen sheep is followed by an unmistakably reverent visit to the baby Jesus. The balance of laughter and prayer is hard to maintain, however, and in a couple of plays about henpecked Noah, low comedy and social satire outweigh the slight spiritual meaning. Chaucer himself maintains such a precarious balance that it is hard to estimate the degree of his reverence for the Bible. His satire of contemporary characters serves a moral purpose, but his Biblical characters never quite emerge from the parodies.

In The Miller's Tale, for example, the flood prediction is designed to procure just such wickedness as the biblical flood was intended to punish. The success of the plot depends on the credulity of the old carpenter, a new Noah who can be counted on to believe such nonsense. "Have you not heard," inventive Nicholas asks him, "how Noah was saved?" Yes, quoth the carpenter, "very long ago." Have you not also heard, pursues Nicholas, "the sorrow of Noah until he could get his wife aboard the ship?" The allusion is not to the Bible the carpenter has not read but to the mystery play he has seen, in which Noah's wife riotously refuses to enter the ark without her cronies. Nicholas's solution to the problem is to hang tubs from the barn roof instead of building an ark. The joke is at the expense of the carpenter rather than Noah (who is called Noel by the ignorant old man), and Nicholas is appropriately punished. Still, the tale hardly leaves the reader with increased belief in this chapter of sacred history.

In a number of the other *Canterbury Tales*, Chaucer portrays popular irreverence and resistance to right thinking about Scripture. It is evident throughout the Prologue to her tale that the Wife of Bath is rejecting clerical inter-

pretations of Scrip-
ture. The Church had
long been aware that
the ignorant might
think they were free
to imitate the marital
customs of the Old
Testament saints.
Back in Anglo-Saxon
times, Aelfric had
warned against pre-
cisely the conclusion
the Wife deduces
from the story of
Jacob. What does she
care, she says, "if folk

MAN OF LAW

speak ill" of those who marry often. She well knows that
"Abraham and Jacob were both holy men," and each of
them had more than two wives, as did many another holy
man besides. Churchmen had insisted from the earliest
days that such passages must be understood figuratively
rather than literally. In fact, the practice of interpreting,
or "glossing," had gone so far by Chaucer's day that the
friars, like the friar in The Summoner's Tale, were accused
of interpreting to suit themselves.

Thad here was no way to keep the laity from suiting
themselves, either. According to Dame Study
in Langland's *Piers Plowman* (Passus XIII), glib
talkers in after-dinner conversations disputed
the justice of the doctrine of original sin. Why should we
suffer for the sin of Adam and Eve? they demanded.
Unlearned men even asked satirically why Adam did not
cover his mouth first, since it was with his mouth that he
ate the apple!

This kind of shrewd and rude questioning not only of interpretations but of the text itself is reflected in the Wife's displeasure with Jesus' rebuke of the Samaritan woman, who, just like the Wife, had had five husbands. The Wife cannot imagine what Jesus could have meant when he said the man then living with the woman was not her husband. "Why was he not?" "How many might she have?" Men "explain and guess," she says, but God never set a specific limit to the number of allowable husbands. The text she approves of is that in which God bade us wax and multiply, without mentioning numbers.

The king she approves most heartily is, of course, Solomon, and she makes a point of his polygamy in her Scriptural defense of frequent marrying. For her the wisdom of Solomon was demonstrated in his taking of many wives. Would that she had been "refreshed" half as many times as he! she cries. And she relishes in imagination the many first nights spent by the great king. In typical medieval style, she has a little list of other Old Testament personages who offer support to her thesis, and she summarily dismisses those presumably cited by her opponents.

The other references to Solomon in *The Canterbury Tales* vary with the context. Both the saintly Parson and the virtuous Prudence quote Solomon as an authority on practical and moral matters, and Chaucer, as the narrator of The Tale of Melibeus, may be thinking of him as the author of the proverbs which adorn his story. This is the official high line. The vulgar low line is taken by the sinners who, like the Wife, recall Solomon's polygamy, and like the Merchant, understand the Canticle of Canticles, the so-called Song of Solomon, in a strictly literal sense.

The contrast between the pious-allegorical and the skeptical-literal view can be observed in the discussions of Solomon's opinion of women in The Tale of Melibeus and in The Merchant's Tale. In The Tale of Melibeus, the husband quotes Solomon's saying that he had never found a good woman. Without questioning the wisdom of Solomon, Prudence prudently replies first, that other men have found good women. Secondly, she "glosses" the text by saying that perhaps Solomon's meaning was that he never found "perfect virtue in a woman" because nobody is perfect except God alone. She speaks no ill of Solomon and praises him frequently.

The same text and gloss appear in The Merchant's Tale, only to be glossed away by Proserpine, that amazing composite of pagan queen of the underworld, queen of fairyland, and biblical exegete. Her husband Pluto, scandalized by the imminent adultery of May and Damian in the presence of blind January, quotes the same memorable words as did Melibeus, that Solomon never found a good woman. But Proserpine sounds more like the Wife of Bath than Prudence as she rejects the authority of Scripture and then outquotes her husband. What do I care about "your authorities," she demands shrilly. Well does she know that "this Jew, this Solomon" found fault with women. More calmly, she makes the same two points as Prudence, even to the same words. Indeed, these lines have a quality of impersonal rote, like a lesson learned in school. But then the tone changes and the tempo quickens as Proserpine launches into her own heartfelt interpretation of Scripture. "Eh! for God's truth," she exclaims, "why do you make so much of Solomon?" With considerable satisfaction she points out that although he made the temple, he also committed the worst sin by making a temple for false gods. Fair as you may "plaster over his name," she says, he was a "lecher" and an "idolater," and in his old age he forsook God. He would even have lost his kingdom, if God had not spared him for his father's sake. Proserpine concludes by justifying her attack on Solomon as an answer to his attack on women.

In this same tale there is a parody of the Canticle of Canticles, the book of the Bible once thought to be by Solomon, still most startlingly in need of allegorization. As St. Bernard of Clairvaux had been at pains to explain, nobody was supposed to see anything in the imagery of the Bride and the Bridegroom but a figure of Christ and the Church, or Christ and the soul, or Christ and Mary. Nonetheless, old January, physically and spiritually blind, could see the sensuality of its language, which he applied to his own bride. There is no mistaking the parody. The scene is set in an enclosed garden such as is described in the Canticle, and many of the phrases are taken directly from the text. "Rise up, my wife, my lady," old January says; "the voice of the turtle is heard . . . winter is gone." "How fairer are thy breasts than wine!" "Come forth, my white spouse." This blasphemous use of Scripture is in keeping with January's misuse of religion throughout the story. No thoughtless youth, this dirty old man manipulates doctrine in a more obscene way than the Wife. Indeed, he may have thought the phrases of Solomon sanctified his lechery. In fact, they point up his disgusting folly, and the critics are probably right that Chaucer intended the parody to express the contrast between January's lust for May and Solomon's love for God.

But what is the significance of the Merchant's comment on January's speech? At the end of the passage borrowed from the Canticle, the Merchant says, "Such old lewd words used he." It is unlikely that we are intended to think the Merchant did not know the source of the lewd words. "Old" implies borrowing, and the Merchant is very knowledgeable about Solomon in the scene between Proserpine and Pluto. The fact that that exposé of Solomon's

189

occurs in the same garden shortly after January's lovemaking may be a development of this comment on the Canticle. That is, the bitter Merchant not only knows the source of the phrases, but is expressing his contempt for both the literal sense and the allegorical interpretation, both of which were probably familiar to him from sermons. Unlike ignorant and lustful January who delights in the lush language of the Canticle, the educated and cynical Merchant is a higher critic who neither enjoys the flesh nor believes in its sublimation.

A briefer series of allusions to the Canticle appears in The Miller's Tale. Standing beneath the window of the room in which Alison is in bed with her lover, amorous Absolon woos her in language borrowed from the Canticle, calling her "honeycomb," "fair bride," and "sweet cinnamon." "Awake, my love," he cries, and then garbles references to lambs and turtledoves. The episode in which the passage appears can be understood as an ironic reversal of the kind of biblical parallelism we saw in The Man of Law's Tale. As falsely accused Constance is like falsely accused Susannah; lascivious Absolon is like lascivious Absalom The biblical character was well known in the Middle Ages, not only in his own right, but as a half-brother of Solomon, son of David by a different mother. The sex life of David's sons sounds more like an x-rated movie than a sermon: besides Solomon with his thousand wives, there was Amnon who raped his half-sister Tamar, and Absolon himself, a family man, who had relations with his father's concubines. Like his biblical prototype, our Absolon has pretty hair; but his amorous pursuits are parallel to those of David's sons only in intention. Asking Alison for a kiss, he sings words from the Canticle of that Solomon whose frequent refreshment was the envy of the Wife of Bath—and kisses Alison's arse instead.

Absolon's folly and vice are beyond doubt; but I find it hard to believe the critical view that his blasphemous use of the Canticle was intended by Chaucer to suggest to the reader the contrasting truth of the spiritual meaning. Whatever Chaucer's intention, he succeeded in showing the aptness of Solomon's language to sensual affairs. And his intention may well have been a satiric recognition of the literal sense, with a comical thrust at the extreme allegorization current in his time. Chaucer could have raised an eyebrow at the story of Noah and the ark, or at the life and works of Solomon, and at the commentaries on them, and still remained in the company of serious and orthodox Catholics. When Gregory the Great warned that the Canticle was not to be ridiculed because it mentions "kisses, breasts, cheeks, and thighs," he was willy-nilly informing us that it was so ridiculed. The faithful have never been obliged to recite exegetical interpretations; Chaucer was bound by the moral teaching of Scripture, and he did not condone the conduct of Absolon.

What is remarkable is not that Chaucer found Noah funny but that he does not seem to have found Moses at all. That is, it was remarkable in the Middle Ages, because so many authors at that time seem to have been writing salvation history which starred the patriarchs and the prophets. In *Piers Plowman,* for example, Langland wrote a particularly beautiful allegory of salvation in which the Dreamer fulfills the Law in his own life (as Augustine said everybody must) by passing through the history of the race. Liturgy and history, past, present, and future all come together as the Dreamer meets Abraham, who teaches him Faith, and Moses, who teaches him Hope. Moses has with him the Law given him on Sinai; it is written on stone to show it will endure for ever. Together they seek Jesus, whose Charity will fulfill the Law.

191

In "Abraham's bosom" the Dreamer sees the souls of all the good Hebrews who lived before Christ, and who are about to be taken up to heaven by Christ after the Resurrection. There was never any argument about these pre-Christian Hebrews; indeed, the writers of plays and poems delighted in the pictorial possibilities of the Harrowing of Hell, and Dante typically portrays Rebecca as the Old Testament sister of Beatrice, the girls sitting side by side in Paradise.

The fate of later Jews was another question. The very reverence for the Scriptures made the Jewish rejection of Jesus a source of difficulty and anger; and the argument was not over as it was with the pagans, since the Jews continued to wait for a Messiah. Like many men of good will, Langland was ambivalent, sometimes scolding the Jews as traitors who brought their misfortunes on themselves, sometimes scolding the priests who, he believed, could convert the Jews if they lived better lives themselves, sometimes portraying the Jewish following of their own law as still pleasing to God.

This is the kind of speculation Chaucer's characters pursue concerning pagans and paganism, but not about Jews and Judaism. Neither Chaucer nor his characters seem to have felt any kinship with the ancient Hebrews; neither he nor his characters speak of "our father Abraham" as other medieval writers and preachers do. Nor do they show any serious interest in the Jews of the fourteenth century.

I think there is some connection, if only a negative one, between Chaucer's treatment of medieval Jews and his handling of Old Testament Hebrews. There is the same difficulty of interpretation because he never tells us in his own voice what he thought, and his characters' speeches are designed primarily to reveal themselves. Nonetheless, a compilation of his characters' references suggests indifference. Reading Chaucer's collected works, one would never guess at the wealth of Scripture, the vision of Isaiah, the power of Moses, or the speculativeness of Job. Noah and Solomon have undue prominence, and they are more parodied than praised. Scripture is recognized as a source of moral teaching, but largely in the form of platitudes and stereotyped examples. The view of contemporary Jews expressed by Chaucer's characters is stereotyped in a worse way, because it reflects only the lowest popular notions of the Jews. We would not guess from Chaucer's works that there were current sophisticated stories such as the one Boccaccio told in the *Decameron,* according to which God alone can tell the difference in the gold content of the three rings of Islam, Judaism, and Christianity. If we pieced together a picture of post Old Testament Jews from *The Canterbury Tales,* we would never guess that among medieval Jews were philosophers, physicians, and biblical scholars who discussed religion with Christian scholars. It should be added hastily that the paucity of references—aside from The Prioress's Tale there are only a few scattered remarks—means that Chaucer was not attempting any such picture. It is nonetheless chilling that with the exception of the reference to Jewish armour makers in Chaucer's Tale of Sir Thopas, Jews are characterized as violently anti-Christ and anti-Christian. Both the Pardoner and the Parson compare blasphemers who swear by the parts of Christ's body to the Jews who rent Christ's body. And in The Prioress's Tale, medieval Jews are Christian-hating usurers who kill a boy for singing a song in praise of the Virgin Mary; it is their forebears who committed ritual murder in the town of Lincoln.

The bleakness of this summary is somewhat misleading. For one thing, we must not identify Chaucer with his characters, not even the Parson. And I think there is enough satire in The Prioress's Tale to indicate that Chaucer found the Nun's anti-Semitism unchristian. For another, it should be remembered that there was no "Jewish problem" in Chaucer's England. The Jews had been expelled in 1290, and although a few bankers and an occasional physician came from the continent in the entourage of a royal personage, no fourteenth-century English city had a Jewish quarter such as is described by the Prioress.

While the Jews were thus not an immediate social problem, they were not an extinct species. There were "Jewries" in the European cities Chaucer visited, tracts about them still circulated in England, and their settlement in England was still remembered as "not long ago" by the Prioress. If we wish to understand The Prioress's Tale and make an educated guess at Chaucer's attitude toward it, we must know this background. The briefest historical survey makes a long preamble to the tale, but without it we run the danger of judging the religion of Chaucer and of the Middle Ages by the standards of the Nun.

The Prioress's Tale gives, in fact, a remarkably accurate picture of the hostility and violence that marked the most notorious relations between Christians and Jews in thirteenth-century England. The atmosphere of the story is heavy with the murder of English Christian children by Jews. The little Hugh prayed to by the Prioress was from Lincoln; the town described as the setting for the murder of another boy suggests Norwich, and Norwich was the location of the first and most famous case of ritual murder. The history of the case not only supplies the background of the tale but also shows that there were levels of Christian-Jewish relations undreamed of by the Prioress and unnoted by Chaucer.

The death of William of Norwich was shrouded in mystery. When the boy was found murdered, the fact that he had been friendly with Jews was not at first considered relevant. The Christians who found the body in a wood were so far from suspecting that they had discovered a martyr that they buried the body where they found it, without any religious ceremony. Sometime later, however, the boy's uncle charged that the child had been tortured and killed by the Jews on the day before their Passover. The majority of the citizens regarded the charge as an imposture, and the Dominicans or Franciscans (it is not clear which) fought to save the Jews who had been indicted on the charge, and all but one were freed. The ugly and sentimental story, however, succeeded among the uncritical; not only did a cult of the boy martyr develop, but later accusations of ritual murder were widely, but never universally, accepted.

They were rejected most consistently by zealous members of the clergy. The point is relevant here because admirers of The Prioress's Tale often assume the contrary; that is, that religious zeal was responsible for medieval hatred of the Jews, and that therefore the Prioress as well as Chaucer ought not to be judged by the standards of a later age. But the cause of anti-Semitism then as now was not piety but ignorance, as well, of course, as lack of charity.

It is difficult to believe that Chaucer himself shared the ignorance. One would think that even if he was not especially interested in the Jews, he must have known of the frequent condemnations of the libel of ritual murder. Pope Gregory X, for example, had pointed out in 1271 that the Law of the Jews expressly forbade sacrifice, even of certain animals. The defenders of the Jews in England, the most famous of whom was Robert Grosseteste, also insisted that the very idea of ritual murder was repugnant to them. Still well-known in Chaucer's day as theologian, philosopher, and scientist, Grosseteste had been bishop of

Lincoln in the middle of the thirteenth century, when tension between Jews and Christians had been severe. In his student days at Oxford, Grosseteste had studied Hebrew with a rabbi; and when he later became chancellor of the university, he encouraged similar studies by the Franciscans there. One of his dreams was the conversion of the Jews; and in his great work on the relation of the Old to the New Law, he stressed the beliefs that were common to both religions. Immediately after his death in 1255, violence broke out in Lincoln as the result of an accusation of ritual murder. Ninety-two Jews were imprisoned, and eighteen were executed because they refused trial by an all-Christian jury. Through the intervention of the Franciscans, who denied the truth of the charge, the rest were released. Had the voice of Adam Marsh, Grosseteste's beloved disciple, been heeded, little Hugh of Lincoln would never have been popularly canonized.

Chaucer could easily have known also the record of friendly religious disputation, since many such dialogues continued to circulate long after the Jews had left England. The *Liber Disputationum Petri contra Symonem Iudeum* of Peter of Cornwall, for example, survives in a manuscript which was written in fourteenth-century England. In the Prologue to this work, Peter tells how he and a certain Jew met and discussed the faith. From the very beginning, he says, their discussion was carried on without any spirit of contention, without any desire to get the better of each other. They promised not to interrupt each other, but instead to reserve questions in silence. With a sincere desire to inquire into the truth, Peter says they discussed every issue in peace and tranquillity.

Scholarly debates like Peter and Symon's consisted mainly of a polite exchange of Scriptural texts. Outside monastery gardens, however, the argument was likely to be marred by insults, blows, and even murder. This style of disputation is reflected in popular fiction like the early Apocryphal Gospels and the medieval Prioress's Tale. Unlike the Prioress's, many of these stories, vulgar as they are, reflect common business interests, camaraderie, a certain amount of religious experimentation on both sides, and joy over the conversions of the Jewish disputants. The Prioress's Tale, refined as it is, reflects only the ugliest part of the controversy. There is no record of Jews murdering Christian boys for singing a hymn to the Virgin, as the scene is described in the tale; but historical documents suggest that it was not unlikely that the Jews would express their annoyance. They were often in difficulty with the authorities for interrupting religious observances with ridicule, and even, occasionally, for attempting to murder converts to Christianity. On the other side, the Prioress's attribution of the Jewish antagonism to the promptings of the devil and her frequent application of the adjective "cursed" to the Jews gives a fair idea of this level of Christian disputation.

What turned insults and episodes into massacres, however, was not theology, however debased, but the social and economic situation which is also reflected in the tale. Nobody loves a creditor, and because of the Church's prohibition of lending money at interest, and the position of the Jews outside that prohibition, the Jews were the only legal creditors in the nation. As is clear from her remark that the ruler protected usury for his own gain, even the Prioress knew that a substantial part of the income from usury went to the king, who let the Jews become rich and then taxed them. But the king was far away while the Jews were close by, convenient to borrow from, inconvenient to repay. The most anti-Semitic groups were such townsfolk as are portrayed in the tale, and the picture of the ghetto is authentic. The Christians in the story are noticeably familiar with the streets and houses of the Jewish section; no doubt they had been there before to borrow money. (And, let us be fair, some of those not mentioned in the story had been there to eat with their Jewish friends and go to synagogue with them, as we know from repeated prohibitions of both practices.) Most unfortunately accurate is the portrayal of the revenge of the Christians, except for one crucial omission. In history, but not in The Prioress's Tale, disturbances, no matter how they began, ended with the burning of the houses of the money-lenders and the destruction of the records of indebtedness.

Voices were not lacking to proclaim that the real reason for hostility against the Jews was not religion but greed. Pope Gregory X said that Christians were so envious of the Jews that they even hid their own children in order to have a pretext to molest the Jews and to extort money from them; and he decreed excommunication for those who stirred up trouble in this way. And in England, William of Newburgh condemned the Christians who attacked Jews as "cruel butchers," who in their desire for the goods of the Jews were "restrained neither by fear of the hot-tempered King nor the rigour of the laws, nor by feelings of humanity."

Now the Prioress would not have hidden children in order to stir up trouble, nor would she have participated in a pogrom; but her feelings of humanity stopped short of the Jews. Her tale reads like an unhappy chapter in the history of thirteenth-century England, seen through the eyes of a sentimental, pious, and bigoted woman; and that may be how Chaucer meant us to read it. The point is worth laboring here because editors have so frequently praised the tale as a beautiful expression of medieval piety. Recent critics have attempted to cope with the anti-Semitism, but there is still a tendency to emphasize the beauty of the verse form and the touching, if quaint, sentiment of the Nun.

The sentiment of the Nun does, in fact, dominate the tale. Chaucer did not invent the story, for which there are many analogues, nor did he tell it in his own voice. He let the Prioress tell it in her own way, a way that exactly suits her character and personality as they are portrayed in the General Prologue to *The Canterbury Tales.* No actively wicked villain like the Pardoner, the Prioress sins by omission, as Chaucer skillfully implies by his own omissions and innuendos. He tells us in the Prologue that she was all "tender heart and pity." Good qualities, we think, for a nun whose life is dedicated to serving the poor. But her charity and pity were so great that she wept if she saw a mouse caught in a trap, "if it were dead," or "if it bled." And she fed her small dogs on "roast flesh" or "milk with fine white bread." Chaucer has spared seven lines for her overindulgence of pets and has not a word about the poor. In the tale, the death of the slain child, unlike that of the mouse, is genuinely pathetic. But the parallel references to blood are rather shocking: in the Prologue, the Prioress cries over the blood of a mouse; in the tale, the blood of the murdered child cries out for revenge. The connection may only be that the little mouse and the little child are both objects of the Prioress's solicitude; however, the juxtaposition of her pity for the child with her approval of the torture of the Jews is an indictment of her Christianity.

The prompt and terrible revenge the Prioress sanctions with a proverb was the kind of lynching without a trial that was condemned by the authorities of both Church and State. She tells us that as soon as the magistrate arrived at the scene of the murder, he promptly ordered each one of the Jews who knew of the murder to be tortured and put to death. He would not tolerate such cursedness: "Evil shall have that evil deserves." Therefore, he had them drawn apart by wild horses and afterwards hanged according to the law. Of course, the Prioress does not see that her prayer for mercy on "us sinners" is inconsistent with this zeal for "justice" against the Jews. But Chaucer seems to have been pointing to the inconsistency when he has her use the word "mercy" three times in two lines of her prayer to Hugh of Lincoln, whose death at the hands of Jews she stresses. The wording of this prayer may suggest also that her hard attitude to the Jews was not simply a reflection of what everybody thought. Is there not an echo of argument against the skeptics who denied that the Jews killed children, in her words, O young Hugh of Lincoln, "slain also by cursed Jews, as is well known, for it happened but a little while ago"?

Even apart from its anti-Semitism, the story lacks spiritual depth because of the sentimentality and ignorance of the teller. The key word is "little": "little" mice and dogs, "small" children, "little" school-boy, "little" son, "little" child, "little" book. Surely Chaucer is being sly when he has the Prioress claim, with well-earned modesty, to know less than a twelve-months-old baby. Nobody knew better than Chaucer the difference between childlike and childish, between innocence and ignorance. If all that remained of medieval Christianity were The Prioress's Tale, we would deduce a "little" religion, suitable for tribal children and their maiden aunts.

The Prioress's sentimental piety is not the cause of her bigotry, but the two qualities are often present in a type of woman we are all familiar with. Chaucer has portrayed the combination with such uncanny accuracy that the Prioress seems a prototype of the pious lady who would not hurt a mouse but who would not stop a lynching of those outsiders she fears and hates. There are many kind and well-mannered ladies in twentieth-century middle America who (like Mark Twain's Emily Grangerford in the nineteenth) write verses for country weeklies about the sad deaths of children. Their hearts bleed especially for those murdered sensationally by Reds or Blacks, but not for Yellow children slain in a pit in My-Lai. And we forgive them because we see that they do not see that they have a double standard; and besides, they are our cousins or our sisters or our aunts.

The clerical descendants of the Prioress bear an even closer resemblance to her. Many of us have known similarly lady-like nuns, who sang the service divinely, who spoke a little French, who wept over legends of child saints—and were anti-Semitic. Probably nobody ever left the Church because of them; they were kindly and knew every child by name; and there was usually a second nun to give reality to the Christian ideal. It is nonetheless embarrassing to find a nun-scholar of our time who is not ashamed to claim the Prioress for her own. She suggests that Chaucer had known personally many sisters and had listened to their touching stories. Wherever he got the text, she says, he may have heard this very tale from the lips of some old nun, some dear old sister, perhaps an aunt or a grand-aunt. Exactly! Chaucer is telling us that this is just the sentimental, bigoted story dear old sister would tell.

This perfect adaptation of tale to teller seems to me to be Chaucer's major intention and achievement. Since everything, including the treatment of the Jews, is subordinated to this end, we can tell only indirectly what Chaucer's attitude toward them was. But it follows from the disparity he shows between the Prioress's vindictiveness and her Christian vocation of love that he at least disapproved of anti-Semitism. And there is one curious detail that may indicate his own doubts of such martyrdoms as are dwelt on here. Unlike all the other extant versions of the story, the Prioress's is set in Asia. That is, the first line mentions Asia; the descriptions that follow all seem to be of an English town. Did Chaucer slip in "Asia" to imply that this story never happened in England?

I should like to think that the Prioress's references to the Old Testament were also slyly inserted by Chaucer as an ironic commentary on the preposterousness of anti-Semitism, but I do not find this suggestion by one of the critics convincing. When the Nun calls the murdered boy's mother a new Rachel, she is following the medieval custom described earlier, of seeking Scriptural parallels for Christians. And her allusion is taken not from the Bible but from the liturgy, as is her reference to the burning bush of Moses, in the Prologue to her tale. The bush that burned without being consumed had long since become a conventional metaphor for the perpetual virginity of Mary, and it suggests the Prioress's clerical style rather than any thought about Moses. Chaucer's own use of the same appellation appears in a hymn to Mary, "The ABC," and I doubt that it suggested to him a link between contemporary Jews and their Scriptural ancestors.

Considering his works as a whole, I surmise that Chaucer was more interested in portraying popular conceptions of both Scriptural and medieval Jews than in discussing the law and the prophets or the conversion of the Jews. An articulate Christian, he recognized the Judaic roots of Christianity, and the anti-Christian character of anti-Semitism. But intellectually and emotionally he was not drawn to the Torah and Talmud. His preference for classical literature may have been a matter of temperament. The humorous detachment that is characteristic of the sophisticated poet is hardly a conspicuous element in the style of Scripture. Perhaps that is why it is easier to imagine him dining with Ovid than with Jeremiah.

That is not to say, however, that Chaucer was choosing paganism over Hebraism. As a Christian humanist, his religious synthesis included both Hebrew morality and pagan philosophy. The Hebraic is rather like the base of an iceberg; invisible but solid, it keeps the tip from breaking off. Chaucer's search for God among the pagans was safeguarded by the knowledge of the answers he already possessed from Revelation.

VII

Pagans and Paganism

f the two major contributors to Christian thought, which Matthew Arnold called Hebraism and Hellenism, Chaucer was influenced far more by Hellenism. I am not suggesting any conflict between the two, and I don't think there was any for Chaucer; but the simple fact is that there are a great many more pagans than Jews in Chaucer's works, and the proportion probably reflects the amount of thought Chaucer gave to paganism and Judaism. Of course, the Scriptures are the acknowledged source of Chaucer's Christian morality; and Old Testament Hebrews, as was noted in the last chapter, are frequently cited as examples of virtue. But these Hebrews do not play major roles in Chaucer's works. It was classical myth and literature that furnished Chaucer with themes, settings, heroes, and literary models. Even his ponderings over the problem of evil are expressed by such pagans as Troilus and Palamon rather than by the biblical Job. Chaucer's very preference for the classical over the biblical tells us something about the flavor of his own

Christianity. His handling of philosophical ideas, pagan gods, and pagan characters tells us a good deal about his broad concepts of God, of the salvation of the heathen, and of the place of the Church in the universal dispensation.

Pagan Trojans, Christian Englishmen, pagan Britons, Moslem Syrians, Roman Christians, God and gods, Jupiter and Jesus, all mix quite freely in Chaucer's work, in a rather bewildering variety of roles. *Troilus and Criseyde,* The Knight's Tale, The Manciple's Tale, and The Physician's Tale are set in ancient Troy, Greece, or Rome. The Second Nun's Tale is set among pagan Romans in early Christian times; The Franklin's Tale is set in pagan Brittany; The Man of Law's Tale moves from Christian Rome to Moslem Syria, to Roman Britain; The Squire's Tale is set in Tartary. The dream poems, *The Book of the Duchess, The House of Fame,* and *The Parliament of Fowls* arise, Chaucer says, from his bedtime reading of old books about legends and temples and from philosophical talk. Part of this interest was antiquarian; Chaucer portrays himself as bookish, as poring over the *Thebaid* of Statius, the *Aeneid* of Virgil, and the *Heroides* of Ovid and enjoying the sense of the past, much as we do. Like most medieval writers, however, he believed, as he said, with St. Paul, that all was written for our instruction, and he explored the old stories for their eternal values and updated them in a broadly humanistic way.

The respect which Chaucer accords pagan ideas astonishes readers newly arrived in the medieval world through Chaucer's poetry. They are astonished because they have been miseducated by a discredited but still influential view of history, according to which medieval Christians sent everybody to hell except themselves. In fact, so far from being unusual in his attitude, or "ahead of his time," Chaucer was following the popular Boethian synthesis of pagan and Christian thought. Both the synthesis and Chaucer's use of it have been misunderstood even by scholars until quite recently. Chaucer was thought naïve because in his poem "Truth," he apparently identified the "truth" referred to in the *Consolation of Philosophy* with the "Truth" that is Christ in the Gospel of St. John. Sixth-century Boethius could not have meant that, opined critics from the eighteenth to the twentieth centuries, because he was a pagan Roman. Further, the critics thought that Boethius was revered as a saint by his medieval admirers because in their provincialism they assumed that anyone who understood the nature of God must have been a Christian. And finally, they were thought to be so ignorant that they did not realize that the *Consolation* was based on the philosophical ideas of the Greeks and Romans. The critics, however, have often been more provincial than the criticized, and contemporary scholarship has confirmed Chaucer's judgment: Boethius was a Christian, exactly the kind the Middle Ages thought he was; that is, a thinker who fused philosophy with Christian doctrine. In his poem called "Truth," Chaucer was making explicit what really was implicit in the *Consolation*.

Why the *Consolation* is not explicitly Christian does not concern us here, but medieval satisfaction with it does. The numerous translations and borrowings from it exemplify not only the eclecticism but the ecumenism of the many medieval Christians like Chaucer, who rejoiced in what they knew of classical philosophy not only because it coincided with their own opinions or because they thought it prefigured Christianity but because it reflected the presence of God. As St. Bernard of Clairvaux put it in the twelfth century, those who do not know Christ may still know and love God by natural law. The four cardinal virtues of Plato were thus called the "natural" virtues because men could presumably discover them without the special revelation of the Scriptures. Plato, Aristotle, Cicero, and Seneca were admired especially because they were not Christians and yet had come to know wisdom and truth. And there was no condescension in this admiration. The French poet Deschamps was paying Chaucer a very great compliment when he called him a Socrates for wisdom, a Seneca in uprightness of life, and an Ovid in poetic language.

This Christian humanism had a long, if sometimes troubled history. "What has Athens to do with Jerusalem?" demanded Tertullian in the second century; and there were always criers of woe to devotees of antiquity. But when pre-puritans objected to the preservation of paganism, the humanists took their defense from the history of the Hebrews who, when they fled across the Red Sea, carried with them "the spoils of the Egyptians." So, it was argued, Christians were free to assimilate the "spoils" of antiquity. Indeed, it was churchmen who were the principal assimilators. From the sixth century on, after the barbarians had overrun the Empire, the major educational goal of the West was the preservation and rediscovery of the learning of the Greeks and Romans. For some of those centuries, only churchmen, who had had to study a little to read the Bible and the liturgy, were literate. Later lovers of books must be moved by the stories of those remote book lovers, usually monks, who painstakingly guarded and copied surviving manuscripts.

Presumably all was for the greater glory of God, but latter-day classicists as well as Puritans can appreciate the temptations that beset Christians who preferred the elegant rhetoric of Cicero to the rude grandeur of Amos. That is the point of the famous story of St. Jerome, who had a vision of himself being whipped in heaven for being a

Ciceronian rather than a Christian. For the most part, the doctrine that all knowledge and beauty must be subordinated to God was not interpreted narrowly by Christian humanists who discussed, say, the intrinsic value of Cicero's *On Friendship*. It was because of the moral beauty of Cicero's work that Dante ranked him with Boethius. And it was Virgil's "beloved feet" that Dante followed on the first two stages of his pilgrimage. Master of knowledge and art to Dante, Virgil was considered by Mussato as one of the Prophets, as a "Christian without Christ." The great storyteller Ovid would seem to need more defense than Virgil, but his enormous popularity apparently carried him beyond cavil. There was a "moralized" version, but the "unmoralized" stories were also widely told.

In pagan art and philosophy as well as in literature, the Church found evidence of the intimations of divinity given to all peoples and clarified by Christ. Most of the parallels were drawn with Old Testament figures such as Isaac; but in the catacombs, Christ was also portrayed as a young man much like Apollo, and on later Christian tombs, miracles of Christ are shown parallel with the labors of Hercules. In twelfth-century churches there are statues of both Hercules and Samson, both attacking lions, both "figures" of Christ attacking Satan. Indeed, recovered sculpture was stored in churches, especially during the Romanesque period, when there was a "Renaissance" of the art, literature, and philosophy of antiquity. It was also at this time, at Chartres, that clerical scholars specialized in Platonic or Neoplatonic studies. The thirteenth century saw the rediscovery of Aristotle, the study of whose works revolutionized the schools, largely under the guidance of St. Thomas Aquinas. So deeply did Christian, Jewish, and Moslem philosophers fall in love with Aristotle that they gave him a place of honor in their religions, and even traded commentaries on his works with each other. All of this is not to say that medieval Christians like Dante and Chaucer thought it was all one whether you were a pagan or a Christian. It did mean that in Chaucer's intellectual tradition, God was not confined to the Church.

St. Augustine had been most explicit that the City of God was not identical with the Church. Wherever the power of divine love moves the human will, he said, there the City of God is being built. Such a view partially explains why Chaucer's characters do not fall into simple categories of good Christian and bad pagan. And the Christian tellers of pagan stories in *The Canterbury Tales* also hold this broad view; the Knight, for example, expects his pagan characters to make moral decisions and to reflect about God and the universe in a more or less philosophical manner. Theseus, in The Knight's Tale, is the most conspicuous example of such a characterization, his description of the first Mover of the universe and of the subordination of fortune to God being derived from Boethius.

It was commonly assumed by medieval writers that this first Mover, who is the one God of the universe, created all men in his image. Some variation of this last phrase is used so casually by Chaucer and his characters that it sounds like a tag to fill in a line; and tags, of course, reflect an author's assumptions. When Aurelius, for example, is attempting to seduce Dorigen in The Franklin's Tale, he appeals "by God that this world made," and she refuses "by God that gave me soul and life." In *The Parliament of Fowls*, Chaucer describes music of such ravishing sweetness that God, "who is maker and lord of all," never heard any music that was better. In one passage in *The Legend of Good Women*, this God who made heaven and earth might himself love Dido for her beauty; in another, the phrase "since God made Adam of earth" is a simple interjection; in a third, Chaucer calls God "giver of the forms, that has wrought this fair world." This God, the "principal former of all" in The Physician's Tale, has made Nature his vice-regent, and with him she is in full accord. The Friar, at the end of his tale about the Summoner, prays to God who made mankind after his image. And Chaucer, on his way to the House of Fame, prays to God who made Adam. One cannot conclude from this compilation of asides and oaths whether the speakers are pagan or Christian. Whatever their belief or morality, they all assume an orderly universe, ruled over by the God who formed all and is master of Fortune and Nature, and is known by pagan as well as by Jew and Christian.

One Christian implication of the assumption is expressed by the Parson in his tale. Because, he says, we all have one father and mother in the flesh, Adam and Eve, and one spiritual father, God in heaven, we should love our neighbor as ourself. The Parson was addressing Christians, but he did mean "all." A further implication was that all were immortal, albeit to live forever after was not necessarily a happy prospect.

It was not for unbelief, however, that the philosophers and theologians sent non-Christians to hell. St. Augustine had explained that the City of God is a transcendent reality, older than the world and eternal, and that in all ages, Christ is the same Son of God. Therefore, from the beginning of the human race, whoever believed in him or knew him in any way, and lived in a pious and just manner according to his precepts, "was undoubtedly saved by Him in whatsoever time and place he may have lived." In the same vein, Aquinas, quoting Gregory, commented that before Christ's coming, men were incorporated in Christ by faith alone, together with the offering of sacrifices, by means of which the fathers of old "made profession of their

211

faith." It was specifically the good pagans whom they respected so highly that the learned desired to save, and the prevailing cosmology was broad enough to include everybody. That this view was widely known is amusingly evident in the addition by medieval students of the name of Socrates to the liturgy of the saints. "Saint Socrates," they chanted half-jokingly, "Pray for us." The most notable voice to the contrary that I happen to know of was that of Wycliffe's, and he was a heretic. His heresy may be relevant, since the modern view of Christianity as an exclusive religion flourished along with nationalism and Protestantism in the post-medieval period.

At the grass roots, however, there must have been many who interpreted literally the doctrine that only the baptized can be saved (with the exception of the Old Testament saints, who had been taken directly to heaven by Christ himself). At least, the Dreamer in Langland's *Piers Plowman* cites "clerks" as saying that neither heathen nor Jew can be saved. The clerks, however, are only foils for a character named Imagination, who dramatizes Augustine. He remarks first that whether or not Aristotle was saved has not been revealed to the clergy. He thinks that since God gave the pagan philosophers the wit to write books which help us to be saved, we are bound to pray for their souls. Secondly, he says that all men, not just the baptized, are created in the image of God, and that that image can be forfeited only by sin. Therefore, good men of whatever time or place who retain the image of goodness will not be excluded by Goodness himself. God is truth, and will reward the true man who lives as his law teaches and would amend if he knew a better. To think otherwise, Langland concludes, would be to dishonor Truth itself.

Langland was more concerned to empty than to people hell. Similarly, Julian of Norwich, another contemporary

212

of Chaucer's, wrote that anything was possible with God, and that all would be saved. More popular with writers of fiction, however, was the provision of diverse eternal abodes. With their characteristic urge to classify everything, many medieval authors worked enthusiastically on maps of the hereafter. Most of these authors, like Dante and Chaucer, knew they were only speculating, and hence free to produce their own versions.

In the *Divine Comedy*, which Chaucer knew well, Dante assigns places in hell, purgatory, and heaven in such a way as to answer theological questions about the fate of good pagans. The ancient Trojan Ripheus is high up in Paradise not only or primarily as a reward for virtue but as a consequence of his mysteriously infused knowledge of Christ. From him mortals are to learn that they cannot judge who are the elect; we do not know, says Dante, how God interprets the dictum that belief in Christ is necessary. It is observed further that many heathen who never knew Christ will be closer to him on Judgment Day than many who call on his name. Further, when the pilgrim Dante is questioned by St. Peter on the sources of his faith, he attributes his acceptance of this most Christian virtue not only to Moses, the prophets, and the Gospels, but to Aristotle, especially to the philosopher's concept of the unmoved Mover, and to his *Physics* and *Metaphysics*.

Why, then, did Dante the poet put the great philosophers not in Paradise but in limbo on the outskirts of hell? One reason was to demonstrate that philosophy can, by its very nature, take a man only so far; Christianity is a revealed religion that cannot be reached through reason alone. Another reason is that nobody puts anybody anywhere in the *Divine Comedy*: everybody chooses his own place, and the philosophers repair to the underworld they had described in their own works. And finally, what would

213

these fictionalized pagans do and how would they speak in a fictional Christian heaven? Pagans of any time, including our own, find Dante's civilized and elegant palace of the philosophers and poets much more to their taste than the company of angels, prophets, and saints who people his Paradise.

With his quite different temperament, Chaucer steadfastly refuses to categorize the hereafter. I suspect that when he insists that he is no "divine" to explain the soul's destination, he is glancing with a certain amount of amusement in Dante's direction. Certainly his borrowings from Dante reveal his admiration for the master, but one of the few times he is named, it is by the devil in The Friar's Tale who tells the Summoner he will soon know more about the details of hell than Dante! Without arguing with anybody, Chaucer does, however, make a broad distinction between pagan and Christian heavens. When Troilus dies, his soul goes to the eighth sphere, before being led to a permanent home, "whatever that may be," by Mercury. Much more precise are the expectations of the newly converted Christians in the legend of St. Cecilia, who joyfully accept martyrdom in the hope of union with Christ in heaven.

Chaucer was concerned less with compartmentalizing the hereafter than with establishing the similarity of pagan and Christian concepts. In the Prologue to *The Parliament of Fowls*, he gives a long, appreciative summary of a favorite book, Cicero's *Dream of Scipio*, which he and his contemporaries read in a commentary by Macrobius. (Macrobius, who lived in the fourth century, was probably a Christian, and devoted his time to making available the classical liberal arts.) In this dream, Chaucer tells us, Scipio's ancestor, Africanus, appeared to him and told him that ignorant as well as learned men who "loved the common good" would go after death to a blissful place of "lasting joy." Africanus then showed Scipio this "little earth," and by contrast, Scipio heard the music of the spheres. From this dream Scipio was intended to learn the insignificance of earth, his own immortality, and the way to enter heaven. Chaucer, like the numerous other admirers of Cicero, apparently learned from the vision confirmation of the Christian belief in immortality.

Similarly, the pagan knowledge of virtue was taken as strengthening the truth of Christian morality. St. Jerome, for example, insists that chastity was not some Christian invention but an eternal good that was praised and practiced by the ancients. Jerome is cited in the Prologue to *The Legend of Good Women* as telling not of a few but of a hundred pure maidens, true wives, and steadfast widows who chose death rather than betrayal of their vows. This constancy, it is noted with admiration, was not the result of Christian holiness, for they were heathen, "the whole pack." The same whole pack is cited by Dorigen in The Franklin's Tale when she is considering suicide as an alternative to adultery.

The Parson remarks that not only Christians but pagans practiced patience, and for the most part, it is simply assumed that virtues like patience and prudence and chastity—and vices like impatience, anger, and lechery—are universally human. Poets, philosophers, prophets, and exegetes, authors and characters alike, are drawn on for moral lessons with little concern for chronology or ethnicity. In The Tale of Melibeus, for example, Prudence cites Ovid, Seneca, St. Paul, Christ, Jesus Sirach, Solomon, Jacob, Abigail, David, Cicero, Gregory, Cato, and Cassiodorus. Hers is a most impressive list, but she is not alone, many of Chaucer's characters being very well educated. Not only does the Clerk of Oxford have twenty volumes of Aristotle at the head of his bed, but the vulgar Host cites Seneca, as does the Wife of Bath, who also quotes Juvenal, Ovid, St. James, and the Scriptures. The Wife also knows well the book read most often by her fifth husband, a book about wicked wives like Eve, Delilah, Xantippe, and Clytemnestra.

Skipping over these lists which bore us as much as they entertained our ancestors, we may miss their significance in Chaucer's religious thinking. Does it not signify that in spite of the unequivocal Christian prohibition of suicide, there is no hint of disapproval in Chaucer's *Legend of Good Women* of heroines who killed themselves? Of course, Chaucer was only following his sources, as St. Jerome was following his. But the very ability to accept the values of pagan sources suggests a sense of what we call comparative religion. So Dante puts Christian suicides in hell, but pagan Cato holds the honored position of guardian in the *Purgatory*, because, noble Roman that he was, he killed himself rather than submit to Caesar's tyranny. Aware of differences in moral codes, Chaucer also admires those who lived up to the highest that they knew, and he does not condemn them for what they did not know.

He sees also that customs are alike in different civilizations, and he sometimes departs from his sources to interchange pagan and Christian names when they represent the same things. Lucrece, for example, was such a good wife, Chaucer says in her legend, that not only pagans commend her, but he who is called in "our legend" the great Augustine, had great compassion on her. At the end of her story, Chaucer remarks that she was considered a saint in pagan Rome, and her day was kept holy according to pagan religion. In many of the stories, that religion is portrayed as part of daily life, rather like going to Mass in Chaucer's day. In *The House of Fame*, the temple is described very much like a church, and when Troilus goes to the temple at the

beginning of *Troilus,* he and the other young men are looking over the girls quite as young men do in church.

An extreme example of this rather offhand respect for
other religious laws appears in The Squire's Tale. The action is set in the land of Tartary, the religion of which was
apparently as vague to Chaucer as it is to most of us. As-
suming the best, however, the Squire says that the noble
king, Cambuskan, excelled in every way. As to the "sect in
which he was born," he "kept the law" to which "he was
sworn," and therefore he was "hardy, wise, and rich, merciful and just, true to his word, benign and honorable."

As Boccaccio explained in his *Genealogies of the Gods,*
unlike the early days when Christianity was fighting for its
life against paganism, now the Church had triumphed
everywhere, and there was therefore little danger in the
study of paganism. When Chaucer calls Jove the "author of
Nature," and Apollo the "god of science and light" in *The
House of Fame,* he is enjoying the sophisticated notion that
God is called by many names. When on the other hand
Chaucer constructs historical fiction in which paganism is
conceived as active idol worship, he treats it seriously. It is
clear in these stories that he did not think that all gods are
equal, or that the sincerity of the devotee, however admirable, proves the truth of his religion.

Chaucer's sharpest indictment of pagan religion appears in a stanza near the end of *Troilus.* The attack is
surprising, coming at the end of a poem in which worship of
the gods is apparently accepted as part of the historically
imagined setting. In summing up his book, however,
Chaucer steps out of the setting, and out of his role as
faithful follower of sources, to address his audience directly.
Having related the unhappy end of the love of Troilus and
Criseyde, Chaucer advises young Christians to turn to
Christ, who died for them. Apparently returning to the

217

story, Chaucer then speaks of the "cursed old pagan rites" of ancient Troy, practiced by Troilus. "Lo, here," says Chaucer, see what all their gods avail! Here is "the reward of travail" for Jove, Apollo, Mars, and "that whole mob!" This juxtaposition is not, I think, an irrelevant contrast of Christianity and a long-dead paganism, but an expression of compassion for Troilus and Criseyde; unlike the young Christians of Chaucer's time, these young pagans of old had no help, hope, or comfort from their gods.

Similar scorn of their uselessness is poured on the mob of gods in The Second Nun's Tale of St. Cecilia. But in this traditional saint's legend of the third century, the emphasis is on the pagans who are converted by the obvious superiority of Christianity as well as by the miracles granted to Cecilia. Appearing to pagan Valerian as an old man dressed in white, St. Paul paraphrases his letter to the Ephesians, "One Lord, one faith, one God without more, one Christendom, and Father of all also, above all and over all everywhere" (Eph 4:5,6). Valerian immediately accepts this basic doctrine, for nobody, he says, might "think a truer thing." Similarly, his brother Tiburtius readily accepts Cecilia's assertion that dumb idols are vain; then Cecilia preaches the Trinity and the life of Christ.

The Prefect, however, is a firm adherent of the old religion. After considerable debate with Cecilia, he says that as a philosopher he can put up with personal insults, but he cannot endure what she says of the gods. When she responds that the people will laugh at his folly in believing in images, for "commonly men know that God is over all in heaven," he becomes angry and sends for the executioners. For her part, Cecilia distinguishes between the religion and the disciple; while she mocks the perfect's belief in idols, she does not threaten him with hell for his belief.

The only other conversion story, The Man of Law's

Tale, concerns Moslems and pagan Britons. When the Sultan of Syria decides he must marry the reputedly beautiful and virtuous Constance, his council discusses the religious impediment. They see that no Christian prince would wed his daughter under the "sweet law" of their prophet, Mohammed. When, however, the Sultan and his barons agree to be christened, the pope is happy to arrange the wedding. The Sultan's mother is not happy, and her words suggest both Chaucer's ignorance of Islam and his belief that a Moslem might be sincere. Angry that her son will end all the "old sacrifices" and the holy laws of the Koran, the lady vows to God that life will leave her body before Mohammed's law leaves her heart. This new law, she believes, will draw them to hell. And when she is planning to pretend to accept baptism, she says that a little cold water won't hurt! At the wedding feast, she orders the murder of just those members of the Council who had been converted willingly.

The description of Roman Britain, Constance's next port of call, strikes us as a fairly accurate historical picture. It is quite different from the prevailing fancies of the romances. *Sir Gawaine and the Green Knight,* for example, begins with a reference to the destruction of Troy, whence came King Aeneas to the Western Isles, and one Felix Brutus, who founded Britain and was the ancestor of King Arthur. Ignoring such popular legends, the Man of Law remarks correctly that when the pagans had conquered Northumberland, the Christians had fled to Wales, except for a few who had remained and continued to honor Christ secretly. He also notes that the natives spoke a kind of corrupt Latin, and so could understand Roman Constance. The natives do not say anything about their religion, probably because the teller of the tale knew even less about it than about Islam. Like good people everywhere, however, the constable and his wife are impressed with Constance's virtue, and the wife is converted secretly, lest her pagan husband have her killed. Ultimately, however, both the constable and King Alla (historic King of Deira, who died in 588) are converted by a combination of miracle and preaching, without any theological debate. The pagan mother of the king rejects Constance because she does not like strangers; nothing is said of her beliefs. She is later consigned to hell by the narrator, not, however, for her faith, but for her wicked deeds.

Long ago or far away must have seemed the Roman Prefect, the Syrian Sultan, and the Northumbrian King to the Parson of the Canterbury pilgrimage. Wholly concerned with the practice of Christian principles at home, he takes no comfort in the theological superiority of Christianity to paganism; for him, the difference must be expressed in deeds. What difference is there, he demands, between an idolater and an avaricious man except that the idolater has only one or two idols while the avaricious man has many? Every "florin in his coffer is an idol," says the Parson, and the man who worships his treasure breaks the first commandment by having false gods.

Remote though they were from the good parish priest, however, Islam and tribal paganism were not dead in the fourteenth century, as Chaucer well knew. As was noted earlier, the Knight is described in the Prologue to *The Canterbury Tales* as having fought in Moslem lands, specifically in "Belmarye" and "Tramyssene," that is, Morocco and western Algeria. Part of his service had been with the lord of "Palatye," a heathen who in 1365 was allied with King Peter of Cyprus. And the Knight had been campaigning in Lithuania, where the people became Christian only in 1386, perhaps just before the Knight joined the Canterbury pilgrimage. None of this experience is referred to directly in his tale of Thebes and Athens, but it may be that his treatment of religion reflects the way a man with the Knight's experience felt about outsiders and their laws.

KNIGHT

While the Second Nun and the Man of Law indicate no interest in the rites of the non-Christians in their stories, the Knight hints at mysteries. He says that he dare not tell the secret rites of Diana, but it would be a "game" to know all, and would do no harm to "him who means well." The passage is ambiguous, but it has been interpreted to mean that the Knight prudently pretended ignorance of heathen religions because the order of Knights Templars had been accused of dabbling in the occult. Certainly many crusading knights were tolerant of the customs of the heathen they admired as valiant fighters, and whom they sometimes knew socially. This Knight, good Christian that he is, identifies so heartily with the knights in his story, good pagans that they are, that he longs to join their noble company at the tournament of Theseus.

The gods in The Knight's Tale appear not as useless idols of stone but as great powers who manipulate the crucial events in the lives of Palamon and Arcite. Saturn, for example, is a dread figure, who, we are told, presides over disasters like stranglings and drownings and secret poisonings, the "ruin of halls" and the "falling of tower walls," treason and pestilence.

221

But while the gods seem vital deities in The Knight's Tale, scholars assure us that in most of Chaucer's works, Mars and Venus are primarily planets. So they are in Dante's *Divine Comedy*, where they are stars in Paradise, and serve as the eternal homes of good soldiers and true lovers. Now it was generally thought that the influence of the planets was determined by astrology. Insofar as astrology was the science of the day, it does not concern us here. When Chaucer describes the seasons according to the position of the planets, as he so often does (in the opening lines of *The Canterbury Tales*, for example), his calculations are in a class with his *Treatise on the Astrolabe* and have nothing to do with religion. But insofar as the planets affected the conduct of men, they came into uneasy "conjunction" with the Church.

From the Christian view, what was (perhaps is) pernicious about casting horoscopes is that the subject may justify his evil conduct as the inevitable result of the conjunction of the stars at the moment of his birth. When the Wife of Bath proclaims that she is "Venerian," she means that the planet Venus decreed her lasciviousness. There is a certain amount of truth behind her manner of speaking. The Parson himself would not have denied that she was highly endowed sexually "by nature"; but he would have added that she could have used her will to resist. St. Thomas Aquinas said that horoscopes often proved prophetic because people did not resist their impulses. Bodily appetites, he conceded, are influenced by the stars; men who are governed by their passions therefore carry out the predictions of the astrologers. If they do not use their free will, they become slaves of Fortune. That was what happened to Troilus and to Palamon and Arcite. However, St. Thomas says, nothing prevents a man from ruling his passions, and astrologers themselves agree that "the wise man rules the stars." A couple of examples will suffice to show how Chaucer indulged his taste for astrology within the orthodox framework. Clever Nicholas in The Miller's Tale misuses the science to make false predictions to further his lechery. Ordinarily, his astrology may be legitimate: with his *Almageste,* the Arabic text of astrology, he studies the heavens, predicting droughts and issuing flood warnings as scientifically as the weather bureau. But Aurelius in The Franklin's Tale hires a magician to create magic effects, a practice condemned by the Franklin as "folly" that in "our" day is not "worth a fly," since faith in the Church allows "no such illusion to grieve us." There is probably a certain amount of satire in the Franklin's overprotesting. Disclaiming knowledge of the terms of astrology, he seems very familiar with the "cursed superstition" based on the Toledan tables which had been compiled by Arabic astronomers. He talks too much of "tables of proportional parts" for computing the motion of planets, of equations, and other observances such as "heathen folk used in those days."

The Man of Law is a firm believer in planetary influence, but in his correct cosmology, stars control events, not character. He remarks that the death days of such great men as Hector, Achilles, and Socrates were all written in the stars, and he laments that no "philosopher" picked an auspicious time for the marriage of Constance. But Constance, as her name suggests, rises above bad fortune. And when she is set adrift on the sea, the narrator prays that He who is "Lord of fortune" will be her guide.

Sometimes natural, sometimes supernatural, such gods as Morpheus and Bacchus are sometimes funny. When in *The Book of the Duchess,* Chaucer cannot sleep, he reads Ovid's tale of Ceyx and Alcyone, in which the god of sleep is mentioned. Still insomniac, Chaucer, who "never knew any god but one," but who is afraid he'll die for lack of sleep, offers Morpheus a featherbed and pillows. At once, desire for sleep overcomes him! The Canterbury Host's mock prayer to Bacchus has more of an edge because it parodies Christian prayer. When the Manciple gives the drunken Cook another drink to soften his anger, the Host laughs and exclaims, "O thou Bacchus, blessed be thy name that so can turn earnest to game! Worship and thanks be to thy deity!"

Many of the diverse strands of thought glanced at in this chapter are woven into a complicated pattern in *The House of Fame.* Unlike a good deal of medieval mixing of pagan and Christian figures, which seems simply ahistorical, Chaucer's combination in this poem of pagan and Christian elements, of story, philosophy, astrology, and religion seems most deliberate. It is almost as though Chaucer was doing what we are trying to do here—look at this aspect of his intellectual heritage and decide where he fit in.

Using a dream technique, Chaucer provocatively juxtaposes materials from different traditions. After expressing devotion to Morpheus, the god of sleep, he shifts to a philosophic appellation for God and a phrase from the Gloria, praying to him who is "mover of all," "that is and was and ever shall be." In the dream story that follows, Chaucer finds himself in a place he recognizes as a temple of Venus by familiar pictures on the walls, such as one of Venus floating naked on the sea. But he suddenly reflects that although the art work is magnificent, he doesn't know who made it or where he is. He therefore physically and spiritually steps outside the pagan temple to pray to Christ to keep him from "phantom" and "illusion."

Chaucer is careful to name his "authorities," his sources and his models. Besides his literary arbiters, Ovid,

Virgil, and Dante, he cites three main lists of Scriptural and classical authorities, one pertaining to visions, two to miraculous flights to outer space. The famous dreamers include Isaiah, Scipio, Nebuchednezzar, and Turnus; those carried to heaven were Enoch, Elias, Romulus, and Ganymede; those who looked down from on high, Alexander, Scipio, Daedalus, and Icarus. After citing these august visionaries, prophets, and heroes, Chaucer carefully disassociates himself from them. He is not one of them, he insists, and we believe him.

The eagle that carries Chaucer aloft is himself an eclectic creature, conceived with the help of Virgil, Ovid, and Dante, and nurtured by Chaucer's comic muse. Traditionally Jupiter's bird, the eagle is a figure of empire in Dante's *Paradise*, where such different rulers as David, Trajan, Hezekiah, Constantine, and Rhipeus are portrayed as "lights" above the eagle's eye. And in mythology, Jupiter himself took the form of an eagle when he carried away Ganymede.

In Chaucer's adventure, as there is nothing glorious about Geoffrey, there is nothing regal about the eagle. "Awake!" the eagle yells at the all but unconscious, cowardly Geoffrey, in the same voice, Chaucer says, as that used by someone he could name—Mrs. Chaucer, we presume. Jupiter's bird, dweller with the god of thunder, the eagle swears by God and by Saints Mary, James, Julian, and Clare. En route he gives Geoffrey a long lesson in physics, in motion and sound, citing Aristotle and Plato in a schoolmaster's voice, and asking at the end if he hasn't done a good job of simplifying the material for an ignorant man. Geoffrey later refuses a lesson on the stars, complaining that he's too old. A most humdrum, uncelestial pair, these two!

But the dream is part "earnest" as well as "game." The

dreamer looks down on little earth like Scipio, wonders like St. Paul whether he is in the body or the spirit, reflects about it like Boethius, and invokes Apollo like Dante. All, however, are filtered through Chaucer's dream-consciousness until they form a new and independent vision. When at one point Chaucer the dreamer is asked if he is seeking fame, he responds rather haughtily that he is not, that he is the judge of his own art, that he himself knows best how he stands. I think Chaucer knew where he stood also in the company of great religious thinkers.

Like many medieval writers, Chaucer did not consider humor incompatible with religion, and humor is a basic ingredient in his own vision of the universe and of his place in it. The picture of terrified Geoffrey sailing through the Empyrean in the claws of a loquacious eagle is at once a witty parody of all the famous flights alluded to and a comically serious analysis of the personality, education, and religion of the author. When Chaucer judges that he is no Isaiah, Scipio, Paul, Boethius, or Dante, he is denigrating neither them nor himself, but recognizing the difference. Chaucer never claims direct communications from God. He has learned about God from the diverse books and traditions described in the poem, and assimilated the knowledge in his own way. That way, he is telling us here, is the sophisticated, eclectic, and humorous way of this particular fourteenth-century Christian gentleman and poet. Surely he recognized his own comic spirit and personified it in his eagle guide; just as surely, his eagle carries him ultimately to the universal God of Plato, Aristotle, and Scipio, of Paul, Boethius, and Dante.

VIII

The Problem of Evil

f there is a just God, why do the innocent suffer and the wicked prosper? Who is responsible for disasters like shipwrecks? If there is a God, what is chance, or fortune? Why do men commit evil? Are they morally responsible or are they products of their heredity and environment? If God foresees the future, does anybody, hero or villain, have free will?

These are the questions of Job and Oedipus and of every thinking human being in every age. They are asked so frequently in Chaucer's works, and his fictional characters so rarely know the answers, that some readers have concluded that Chaucer was a skeptic or a determinist. Speaking in his own voice in poems of personal piety, however, Chaucer expresses entirely orthodox views on Providence, the justice of God, and free will; in poems on these subjects, his thinking is very close to Dante's. And he certainly knew the philosophical answers: they are all in the *Consolation of Philosophy* of Boethius which he translated. Why, then, does he leave his doubters in doubt? We might as reasonably ask why Sophocles did not supply footnotes to the *Oedipus* explaining how far Oedipus was a puppet in the hands of the gods and how far a responsible individual choosing his destiny. Like Sophocles, Chaucer does not simplify experience in order to prove a thesis; he was not primarily a philosopher or a theologian but an artist who saw life creatively rather than categorically, and even thought some of the categorizing funny.

In Chaucer's real and fictional worlds, just as in Job's time, people wanted immediate justice, and thought misfortune was—or should be—a punishment for sin. Then as now, plain folks tended to confuse God, fortune, and chance. Then, much more than now, theologians argued warmly over predestination, while witty students mocked the whole dispute. The range of ideas is well represented in Chaucer's works, and it is true that in the complex world he creates, as in the world we all inhabit, the questions are better known than the answers. Finally, however, God does not forsake Chaucer's unphilosophical characters, who come to understand not through dialectics but through prayer and morality.

The dialectics are important for our understanding, however, and are supplied by Boethius, whose *Consolation of Philosophy* was enormously influential throughout the Middle Ages. The very phrases of the *Consolation* appear in numerous passages in the *Romance of the Rose* by Jean de Meun (who also translated the work), in the *Divine Comedy* of Dante, and in the *Troilus* and The Knight's Tale of Chaucer, to mention just the best known. Further, Chaucer's translation of the work from Latin to English makes it one of his own works.

Chaucer's admiration for this noble Roman's response to the evil that befell him tells us as much about Chaucer's views as the words he borrowed to put in the mouths of his characters. For Boethius was revered in the Middle Ages as a saint who was unjustly sentenced to a death which he accepted with dignity, and who thus turned evil into good. A member of a distinguished Roman family, a classical scholar and a Christian, Boethius served as sole consul under the emperor Theodoric in the year 510, and in 522 his two sons had the unusual honor of being consuls together. Soon after, however, Boethius was falsely accused of treason and imprisoned, and in 524 he was put to death. During the last months of his life in prison, he wrote the *Consolation*, a much loved work, translated into English by such diverse persons as King Alfred, Chaucer, and Queen Elizabeth.

Gifted with poetic imagination, Boethius dramatized his experience in the form of a dialogue between himself and Lady Philosophy, in which he raises the problem of the existence of evil in a God-created world, and Lady Philosophy answers him. Boethius portrays himself complaining bitterly of the injustice of his fate to Lady Philosophy, who has appeared to him in his cell. He took part in public affairs, he says, because he followed Plato's counsel to spread wisdom; he has defended the poor and fought against the greed of rulers. Indeed, it was precisely because of his love of righteousness that he was accused and condemned. Why, he demands, are the innocent rather than the guilty punished? Why does the Master of all fail to control the works of men? If God exists, whence comes wickedness?

These are universal questions; it seems "natural" for Palamon in The Knight's Tale to ask them, although of course, it is Chaucer's art that adapts the very phrases of Boethius to the style of the Theban knight. The answers of Lady Philosophy are less obvious, and presuppose an uncommon interest in philosophy, and patience with dialectic. Only such unusual fictional and real personages as

Theseus in The Knight's Tale and Chaucer himself in "Truth" seem to have absorbed the Lady's full teaching. But the reader who knows Boethius, as many of Chaucer's readers did, can see just where the other characters go wrong in their thinking and attitudes.

In the course of the *Consolation*, Lady Philosophy gradually leads Boethius, from one question and answer to the next, to an application of the general truths of philosophy to his own plight. Comparing the smallness of the earth to the greatness of the heavens, she points out the insignificance of glory and fame. Boethius begins to see that in his pain he has forgotten the transitory nature of both prosperity and adversity. Even if there is no afterlife, he sees that death makes highest and lowest equal. And if there is a heaven, earthly honors are hardly worth noting. Still, how are these honors distributed? If God gives them out, how can vice triumph and virtue fail? Or are success and failure the result of chance or fortune, without God?

Good and bad fortune was a subject much discussed by medieval men and women, both in and out of fiction. Probably men have always blamed their woes on what we call "bad luck" and wished each other "good luck" without thinking much about what they meant. When they do brood over, say, the falling brick that kills one man and spares his companion, or the winning lottery ticket that is only one number away, they find it so difficult to conceive of random chance that they personify or deify the notion. The Romans talked about the Goddess Fortune, and medieval illustrators delighted in portraying the lady with a wheel, on which are bound poor mortals, who go up or down with every seemingly whimsical turn. Historically and popularly, she was more to be railed at than prayed to, her very nature being capricious changeability. Boethius and Dante, followed by Chaucer, however, adapted the

230

pagan goddess to Christian cosmology by subordinating her to the role of executor of God's will, and thus rather extending her range to moral matters.

Lady Philosophy explains that when men intend one thing and something else occurs, they call it chance, but that is only because they do not know the cause. In fact, good and bad fortune are under God and are given to punish or support, or to test or exercise the will. Further, since what is good for one man's soul is not good for another's we cannot judge by appearances; what looks like bad fortune may, in the light of eternity, be good. Stripped of worldly pride, the man stricken by so-called misfortune may seek the truth of God. When the seeker sees that all truth is within, then the darkness that hides the truth will be dispelled and the sun will light him.

There is no doubt that Lady Philosophy thinks Boethius's "bad fortune" is good for him, and will lead him to that fair otherworld in which there will be no tyrants. The heart of that otherworld is love, she says; it is love that governs earth, sea, and heaven; love holds together people joined in holy marriage; and love would make all men happy if they allowed it to govern their hearts.

The last major questions of Boethius concern free will and foreknowledge, a subject which troubles Chaucer's characters and is discussed at length by Troilus and in brief by Chanticleer. Boethius asks, If God knows all the future, are we not constrained to act as we do? If we are so constrained, there is no free will, he says, and there is no vice or virtue, no reason to hope in God or pray.

In a Platonic argument, Lady Philosophy says that all men desire what they think is good, but they do not choose wisely. Reasonable creatures use their free will to choose correctly what to flee and what to desire, but souls enslaved by vice lack the light of proper reason and choose falsely

231

because they are darkened by ignorance. Further, ignorance of eternity is a built-in limitation of our nature, and it is this limitation that makes it difficult for us to reconcile the idea of free will with that of God's foreknowledge. As Lady Philosophy explains, things are known according to the nature of the knower, not according to the thing itself: creatures who creep on the ground do not understand the earth as well as men who stand and look down on it. Similarly, men living in time cannot comprehend eternity, which has no past or future. God is not "older" than things by time; he knows by a different property of his nature. To God in his eternal and ever-present state, all things are right now. With our limited vision we can see two actions which occur simultaneously in the temporal present; God sees all actions, past, present, and future, in the eternal present. If you change your purpose, says Lady Philosophy, you do so by your own will, and God sees you changing in the present. Therefore, exhorts the Lady, turn by free will to divine actions; love virtue and pray.

Apparently Chaucer did not find this defense of free will suitable for his fiction. No doubt he was right. Not only is the argument rather difficult, but it gains its effectiveness in the context of the Socratic dialogue, if one likes that sort of thing (as Chaucer apparently did); but it would offer pale comfort to men and women in Boethius's trouble without Boethius's temperament and training. Instead of versifying Boethius's whole argument, Chaucer dramatically exploits the negative arguments by putting them in the mouths of characters who do not know the answers, and who, Lady Philosophy would say, do not know because they are blinded by sin or ignorance. What this means in fictional terms is that Chaucer's characterizations are so convincing that we cannot imagine the poor souls heeding Lady Philosophy if she did appear to them. Chaucer did heed, in his own way. As we shall see, phrases borrowed from her are usually incorporated in less philosophical but equally fervent affirmations of a loving God whose creatures behave as though they have freedom of choice.

In The Knight's Tale, the problem of evil is discussed in terms which accord with the circumstances of the characters. Palamon and Arcite blame their misfortunes on the gods, Theseus recognizes Providence in all, and all is seen through the eyes of the good, not especially learned, Knight. In this medieval romance told on the pilgrimage to Canterbury, Palamon and Arcite are presumably two knights of ancient times who were captured in the battle of Thebes by Theseus, King of Athens. No ransom is allowed and they are sentenced to life imprisonment. Blaming their adversity on Fortune, Arcite at first seems willing to endure it. But when they become bitter enemies in their contest over the fair Emily, whom they have seen walking in the garden below the prison window, they rage against their fate and each other. When Arcite is exiled, free but deprived of the sight of Emily, and Palamon remains, imprisoned but hopeful of an occasional glimpse of the lady, each envies the other's unenviable plight. To Arcite the prison of Palamon is Paradise and Palamon is favored by Fortune. Pondering the quirks of chance, he sees that wishes granted (like his for freedom) often lead to harm, and that Fortune serves us better than we could devise ourselves. In applying this argument of Lady Philosophy on the hidden causes of Fortune to Palamon, however, Arcite fails utterly to see its application to himself.

Palamon, meanwhile, pronounces a diatribe against the gods which echoes, but goes far beyond, the complaints of Boethius in prison. "O cruel gods that govern all this world," he cries, "what is mankind to you more than sheep?" Men are "slain like other beasts," they "dwell in prison and in sickness," and yet are often guiltless. "What kind of governance is this that torments innocence?" And what increases his misery, Palamon says, is that man is "bound in duty to God to curb his desires," whereas a beast may fulfill all his wishes. And when a beast is dead, he has no pain, but man, even after death "must weep." The explanation of this injustice, Palamon says, he leaves to the theologians; the pain he feels himself. And he ends with a passionate outburst against the unfairness of the world and the gods.

The way in which Chaucer selects and transforms material from the *Consolation* in this passage is most revealing of his mind and art. In the *Consolation,* Lady Philosophy had spoken contemptuously of thoughtless beasts, and surely she would scorn Palamon for envying their ignorance. But surely Chaucer does not intend us to feel contempt for the poor knight Palamon. It is true that he is blinded by passion, but it is also true, as he says, that the wicked go free while he (like Boethius) is in prison because he served his country honorably. His cry from the heart touches us and we do not hold it against him that he is not a philosopher and that Lady Philosophy has not visited him in prison. Chaucer portrays his despair with sympathetic understanding and does not turn him into a peg on which to hang an argument.

The generally admirable Knight who tells the tale is not much of a philosopher either, and his sole response to Palamon's outburst is to ask whether Arcite or Palamon had the harder lot! And while he calls Palamon's imprisonment a martyrdom, his basic view of the forces controlling the action is optimistic. He believes in "destiny," but a Christian destiny that, like Fortune, has been subordinated to God. It is to this destiny, "the minister-general" of Providence, that he attributes the coincidence of Theseus's going hunting in the same grove at the same moment that Palamon and Arcite are duelling. Though the world may deny it, says the Knight, destined events happen according to plan; our appetites and fears, "our hates and loves" are governed by a providence above.

The cheerfulness of the Knight's determinism may be related to the fact that he thinks the story has a happy ending. Perhaps it's as happy as it could be; given the situation of two fanatical lovers, one has to die and the other get the girl. And since they are both equally brave and honorable, winning and losing depend not on the exercise of their will but on the will of the gods. When Arcite sacrifices to Mars, and Palamon to Venus, there is strife in heaven until a compromise is reached. The devotee of Mars wins the battle, but when his horse is tripped by Pluto he dies so that the devotee of Venus can win Emily. Even Arcite's deathbed rejection of jealousy is so standard a scene as hardly to reflect a moral choice, not to say concern with the hereafter.

The Knight professes to be more interested in the medical details of Arcite's death than in the destination of his soul. When Arcite cannot rid his body of corruption, "neither vomit upward nor laxative downward," the Knight gives him up. Observing that Arcite's spirit "changed house," the Knight refrains from further speculation. There is a shadow of doubt about the universe here, but the Knight is basically untroubled, and his tone suggests that everything will work out in this best of all possible worlds of knights and tournaments.

That is the substance also of the elaborate speech of Duke Theseus, the official moralizer of the story. The Providence that the young lovers, blinded by jealousy and misfortune, could not see, is obvious to the mature and successful ruler. He says in Boethian language that the

"First Mover of all above" made the "fair chain of love," by which he bound fire and air, water and land. That same "Prince and Mover" established in this "wretched world" the "time span for all." Theseus says he need not cite authorities, since it is proved by experience that this Mover is "eternal and unchanging," and that every part derives from the whole. Like the oak, so men and women, "king and page," all perish. And since everything is controlled by the King, it is wise to make "virtue of necessity," and "take well what we cannot avoid." Applying his philosophy to the events at hand, Theseus says it is folly to grumble about the death of Arcite. Arcite was the "flower of chivalry," and he departed with honor out of the "foul prison of this life." Furthermore, after grief, there should be bliss and praise to Jupiter. From two sorrows, one joy can be made; let Palamon wed Emily.

For all of its borrowing from the *Consolation,* this counsel to make the best of things sounds rather like Ben Franklin; it is Lady Philosophy adapted for Theseus by the Knight conceived by Chaucer. I am not implying that Chaucer was satirizing the Knight, Theseus, or Lady Philosophy, but rather that in presenting them as admirable in their own ways, Chaucer conveyed shades of personality.

Many of the same allusions to Fortune and Providence recur in *Troilus and Criseyde,* but there are no pat answers and no minimizing of either woes or joys. The fact that the joys are overshadowed by a sense of impending doom has been taken as evidence of Chaucer's pessimistic determinism. But recognition of the inevitability of catastrophe is not a denial of free will. Sophisticated Christians such as Chaucer and Boethius saw that men have little control over the circumstances of their lives. Riches, success, brains, and beauty are gifts which may be lost. The area of free will is small, but not less real for being confined mainly to the inner life. It is exercised not in what happens to a man—witness the imprisonment and execution of Boethius—but in the way he responds.

The whole interest is in the response in a story like the *Troilus*, in which the outcome was predetermined for Chaucer and his audience. While the inventor of a new plot, the end of which is a surprise to the reader, resembles a creator standing in the garden watching his creatures to see what they will do, the reteller of an old tale is a judge standing outside time evaluating their motives for behaving as they did. One of the advantages of such a "given" plot is that this sense of inevitability lends a certain cosmic significance to what otherwise might seem an irrational or trivial plot; bound to it as he is, the author is the freer to concentrate on character and personality, and meaning. The infidelity of Criseyde, which Chaucer announces in the opening lines, was as much a foregone conclusion as the death of Hector in the *Iliad* or the fulfillment of the oracle in *Oedipus Rex*. When Shakespeare dramatized the story, it suited his purpose to make Criseyde's character the cause of her conclusion. She evokes no sympathy, not only because she is a wanton whose very body language invites lechery but because she seems to be choosing her own role. Chaucer, however, interweaves her character with her destiny in a way that gives us leave to pity her without condoning her crime.

He shows us the difficulty of her position in Troy, her vulnerability to social pressures, and the weakness of her character. And her uncle, Pandarus, uses her circumstances and her character to influence her conduct. Still, conditioned as she is by heredity and environment, she nonetheless makes choices. This interplay of forces is evident in the prologue to the famous bedroom scene. When Pandarus invites her to his house for dinner, he carefully selects a night when the weather forecast is for clouds and darkness. However, when Criseyde is kept from leaving by a heavy rain, Chaucer tells us the downpour was caused by the will of the gods. But—it was already raining when Criseyde left home. And when she later yields to Troilus, she herself says that if she had not already yielded in her mind and heart, she would not just happen to be in bed in Uncle Pandar's house. Similarly manipulating destiny, but for the opposite end, Chaucer makes Aeneas look worse in *The Legend of Good Women* than he does in the *Aeneid* by omitting Virgil's comment that the storm that kept Aeneas and Dido in the cave was arranged by Juno and Venus.

On most occasions Criseyde does not so clearly distinguish the real from the good reason, but she knows the good, Boethian ones. To persuade Troilus that it is best for her to follow the decree of the Council that she go to the Greek camp, she says that it is useless to blame Fortune. Rise above it, she advises Troilus, be "lord of Fortune," use reason and moderation, and "make virtue of necessity." The very words of Theseus on the lips of Criseyde! Apparently Chaucer saw that platitudes could be used to justify situation ethics. For, alas, in the Greek camp the immediate necessity is the warrior Diomede, and Criseyde half convinces herself that loving him is necessary. She also knows, however, that it is not virtuous and that "till the end of the world, no good word of her will be said," that she will be hated for her infidelity to Troilus. . . . But since there's no better way, and it's too late to be sorry, she'll be true to Diomede. So Chaucer shows Criseyde making a series of wrong choices. But he does not judge her harshly, and he has no heart to punish her. Anyhow, he considers her ill fame sufficient for her guilt.

Troilus, on the other hand, is portrayed in part as a kind of deterministic cry-baby who blames everything on fate. He is not, however, a puppet set up to prove a point out of Boethius, and Chaucer allows a certain measure of truth to the views of this unhappy young lover. Falling in love, remarks Chaucer, is a condition of nature. When proud Bayard (a common name for a horse) feels the whip, he realizes he is but a horse "who must endure horses' law." So Troilus, though he is a king's son, is subject to the stirrings of love. And in the Proem to Book IV, Chaucer acknowledges that Fortune is about "to turn her face away from Troilus"; "how she forsook him must henceforth be the matter of this book"—as it has always been written.

The exigencies of the traditional plot partly explain why Troilus blames Fortune in every difficulty instead of taking action. After all, if he were an aggressive sort, he would carry off Criseyde instead of watching her go to the Greek camp. But that was not the way it had always been written. As Chaucer convincingly creates him, Troilus, we feel, is exactly the kind of man to whom what did happen would happen.

It is not only the weakness of his character, however, but the strength of his passion that destroys his freedom. Brave, handsome, well-born, rich, once he is bound to lust he hands himself over to Pandarus and increasingly sees himself as a victim of fate. When he first complains that Fortune is his foe, nothing has happened to him besides falling in love. When he hears the news of Criseyde's appointed departure, he wails, What have I done wrong? How can Fortune, whom he "has honored above all the gods," be so cruel? Apparently Troilus did not know that cruelty and change are quintessential characteristics of Fortune, and Chaucer does not enlighten him.

We know that Troilus is not speaking for Chaucer here because Chaucer spoke for himself in a short Boethian poem in dialogue form entitled "Fortune." In her own defense, Fortune says that no man is wretched except through his own fault. Indeed, she has done the complainant the favor of showing him his true from his false friends. And anyhow, he has only been driven around the wheel like everybody else; her mutability is part of her nature. Blind beasts don't see that Fortune is under the righteousness of heaven, she says, but wise men like Socrates are never either tormented or pleased by her.

Troilus, of course, is no Socrates. And as Chaucer leaves him in the toils of Fortune, so he lets him embroil himself also with the predestinarians. Fallen in despair and anxious to die, Troilus concludes that all things happen by necessity and that free will is an idle dream. His numerous arguments resemble those advanced by Boethius, but the answers of Lady Philosophy are not given. One reason for this one-sided argument is that Troilus could not have understood or accepted the other side. Lady Philosophy had said that things are known according to the nature of the knower, and that souls enslaved by vice cannot know truly because they are clouded by ignorance. Troilus thinks the sun rises with Criseyde, and when he expects to lose her, he says he will end his life in darkness like Oedipus. How could he imagine the light of eternity?

But there must be another reason for this extraordinary speech of 132 lines. Not only is the length ridiculously inappropriate to the circumstances, but it is hard not to laugh at its style, at the yeas and nays, at the way Troilus begins all over again with the different kinds of necessity when we think he has finished, at the pedantry with which he announces his points. He says, for example, "Right so is it of the part contrary, as thus—now hearken for I will not tarry." Praying alone in the temple for death, whom is he addressing in this schoolmaster's voice?

I guess that he was addressing that "philosophical

Strode" to whom the *Troilus* was in part dedicated, and that the whole passage, which seems to have been inserted after the poem was finished, was a satire of the endless arguments of the day over free will. Chaucer's friend Strode was a defender of the doctrine of free will and had disputed the subject many times with Wycliffe. But Strode was an

NUN'S PRIEST

apologist who didn't like controversy; and Chaucer, for all the words expended here, deals not with the deeply serious part of the controversy, but only with its futility.

Strode was reputedly so civil a disputant that even fiery Wycliffe was restrained with him. Further, his theme was peace in the Church, and he thought that charity should be put ahead of differences. As a Thomist who believed that Christ was the head of all men, he argued against Wycliffe's doctrine that Christ was "head only of the predestined elect" and his view that "no word in Scripture justifies a belief in universal salvation" (a belief held by fourteenth-century Julian of Norwich, for example). What especially troubled Strode was Wycliffe's assertion that a man could be damned "for the good of the Church." On this level, the argument touched on the ultimate issue of whether God is responsible for evil and for the damnation of sinners. This is not Troilus's level.

Chaucer emphasizes instead the technical language that characterized the scholastic argument, and was itself familiar. This same Ralph Strode was well known for his

treatises on logic, in which he discussed syllogistic reasoning and gave a series of formal exercises in dialectics.
Strode would undoubtedly have been amused by the way
Troilus bumbles the middle term of his syllogism on the
order of causes. And schoolmen and former students alike
would have recognized the way Troilus, having lost the
thread of the argument, tries to save himself with thuses
and therefores, and repeats the same "proof" four times.

Furthermore, free will was traditionally the subject of
ecclesiastical humor. Facetiousness was stimulated not only
by the technical language used but by the impracticality of
its practical application. Wycliffe, for example, held a rigid
predestinarianism according to which every act is predestined from eternity. Every act? No free will? If it would take
a miracle to prevent a man from committing adultery and
God does not provide the miracle, has God predestined the
act, which is therefore not a sin? So went a contemporary
joke. Similiar sophomoric fun was provided by the students
at the University of Paris who attached the label "Buridan's
ass" to the teaching of a well-known philosopher. Buridan
taught that if the intellect presents two equally desirable
alternatives, the will is free only to suspend choice. College
wits added the story of the ass who starved because he could
not choose between two loads of equally distant, equally
choice hay.

The same parodic spirit fills the barnyard in The
Nun's Priest's Tale. The Priest-narrator is a moderate
determinist whose exposition of the various kinds of necessity is occasioned by the dilemma of Chanticleer, who
had been warned in a dream and whose fate seems as inevitable as that of Troy. What God foreknows must needs
be, the Priest says, according to the opinion of the clerks.
Everybody knows, he adds sagely, that there is "great alter-
cation and disputation" in the schools, by a "hundred

thousand men." He names three of the most famous, Augustine, Boethius, and Bradwardine (an early mentor of Wycliffe). He complains, however, slipping into scholastic jargon, that he himself cannot tell whether God's foreknowledge forces him to do a thing by necessity or if free choice be granted him to do that same thing or do it not; or if God's knowledge does not constrain him except by conditional necessity! "Well," says the Priest, giving it up, "my tale is about a cock."

When the fox carries off Chanticleer, the Priest laments the destiny that may not be escaped. The manly cock, however, does not accept what seems his inevitable fate of being eaten. By tricking the fox into opening his mouth, he escapes. Sitting high on a tree, Chanticleer does not blame his mishap on Fortune or predestination but on his own susceptibility to flattery. And with a final wink at the theologians, he punningly moralizes that he who closes his eyes "all *willfully*" when he should see deserves what he gets. In its humorous way, the tale expresses the ordinary man's unphilosophical acceptance of the inexplicable working of destiny, according to which, necessity or not, a man is responsible for his deeds.

Surely Chaucer's sophisticated and knowledgeable audience would have understood Troilus's soliloquy as a similarly light-hearted spoof of the quibbling of the hundred thousand men, as useless to him as it was to the cock. As with the cock, the point can be deduced from the action which follows the words. A believer in free will, Chanticleer saves himself. A believer in predestination, Troilus (like Buridan's ass) logically takes no action. When Pandarus bustles in to assert that the weeping Troilus is his own foe, the argument for necessity falls to the ground, because Criseyde is still at home waiting for Troilus to do something. His will is not free, not because he is constrained by

243

necessity but because his eyes are closed "all willfully."

Only death, that most effectual conclusion of corporeal attachments, can open his eyes. It is, in fact, the sudden end of his body that accounts for the sudden shift in his views at the end of the poem. After he is slain by Achilles, his spirit goes up to the eighth sphere; there he understands Lady Philosophy's views, not by argumentation but by illumination. Having seen the stars and heard the heavenly harmony, when he looks down on this "little spot of earth embraced by the sea," he begins to "despise this wretched world" and to hold all "vanity by comparison with the felicity of heaven." He even laughs at the sorrow of those who weep over his death. Now, instead of blaming Fortune and the gods, he condemns the "works that follow blind lust" and which "cannot last." Now he knows the Boethian truth that we should place our hearts in heaven in order to free our will.

The same point is given Christian form in the final address of Chaucer to his readers. Chaucer makes no concession here to the inevitability of falling in love; on the contrary, he assumes unusual power to exercise the will. "Turn home from worldly vanity," he says to the young folks; turn to God and remember that this world passes as soon as a flower. Turn to Christ and you will need no other loves, and nobody will betray you. Finally, after asking "moral Gower" and "philosophical Strode" to correct any errors in this book, Chaucer offers a prayer to the Trinity, asking for help against "visible and invisible foes."

This combination of homily and prayer forms a devotional rather than logical answer to the questions about evil and free will raised throughout this long poem. The love of Christ and his mother and the protection of the Trinity are answers to the inequities and faithlessness of the world as the Passion of Christ is the answer to the suffering of Job.

Evil remains a mystery, but a greater mystery is the Trinity—which defends us against evil, visible and invisible. Through the willing sacrifice on the cross of the most innocent, even the guilty are free to turn from vanity and receive not justice but mercy.

Browsing through the works of Chaucer, we find numerous examples of the same theme with variations, usually with less discussion. *The Legend of Good Women* and several *Canterbury Tales* confirm the impression of the Knight's Tale and *Troilus* that Chaucer was either troubled himself or sympathetic with those who were troubled by the presence of evil in God's world; and in these works also he does not oversimplify the interrelations of Fortune and Providence, character and destiny. In the homilies and legends of Constance, Cecilia, and Prudence, the omnipresence of Providence and the freedom to choose wisely are taken for granted; the same orthodox solution is more subtly in the background of The Franklin's Tale. In The Friar's Tale, The Pardoner's Tale and The Parson's Tale the Devil is subordinated to Providence; although he goes to-and-fro on the earth, he is an instrument of God, testing and offering choices. And in a number of short poems, Chaucer makes it clear that whatever their social or economic class, men and women are free to choose virtue.

The most agonizing question is always, Why does God permit evil? The suffering of the innocent apparently brought the question to the surface of Chaucer's mind, even when it was not part of his literary plan to deal with an answer. In *The Legend of Good Women*, for example, Chaucer tells the story of Philomela, who was raped by her brother-in-law Tereus, who then silenced her by cutting out her tongue. The legend opens by querying God in philosophical terms: "Thou giver of the forms that made this fair world," and bore it "in thy mind eternally before the world began," why did you make this Tereus to the scandal of men? Why did you allow him to corrupt the world so? At the end of the story, Chaucer says only that "thus" was Philomela served, she who deserved no harm. The moral, as befits these legends, is that women should beware of men, who may not be quite like Tereus but are not to be trusted. The larger problem is left untouched.

Sometimes question and answer have a tired note, as if brought in to fill out a passage or finish a platitude. The Merchant, for example, telling how May decided to love Damian, says he does not know whether her decision was influenced by destiny or chance or constellation, for all things have their times, as clerks say. But great God above knows that "no act is without cause." A few lines later, when January loses his sight, the narrator apostrophizes Fortune as unstable and deceitful. Why have you deceived January? he demands rhetorically and thoughtlessly.

In the explicitly Christian moralities, the same questions are raised, but here answers are given or implied. Why, Melibeus asks his wife Prudence in The Tale of Melibeus, why did God permit the wounding of their daughter by his enemies? Prudence is careful not to oversimplify: she cites St. Paul as saying that the ways of God are deep. Nonetheless, she believes that the "God of justice" permitted this evil "for good reason." Melibeus, she says firmly, has drunk so much of temporal delights that he has forgotten Jesus. His three enemies are really the world, the flesh, and the devil, and he has let them enter by the windows of his body. Melibeus, like so many of the confused sinners, thinks Fortune will help him, but Prudence convinces him that his only recourse is to God the Judge.

Unlike Melibeus, Constance in The Man of Law's Tale is entirely virtuous, so that the correction of vice is not a possible explanation of her misfortunes. That is why

246

the Constable, recently converted to the Christian religion of justice and mercy, is shocked when he receives orders in a letter from his recently converted king to set Queen Constance and her baby adrift on the sea. "O mighty God," he asks, since you are a "righteous judge," how is it possible that you let the innocent die and the wicked prosper? While an ordinary Christian may thus reasonably ask Job's question, a saint like Constance takes all as the will of Christ. Kneeling on the shore, she says, "Lord, welcome be whatever you send!" She laments the hardness of the child's father who has sent the message to slay the child, but she does not blame God. Instead, she prays to Mary, who also saw her child slain, to have mercy on her.

In the background of The Second Nun's Tale is the persecution of innocent Christians for their faith, but Cecilia's zeal is so great that she courts what most men consider the ultimate evil, and she has no qualms about taking her friends with her. As a result of their recent enlightenment, her newly converted husband and his brother realize that they must now reverse ordinary judgments. Still, when the brother foresees martyrdom, he shrinks from what he has always considered the worst possible misfortune. Cecilia, however, understands by the light of faith what Troilus had to die to see; that is, that there is a better life elsewhere. And she laughs at the judge who says he has power over her, because in her philosophy, evil has power to kill but not to give life, and she is going to life. Granted the view expressed by the Nun-narrator that this life is only a preparation for eternity, Cecilia's cheerful choice of death over defection is reasonable. Since death is the only entry into that "fair country" of Boethius, it cannot be evil.

Lady Philosophy had also said that what seems bad fortune may be a test of virtue, and this is one of the thoughts behind The Franklin's Tale, a story in which the connections between character and destiny, Providence and Fortune, are carefully worked out through the medium of an old folktale. Loving and faithful Dorigen, watching for the return by sea of her husband, is made uneasy by the rocks on which ships founder. Like so many of Chaucer's characters, she generalizes her fears, and questions what she has been taught about God. "Eternal God," she says, "who through thy providence leads the world by sure rules," men say you "make nothing in vain." Why then has the Lord made these "grisly, fiendish black rocks" that seem rather a "foul confusion" than a "fair creation"? Don't you see, she demands of God, how these rocks destroy thousands of men, men made in God's own image? Why did God make such things which do only harm? She knows, she says skeptically, that clerks argue that all is for the best, but she doesn't know their reasons. Leaving "disputation" to clerks, she then wishes to God that all the rocks were sunk in hell for her husband's sake! Dorigen's complaint follows the pattern familiar to us from The Knight's Tale and *Troilus:* a presentation of the problem of reconciling the goodness of God with the misfortunes of men; professed ignorance of, and distrust of, the answers of the experts; and a final cry for personal help. In this tale the theoretical argument is not picked up later, but I think the events that follow demonstrate that all is for the best in the worst possible way.

In a nice bit of psychologizing, Chaucer has Dorigen's deep fears about the rocks surface in a careless speech. When she makes her rash promise, she is not flirting with the lovesick Aurelius. Her promise to love him when he removes the offending rocks is a courteous refusal, predicated on the impossibility of the task, and its seeming desirability. The sequel is a little reminiscent, in a minor way of course, of the *Oedipus* of Sophocles. In the play, Jocasta scorns the oracles just before their fulfillment proves their validity: she attributes all to chance when in fact there is an order she cannot see. So Dorigen questions the providence of God and cannot see the use of the rocks. Not the rocks, however, but the rash promise that arose from her desire to improve on Providence almost destroys her husband and herself. She had not, as she says, believed possible a miracle which is "against the process of nature"; when the miracle happens, she complains against Fortune and sees death as her only escape.

Her husband Arveragus, however, is not Fortune's slave. He does not question the seemingly capricious act of the gods. He does insist that although Dorigen spoke lightly, she must take responsibility for her words and carry out her promise. Arveragus has said that Truth—here with the meaning of keeping one's word—is the highest good. The evil permitted thus turns out to be a test of his truth, and he passes splendidly. He follows his doctrine to its logical conclusion with as little hesitation as Cecilia follows hers, and with as little counting of the cost.

Evil may be identified with falsehood or falseness, and may be personified as the devil, who is the father of lies. The "foes visible and invisible" against whom Chaucer prays the Trinity to protect us are no mere allegory, but they play only a small part in Chaucer's discussions of evil. References to the devil in *The Canterbury Tales* often reflect the personality of the pilgrim-narrator; from the stories we can deduce the conventional notions of the powers and limitations of the fiend.

The Man of Law refers quite simply to Satan as the serpent. The Nun Prioress also calls Satan serpent, our first foe, and shows him slyly inciting the Jews to murder the Christian boy by telling them that the boy sings in praise of Mary just to spite them. The Pardoner and the Parson are more sophisticated. The Pardoner calls the tavern the "devil's temple" because there sinners "sacrifice" to the devil by dancing, dicing, and rioting. The Parson, too, uses the concept of the devil metaphorically. He says that anger destroys the image of God, that is, virtue, in man's soul and puts in him the "likeness of the devil." Anger is "the devil's furnace," destroying spiritual things. Elsewhere he says that the devil blows in man the fire of fleshly concupiscence. He is quick to add, however, that men decide whether or not to fall into temptation.

The devil's role in the world's evil is amusingly dramatized in The Friar's Tale. The devil's presence does not explain the corruption of the Summoner, who is the real villain of the piece. Like the sinners in Dante's *Inferno*, this Summoner chooses his hell by his conduct on earth. When he meets the fiend, the Summoner is making his rounds, extorting money from the innocent by blackmail and threats, instead of summoning the guilty to court as he is supposed to do. He is at once comfortable with the devil, with whom he swears brotherhood. Indeed, he is more interested than disturbed and he asks questions about the forms devils take in hell and on earth, and whether they can make new bodies from elements.

These are not the questions the devil chooses to answer. Obviously no pitchfork-wielder, this ancestor of C. S. Lewis's Screwtape gives intelligent and knowledgeable moral information. He does not expect the Summoner, who is "bare of wit," to understand, but he explains nonetheless that the fiends are "God's instruments." Without God, he explains, they have no power; sometimes they have leave to test only the body, as with Job, sometimes the soul. If the person withstands temptations, the devils are the cause of his salvation, although that is not their intent.

At the climax of the story, we see how limited the

devil's range is. Unlike the Summoner, he can take only what is freely given. When the falsely accused old woman wishes the Summoner to the devil, the courteous fiend asks, "Now Mabel, my dear mother, is this your will in earnest?" Yes, she replies, the devil fetch him, unless he repents. Since repentance is not his intent, the devil takes him to hell. The Pilgrim-Friar concludes the tale by advising the pilgrims to dispose their hearts to withstand the fiend, who "cannot tempt them beyond their strength," for Christ will be "their champion and knight." For all the fun, the moral is the same serious one voiced by Chaucer at the conclusion of his *Troilus*. The Friar, however, is hardly a trustworthy spokesman for the author. While his shrewd assessment of the devil's powers and limits is sound enough, the rough justice of the tale reflects mainly the teller's delight in the summoning of the Summoner, his personal enemy. Chaucer himself, as we have seen in *Troilus*, does not reduce the problem of evil to a system of prompt rewards and punishments.

Reviewing the stories, we see that the force of circumstance is strong, but that the characters are responsible for their handling of the evil that descends upon them. Even the unfortunate Philomela, helpless in the hands of the villain Tereus, resists as far as she can and then embroiders her story in a tapestry that she contrives to send to her sister. Live or die, those who master Fortune do so by choosing the good, whatever the cost.

Chaucer's view that men are free to choose, and that they are not simply products of heredity and environment is supported also in his famous short poem called "Gentilesse," that we have glanced at in other contexts. The idea that true nobility must be chosen rather than inherited is central to Chaucer's handling of will and fate. Without the freedom to choose virtue, men would indeed be bound

251

to Fortune. As the lady in The Wife of Bath's Tale puts it, if gentilesse were "planted naturally according to lineage" then people could do no wrong. Behavior would be controlled by natural law, like fire, which burns until it dies. But, she reasons, folk do not follow laws of nature as does fire. A lord's son does not necessarily do noble deeds like his ancestors; and if he does villain's deeds, "he is a churl." Likewise, she whose ancestors were rude can choose gentilesse, which comes from God, not from blood or place in society.

This Christian principle of free choice runs through Chaucer's works, but it concerns moral choice only. There is no suggestion that gentilesse leads to success at court; indeed, the contrary may be true. Rewards and punishments are distributed not here but hereafter. It is only from the vantage of eternity that it can be proved that the universe is run by a just God. Nor is the line between good and evil easy to draw in this false world. Looking at the human race, Chaucer does not apply his principle of free choice rigidly. He sees that the choice of evil is not simple, that what men desire they think is good, and he pities their blindness. And not only sinners but virtuous men and women ask the questions of Job and suffer similar pain and frustration. Evil is part of the human condition, and questioning is, as God made clear to Job's friends, the prerogative of the creature made in his image. Men can understand the nature of God only in terms of their own nature, and they may not understand Boethius. Still, it is part of their created nature that they are free to choose gentilesse, and so be masters rather than victims of Fortune.

IX

Reconciliation

A non they kissed, and rode upon their way." "They" are not Troilus and Criseyde, or Arveragus and Dorigen, or Palamon and Emily, but the Host and the Pardoner, the one a foul-mouthed innkeeper, the other an evil purveyor of false pardons. They have quarreled with such violence and bitterness that there could ensue only eternal enmity, we would think. But the Knight intervenes. "No more of this," he says. "Sir Pardoner, be glad and of merry cheer. And you, Sir Host, who are so dear to me, I pray you to kiss the Pardoner. And Pardoner, I pray you, draw near, and, as we did before, let us laugh and play." Without further ado, the two rogues kiss and make up and continue on the pilgrimage.

This brief episode at the end of The Pardoner's Tale dramatizes the theme of reconciliation that is an integral part of Chaucer's Christian interpretation of life. Typical of Chaucer's religious as well as literary style, the scene does not minimize man's wickedness, but neither does it limit

253

God's forgiveness. The Pardoner has been called by commentators the one lost soul among the pilgrims, but the Knight's act suggests that Chaucer did not finally damn the man, strongly as he condemned his sins. The good Knight has heard the Pardoner bragging of his wickedness, but unlike the righteous reader, he does not ostracize him. And the courtesy of this peace-bearing Knight to this crude hustler is proof of his own God-given gentilesse. It is because of his Christian respect for every soul that he can call the Pardoner "sir"; and Host and Pardoner can be reconciled because all are pilgrims on the same way, all in need of mercy.

In a great many medieval works besides Chaucer's, this view that sin is the one activity shared by the whole human race leads more often to kisses than to tears. At a first glance, *Piers Plowman,* for example, with its extreme condemnation of a wide variety of sins and sinners, may seem closer to the *Contempt of the World* than to *The Canterbury Tales.* But Langland's cry for repentance is closely allied to his belief in mercy. Indeed, he goes so far as to say that on the Day of Judgment, all sinners will be pardoned by the King, and only the devils will remain in hell. And for all of his criticism of the clergy, he saw Christ and the Church as the great reconciler—of Old and New Law, of Jew and Gentile, of man and God.

Most of the happy endings of fictional pilgrimages, histories of the world, mystery and morality plays, are the result of this double theme of repentance and reconciliation. Dante must go through Hell and Purgatory, but his work ends in Paradise. And it is predictable that in the white radiance of eternity, he will be reconciled not only with Beatrice but with God. The same theological certainties and inferences shape the ending of *Sir Gawaine and the Green Knight.* In this seemingly worldly story, replete with elegance and magic, Gawaine's adventurous quest turns out to be the painful education of a Christian knight. What mitigates the pain is the sharing of the burden of confessed guilt. "Cursed be cowardice and covetousness!" cries Gawaine when the Green Knight explains why he nicked his neck; in a storm of shame, Gawaine acknowledges his fault. When he returns to the court of King Arthur, he tells them his fault at once, and explains that he wears the girdle as a memorial, to remind him of his sins when he is riding proudly. The court responds with perfect gentilesse. Amid much kissing and laughing, they all agree to wear a similar girdle as a token of their common sinfulness and their common need for mercy.

This same pattern is clearly delineated in Chaucer's works. In Chaucer's view, justice would condemn not only the Pardoner but all of us. As the Parson puts it, if our Lord Jesus Christ had not had pity and spared us in our follies, we might all sing a sad song. It is a conspicuous mark of their Christian failure that the least perceptive of Chaucer's characters think this general truth applies to everyone except themselves. The Reeve "quits" the Miller, the Summoner gets even with the Friar, by telling tales in which a rough justice is visited immediately—on the other wicked one. Evil should have what evil deserves, says the Prioress of the Jews, meanwhile asking for mercy for herself and her friends. Chaucer does not continue the cycle by condemning these judges in turn. Instead, he portrays them as seeing the world and themselves in a severely limited way. Blinded by sin or ignorance or childishness, they have so narrow a margin of free will that only God can tell finally whether they have used it well or ill.

The enlightened characters are all men and women of mercy and forgiveness. Dame Prudence sees forgiveness of

enemies as central to
the teaching of Jesus,
and the necessity pro-
logue to reconciliation
and peace. The Parson,
too, says that the
"neighbor" we are
obliged to love includes
our enemies. Chaucer
himself may have been
against war, but he
was not against war-
riors. It is one of his
paradoxes that the

PARSON

Knight is also the peacemaker. It is one of his simplicities
that his virtuous women—Constance, Griselda, and Cecilia—in one way or another make peace, reconcile man
with man, and man with God.

The same spirit of reconciliation pervades Chaucer's poems of prayer. When Chaucer considers the role of Christ in history, it is as
healer of the breach between man and God,
and Mary is the sinners' advocate. In the "ABC," the poet
rejoices that the "bow is bent" not toward the justice of
the Father but to the mercy of the Son, the mercy we need
when we come before the judge. The "I" of the poem
asks Mary to remind Jesus how with "his precious blood"
he wrote a bill of "general acquittal" for all penitents.
This "ABC" was an early work, but the same theme
recurs in later works; for example, in *Troilus* and the Retraction of the *Tales*.

Chaucer assumes that the cry for mercy is supported by
a promise of amendment. Penitence, says the Parson, is
true repentance for sins which the sinner confesses orally

256

and intends never to commit again. It is for Chaucer a mark of the wickedness of the hypocritical Friar that he gives easy penances, and worse, that he says that if a man can't feel sorry for his sins, he can show his good intentions by giving money to the Friar's order. Chaucer's good Parson is strict; he insists that contrition requires the proper inner disposition of heart and will. The detailed examination of conscience which he recommends sounds like a gloomy exercise, but the threat of hell hangs over only those who fail to perform it. Penance is by definition the "sacrament of reconciliation," and that is why it is the subject of the last tale on the pilgrimage.

The Parson says that Christ died to make concord, and that he pardoned the thief on the Cross. Penance was devised, he says, by our Lord Jesus because he wants no man to perish. The Parson, for all his strictness, wants no man to despair, and he reminds sinners that the Passion of Jesus is "stronger to unbind" than sin is "strong to bind." As often as he falls, the sinner may rise again by penitence, for the mercy of Christ is always ready to receive him. And the fruit of penance is the endless bliss of heaven, where joy has no contrariety of woe or grief, where all the pain of this life has passed, where souls will be "refreshed" with the "perfect knowledge of God."

In the light of The Parson's Tale which it immediately follows, Chaucer's Retraction appears as his own act of reconciliation, a sincere acknowledgement of sin, coupled with an equally sincere confidence in the mercy of Christ, who, as he says, redeemed all mankind with the precious blood of his heart. Chaucer apparently had no reason to think he would not be saved with all other penitents on that day of judgment. Both grim and hopeful, such talk of death and judgment was quite compatible with the lighthearted laughing and playing that accompanied the pil-

grims to the shrine of the martyr in Canterbury. The belief
in judgment is also compatible with, if not the cause of,
Chaucer's wide tolerance. As Chaucer is quick to judge
himself rather than others, so he is slow to judge the
stranger and the dissenter. In the fourteenth as in other
centuries, there were narrow Christians who wanted the
literal sense of the Bible to be the measure of all things.
There were other self-righteous Christians who wanted to
lock God in the sacraments of the Church. Chaucer instead
expressed the broadest insights of the Church. Like Augustine, he sees the hand of God in other times and places,
and he has a strong sense of all humanity's descent from
Adam, all created in the image of God. And his faith is
enriched rather than troubled by the literature of antiquity.
As he remarks in the Prologue to *The Parliament of Fowls,*
"out of old fields" comes "new corn from year to year"; from
the old philosophies and the old stories, Chaucer gleaned a
rich and diversified harvest.

Chaucer's ecumenism included Lollards as well as pagans. The Lollards, like Wycliffe himself, excluded too
much of history and tradition for Chaucer's taste; even
their heaven admitted only the elect. The pilgrimages, the
invocations of saints, the popes and bishops, and the oral
confession that the Lollards rejected were aspects of religious life valued by Chaucer. But Chaucer does not exclude
the Lollards for their exclusions. Apparently differences in
theological opinions, at least within the bounds kept by his
Lollard friends, seemed less important to him than the
moral views they shared.

The ones he judges severely are those closest to him.
He apparently felt (as did Newman in the nineteenth century) that the proverb *Corruptio optimi est pessima* applied to
the Church. His clergy sin with a depth and intensity that
laymen are spared; and there is more blasphemy within the

Church than without. That is because there is more light to sin against. The light is still there in Chaucer's portrait, not only in the good clerics, but in the good teaching of even the bad ones, and in the beauty of the liturgy and the traditional morality of Mother Church. Behind all the sinners is a positive vision of an ideal Church, and of the power and goodness of God—a God of love and forgiveness; a God who dispenses gifts of nature, beauty and health, brains and wit, and gentilesse; a God who blesses marrying and not marrying, and, indeed, blesses all noble thoughts and deeds.

Chaucer's God of love also loves laughter and humility. Chaucer would have been funny whatever his religion, but his Catholicism specifically blessed laughter as a means of reconciliation. How much of the poet's modesty is related to his religion is hard to say. Of course there have been arrogant Christians and humble atheists, but Chaucer himself admires humility as a religious trait in his characters, and to judge from his prayers, it was a virtue he himself cultivated through penitence. Combined with humor and with a sense of community with poor sinful creatures, this rare modesty moderates the sting of satire and saves the philosophic, intellectual poet from snobbishness and self-righteousness. The people laugh while the *gentil* Knight reconciles the Pardoner and the Host, all on pilgrimage with the observant poet. The Pardoner can be pardoned, the Host is on the altar, the Knight brings the kiss of peace, because finally all share with Chaucer in God's plenty.

SELECTED BIBLIOGRAPHY

Basic Text

Robinson, F. N., ed. *The Works of Geoffrey Chaucer.* 2d ed. Boston: Houghton Mifflin, 1957.

Translations and Dual-language Edition

Coghill, Nevill, Trans. *The Canterbury Tales.* 1951. rept. Baltimore: Penguin, 1975.

Hieatt, A. Kent and Constance Hieatt, eds. *Canterbury Tales/ Tales of Canterbury.* New York: Bantam, 1964.

Morrison, Theodore, ed. and trans. *The Portable Chaucer.* New York: Viking, 1975. (Includes *Troilus and Criseyde*)

Sources and Background Works

Anthologies

Loomis, Roger Sherman and Laura Hibbard Loomis, eds. *Medieval Romances.* New York: Modern Library, 1957.

Mack, Maynard, ed. *Norton Anthology of World Masterpieces*, 4th ed. New York: Norton, 1979, Vol. I. (Selections from Virgil, St. Augustine, Dante, Boccaccio, *Sir Gawaine and the Green Knight,* Chaucer)

Miller, Robert P., ed. *Chaucer: Sources and Backgrounds.* New York: Oxford Univ. Press, 1977. (A most useful collection of selections from works Chaucer is known to have used)

Single Works

Andreas Capellanus. *The Art of Courtly Love*. Trans. John Jay Perry. New York: Norton, 1969.

Boccaccio, Giovanni. *The Filostrato*. Trans. Nathaniel Edward Griffin and Arthur Beckwith Myrick. New York: Biblo and Tannen, rept. 1967.

Boethius. *The Consolation of Philosophy*. Trans. Richard H. Green. Indianapolis: Bobbs-Merrill, 1962.

Dante Alighieri. *The Divine Comedy*, 3 vols. Trans. Allen Mandelbaum. Berkeley, California: Univ. of California Press, 1980–82.

De Lorris, Guillaume and Jean de Meun. *Romance of the Rose*. Trans. Charles Dahlberg. Princeton: Princeton Univ. Press, 1971.

Jerome, Saint. *The Epistle against Jovinian. The Principal Works of St. Jerome*. Trans. W. H. Fremantle. Nicene and Post-Nicene Fathers. New York: Christian Literature Co., 1893.

Julian of Norwich. *Revelations of Divine Love*. Ed. M. L. Del Mastro. New York: Doubleday, 1977.

Langland, William. *Piers the Ploughman*. Trans. J. F. Goodridge. Baltimore: Penguin, 1959.

Letters of Abelard and Heloise. Trans. Betty Radice. Baltimore: Penguin, 1976.

Ovid. *The Art of Love*. Trans. J. H. Mozley. Cambridge, Mass.: Harvard Univ. Press, 1929.

Critical and Historical Studies

Bennett, J. A. W. *The Parlement of Foules: An Interpretation*. Oxford: Clarendon, 1957.

Brewer, D. S. *Chaucer and Chaucerians: Critical Studies in Middle English Literature*. University of Alabama: Univ. of Alabama Press, 1966.

————. *Chaucer and His World*. New York: Dodd, Mead, 1978.

Corsa, Helen S. *Chaucer: Poet of Mirth and Morality*. Notre Dame, Indiana: Univ. of Notre Dame Press, 1964.

Curry, W. C. *Chaucer and the Mediaeval Sciences*. 2d ed. New York: Barnes and Noble, 1960.

Curtius, Ernst Robert. *European Literature and the Latin Middle Ages*. Trans. Willard R. Trask. Princeton: Princeton Univ. Press, 1973.

Donaldson, E. Talbot. *Speaking of Chaucer*. New York: Norton, 1972.

Fisher, John H. *John Gower: Moral Philosopher and Friend of Chaucer*. New York: New York Univ. Press, 1964.

Fleming, John V. *The Roman de la Rose: A Study in Allegory and Iconography*. Princeton: Princeton Univ. Press, 1969.

————. *From Bonaventure to Bellini: An Essay in Franciscan Exegesis*. Princeton: Princeton Univ. Press, 1982.

Gilson, Etienne. *History of Christian Philosophy in the Middle Ages*. New York: Random House, 1955.

Howard, Donald R. *The Idea of the Canterbury Tales*. Berkeley: Univ. of California Press, 1976.

Huizinga, Johan. *The Waning of the Middle Ages: A Study of the Forms of Life, Thought, and Art in France and the Netherlands in the Fourteenth Century*. London: Arnold, 1924.

Hussey, Maurice. *Chaucer's World: A Pictorial Companion*. Cambridge: Cambridge Univ. Press, 1965.

Hussey, Maurice, A. C. Spearing, and James Winny. *An Introduction to Chaucer*. Cambridge: Cambridge Univ. Press, 1965.

Kelly, Henry A. *Love and Marriage in the Age of Chaucer*. Ithaca, New York: Cornell Univ. Press, 1975.

Leclercq, Jean. *The Love of Learning and the Desire for God: A Study of Monastic Culture*. Trans. Catherine Misrahi. New York: Fordham Univ. Press, 1961.

Leff, Gordon. *Medieval Thought: St. Augustine to Ockham*. Baltimore: Penguin, 1958.

Lewis, C. S. *Allegory of Love: A Study of Medieval Tradition*. London: Oxford Univ. Press, 1936.

————. *The Discarded Image*. Cambridge: Cambridge Univ. Press, 1968.

McFarlane, K. B. *Lancastrian Kings and Lollard Knights*. Oxford: Clarendon, 1972.

McKisack, May. *The Fourteenth Century, 1307–1399*. London: Oxford Univ. Press, 1959.

Makarewicz, Sister Mary Raynalda. *The Patristic Influence on Chaucer*. Washington: Catholic Univ. of America Press, 1953.

Mâle, Emile. *The Gothic Image: Religious Art in France of the Thirteenth Century*. Trans. Dora Nussey, 1913. Rept. New York: Harper and Row, 1958.

Matthew, Gervase. *The Court of Richard II*. New York: Norton, 1968.

Muscatine, Charles. *Chaucer and the French Tradition*. Berkeley: Univ. of California Press, 1957.

Owst, G. R. *Literature and Pulpit in Medieval England*. Oxford: Blackwell, 1966.

Power, Eileen, *Medieval People* London: Methuen, 1924. Rept. Barnes and Noble 1977.

Robertson, D. W. Jr. *A Preface to Chaucer: Studies in Medieval Perspectives*. Princeton: Princeton Univ. Press, 1969.

Roth, Cecil. *A History of the Jews in England*. 3d ed. London: Oxford Univ. Press, 1979.

Rowland, Beryl, ed. *Companion to Chaucer Studies*. Toronto: Oxford Univ. Press, 1968.

Ruggiers, Paul G. *The Art of the Canterbury Tales*. Madison: Univ. of Wisconsin Press, 1965.

Smalley, Beryl. *The Study of the Bible in the Middle Ages*. New York: The Philosophical Library, 1952. Rept. Indiana: University of Notre Dame Press, 1964.

Thomas, Mary Edith. *Medieval Skepticism and Chaucer*. New York: William-Frederick Press, 1950.

Utley, Francis Lee. *The Crooked Rib*. Columbus: Ohio State Univ. Press, 1944.

Workman, Herbert B. *John Wyclif, A Study of the English Medieval Church*. 2 vols. Oxford: Clarendon, 1926. Rept. Shoe String, 1966.

INDEX